UFO POLITICS AT THE WHITE HOUSE

UFO Politics
at the
White House

Citizens Rally 'Round Jimmy Carter's Promise

Larry W. Bryant

2015
Galde Press
Lakeville, Minnesota U.S.A.

Galde Press
PO Box 460
Lakeville, Minnesota 55044–0460

For Gretchen B. Condon—
that Daughter of Daughters who continues
to champion her father's voyage toward UFOtruth.

Contents

Acknowledgments

In the ocean of authorial pursuits, no person is an island. (S)he per force accumulates varying degrees of supportive debt (cum commensurate gratitude) as a given project moves from idea to research to manuscript to printed page. In the case of this long-delayed effort, some of those supporters' names and deeds have faded from the author's memory—but not from his enduring gratitude.

During the book's summer-2001-long e-serialization upon the Internet website of the Norfolk, Virginia, daily newspaper *The Virginian-Pilot*, a number of colleagues and other champions of UFOtruth—too numerous to list here—lauded the project. Chief among them: Grant Cameron, whose own research into presidential UFO awareness serendipitously complements this work (see *www.presidentialufo.com*).

On the personal level, my life-traveling companion, Evelyn J. Goodwin, receives eternal thanks for her empathy, faithful acceptance, and wise counsel.

And, without fail, I acknowledge the continuing, nearly life-long support of Patrick Huyghe—confidant, colleague, and pathfinder for the uninitiated author in the swamp of cyberpublishing.

Author's Note:
The Story Behind the Story

In the world of publishing, the story of a book's origin can be almost as compelling and stimulating as the book's thesis.

In the case of this compilation of UFO-related letters to President Carter, the story begins in my late thirties, runs parallel to my thirty-six-year federal-employment career (mostly as a writer-editor for military publications), proceeds on past my retirement (on June 1, 1994, during my last assignment with Army headquarters at the Pentagon), and continues to this day with a phoenixoid life of its own. Along the way, various delays, detours, serendipitous discoveries, and pockets of irony intervene to shape the book's destiny.

Of course, part of the story reflects my yet-to-be-crafted final entry in this trilogy of historic reviews (to be titled *UFO Politics at the Pentagon: An Insider's Three-Decade Struggle Against UFO Secrecy*). In the meantime, Volume II's production also awaits my attention: its title will be *UFO Politics in Congress: Citizens Add to the Congressional [UFO] Record*, which will compile various UFO-related letters written to representatives and senators during the heyday of public UFO awareness. The idea for the current work extends back to an original 1967 paperback produced by the prolific hand of Bill Adler: *Letters to the Air Force on UFOs*, which contains an assortment of citizens' letters sent to USAF headquarters as part of public discussion of the now-defunct USAF UFO-investigation program called "Project Blue Book," whose records now repose at the U. S. National Archives and Records Administration in College Park, Maryland.

"Why shouldn't I seek access to citizens' UFO-related letters to President Carter?" I casually ask myself on the way to work one day. The answer becomes obvious to me, a keen follower of veteran talk-show host Barry Farber's dictum of "Keep asking questions!" And what better way to pose the key question than by firing off a freedom-of-information request to USAF headquarters? Give me, please, a copy of all citizens' letters written to Jimmy upon his taking office as the "UFO President"— that's the substance of my FOIA request (a precursor, incidentally, to my numerous other such FOIA forays/lawsuits during subsequent years). To my pure activist's de-

light, the secretary of the Air Force proceeds to cough up several hundred speci-
mens of Carter's one-way (mostly) UFO-correspondence exchange—all presented
to me as privacy-sanitized printouts from microfilm. I leisurely set about sorting,
editing, and commenting upon this historic material (albeit a fraction of the volume received at the White House). As I sit in a bus seat next to a fellow Pentagon
employee on the way home from work, he notices my editorial scribbling upon a
handful of the Carter letters. "Oh, I'm editing this presidential UFO correspondence
for a book-length compilation of it," I happily explain. "The laborious part of the
project will be my having to use a manual typewriter to produce the final manuscript." Whereupon, he mentions that his wife, a proud owner of an IBM-Selectric
typewriter, happens to ply a home-office job as a manuscript typist. For a reasonable rate, she could do my project. We seal the deal, and a few weeks later, I possess
the fruit of our joint labors. But this glowing plum of a creative venture begins, with
the agonizing passage of time, to acquire the tell-tale wrinkles and coarse skin of a
neglected prune. Unable to find a publisher, disinclined toward self-publication,
and disheartened over my literary embryo's self-aborted debut, I let the manuscript
gather dust among all the other UFOana then crowding me out of my little apartment in Arlington. Thus I fail to achieve my freelance career goal of having my first
book published by the age of forty. Fast-forward to the mid-eighties. And enter one
Phil Reynolds. Because of my series of "UFO-coverup-whistleblower" solicitation
advertisements placed in the Pentagon's Army weekly newspaper (*The Pentagram*),
fellow Pentagonian Phil tracks me down to my new residence in Alexandria, Virginia. Our mutual interest in UFOlogy begins to fuel a camaraderie that flourishes
to this day.

Years after my retirement, Phil telephones me for an update on projects and
plans. He reminds me of his now-realized plan to help found a specialized publishing house, drawing on the emerging, economic digital technology of print-on-
demand publishing. The house's name—the Invisible College Press (*http://www.in-
vispress.com*)—alludes to the late Dr. J. Allen Hynek's characterization of the small
body of scientists privately (and undeclaredly) committed to serious UFO research.
At some point in the conversation, the proverbial light bulb activates: would Phil
like to see my unborn book? Phil's simple "Yes, go ahead and submit it to us" ig-
nites the spark of resurrection, and publication ensues in late 2001.

Alas, few PoD books enjoy high-volume sales. (Ironically, because of that draw-
back, some of them can become instant collector's items.) But they do put the first-
book author on a relatively easy track for eventually breaking in to conventional
publishing. Such becomes the case with this tome. Now that my ICP contract has
expired, you'll be reading this updated version from both a deeper perspective and

a different publisher.

How does this come to pass? Well, FATE magazine publisher-editor Phyllis Galde and I renew our acquaintance at the annual X-Conference near Washington, D. C., in mid-April 2004. She's sitting at a display table in the vendors' room, jauntily flaunting her literary wares (including various back issues of the magazine). I approach the table as if I were a honeybee spying a field of ripe clover. At the end of our conversation, with the ICP flyer on my book now duly presented to her, I sample some "honey" and proceed to pollinate her cerebral seeds by pointing out that vendor Bob Girard of Arcturus Books, Inc., happens to have a few copies of my book for sale on his table. Lo! Near the end of the conference, Phyllis seeks me out to propose that Galde Press adopt a new-and-improved version of my book. At this development, I go over to Bob, purchase a copy of the book, and autograph it to Phyllis. (You know that an author has reached sheer marketing desperation when (s)he resorts to paying retail price for a give-away copy of the book!) As you explore this version's contents, consider that you're at least one step ahead of Jimmy Carter on the scale of public UFO awareness. For he possesses a copy of only the ICP original, which I mailed to him back in 2002. Not long after that mailing, the Carter presidential library in Georgia sent me a thank-you note for the donation (based on, evidently, Carter's passing it on to the library, read/unread).

By the way, my inscription in his copy reads: "For Jimmy Carter, whose closeness to UFOtruth became the proximity fuse for igniting the public's right-to-know—and the government's duty-to-tell."

Foreword

I have known the author of this book, Larry W. Bryant, for a number of years. Our contact grew from our common belief that a republic's citizenry has a fundamental right to know what its government representatives are doing with hard-earned tax dollars.

Second, we further commonly agreed that when it comes to UFO reality the government is not as ignorant as it claims to be, and that certain official files exit somewhere pointing to answers to the mystery of the flying saucers that have been haunting our skies since at least 1947. Third, Larry and I shared the belief that the government appears to have no imminent plan to wave the white flag of disclosure, and that more pressure would have to be applied by us (and others) to gain the desired results. We both, therefore, have worked unceasingly to search out and demand the withheld files from whoever it appeared was illegally suppressing them from public view.

Until he corrected me, I thought Larry had a legal background, as he was regularly dragging government agencies into court over various Freedom of Information Act requests in hopes that the judicial branch of government could force the executive branch to cough up the files that rightly belong to "an informed citizenry." As it turned out, Larry was nothing more than a federal employee who'd taken it upon himself to be the conscience of a government gone bad.

Before I actually met the man at the Washington, D. C., X-Conference in the spring of 2004, I also had characterized him as a serious, hard-nosed researcher whom one had better not cross unless assured of one's facts. It turned out Larry actually happens to be a laid-back, humorous fellow who merely had decided not to accept, out-of-hand, much of what his government has been saying on the subject of UFOs — and had decided not to let fear interfere with his asking for a proper accounting.

His compilation "UFO Politics at the White House" constitutes one of his latest efforts in that accountability quest. This historic work in UFOlogy achieves its importance partly because of Larry Bryant's chutzpah in investigating, and reporting upon, the knowledge and actions of the chief U. S. executive officer vis-a-vis the "UFO problem."

What's more, this book will remain important because it focuses on the Jimmy Carter presidency — one that always has been considered a critical era in UFO history. The Carter administration gained its UFO notoriety first from Jimmy Carter's public testimony that he too had seen a UFO, and that he'd filed an official UFO sighting report to the International UFO Bureau headquartered in Oklahoma City, Okla.; and, second, from his promise to release the truth if elected president.

Simply put, this book looks at how the most powerful man in the world during the late seventies publicly handled the most important issue of the 20th century — the appearance of extraterrestrials here on this planet.

As a presidential UFO historian looking at all the presidents, I take delight in seeing that someone else has recognized the importance of the presidential UFOtruth issue, and has chosen to write about it.

Sad to say, however: only Larry and I have chosen to take on the White House by demanding answers from the man who theoretically should have the combination to the UFOsafe. The topic of presidential UFO awareness remains generally neglected by other UFO researchers. Even sadder is the fact that the UFO issue has received absolutely no attention from any of the other presidential historians that have written about the presidents. The mainstream press, which would have us regard it as the fourth branch of government, has failed miserably at the mission of putting the president's feet to the fire on this critical issue. Records show that the news media have addressed only two on-the-record UFO questions to the president since the birth of modern UFOlogy 1947. As one White House press corps member said of the White House press corps when they got a chance to ask a UFO question of President Clinton — "They rolled over and played dead."

The Congress also has failed to question the chief executive on the UFO issue, figuring that the matter simply lies not on the line drawn by the "shortest distance between two votes." As a paper tiger of immense immobility, the Congress has shown inability to prompt even its own staff persons to tell what they know about UFO reality. Congress instead has chosen to dwell on issues like presidential sexual dalliances, which are much more effective at stirring up the voting masses at election time.

The public has done its part to question the president, and that fact is the main focus of this survey of public interest. Contrary to wide opinion, people throughout the United States have written their top elected leader to relate their personal UFO sightings, or to seek official answers to various aspects of the UFO mystery. As Larry's book skillfully points out, however, these now-public citizen letters basically have been ignored. Participatory democracy, it appears, is not all it's cracked up to be.

The president is the key person in the UFOgame, or at least he should be. Consider the following:

(1) The president is the most powerful person in the country, if not the world. All U. S. intelligence agencies report their findings through the Director of Central Intelligence to the president. Therefore, the president should have access to the latest intelligence on UFO material being studied by the various intelligence agencies.

(2) Many believe that the military plays a major role in gathering and analyzing UFO information. Since the president serves as the commander-in-chief of all branches of the military, the best evidence in their possession theoretically would be placed on the president's desk.

(3) If the UFO secret is held not in the military but in an agency like the U. S. National Security Agency, then the president still should be getting the best information as he heads up the executive branch, which employs most of the U. S. government's personnel.

(4) Constitutionally, the president is responsible for negotiating all treaties with foreign nations, an authority that would include dealings with extraterrestrial aliens. He thus should be fully briefed on any proposed contacts, contracts, or deals with the extraterrestrials.

(5) If abductions are real, or if aliens represent some other threat to the United States, the president should be getting briefed, as he is constitutionally responsible for the protection of the American people.

The president therefore should know what's going on — and if he does know, his is the final word. Unlike the case with answers from any other government or military official, if the president receives a UFO question and even hints at its seriousness, the cover-up finds itself in deep trouble, because the president is the ultimate authority. No-one safely can stand up later and say the president shouldn't have said what he said, or that he didn't know.

It is probably for this reason that searches of files at the various presidential libraries have produced no UFO files other than some scattered citizen letters to the president on the subject. After a couple of library searches, a researcher easily could conclude that the president never has been involved in the UFO mystery. Nothing, however, could be farther from the truth. The probable reason for the absence of UFO-related records in presidential archives is to conceal the president's knowledge and involvement in the subject. "UFO Politics at the White House" clearly illustrates how this protective concealment ensued in the case of President Carter. The letters were farmed out to other agencies for reply. The president was purposely pulled out of the loop.

The government always has disclaimed any foundation for stories of space ships from other planets, as well as has denied any contemporary serious interest or study on the part of the government. If it be admitted that the UFO problem is one of the subjects on the president's desk, this whole government argument would fade quickly. Remember, too: much of the presidency is about image. Daily care is taken by White House handlers who choreograph a president's every move. As the agent who handles the UFO files at the CIA said, subjects such as UFOs are "controversial and misunderstood" items that carry with them "the ridicule factor." You simply don't want to drag the president down into what is perceived as a no-win issue.

For these reasons it's quite important if and how the president handles the UFO problem. It is this "handling" or "non-handling" of the UFO problem that Larry Bryant has chosen to investigate and expose.

"UFO Politics at the White House" takes careful aim at the extraterrestrial politics of the Jimmy Carter era. In 1976, Carter, then a naive campaigner for the Oval Office, made a promise. In an interview with the National Enquirer, and during a campaign stop in Wisconsin, he promised to release the collection of official UFO data being withheld by the government. That UFO promise led the National Enquirer to publish a related piece in June 1976. This article, in turn, led to a deluge of 9,000 citizens' UFO-related letters into the Carter White House. Larry embarked on a search and found several hundred of these letters. He analyzed them to see how Carter and his executive staff responded to the public UFO queries, and he has presented some of the key letters for all to read. Unfortunately, Larry's accounting of the record shows that Carter did nothing to address the letters that flooded the White House. Most of them never got close to this national leader who had promised never to lie and to tell all about UFOs.

It is my hope that this edition of "UFO Politics at the White House" will reawaken the call for presidential accountability on the UFO issue. If it does, we will have come closer to getting an official, definitive answer to the UFO mystery. If it doesn't, the book still will stand as a truthfully written historical account of government inaction — one that will be read with shame by our children's children.

—GRANT CAMERON
Creator of the Presidents UFO Web Site:
http://www.presidentialufo.com

Introduction

On February 6, 1977, when I addressed my own letter to President Jimmy Carter—the only U. S. president ever to admit having sighted a UFO and the only one ever to endorse in an election campaign the notion that all government UFO data and findings should be released to the public—I had expected to receive no substantive reply. I wasn't disappointed.

After all, considering my then-already twenty years of needling officialdom on its multifaceted failure to grasp the seriousness of the so-called "UFO problem," how could I expect to receive any more than the dismissive, formula response that I've always received? I can understand that I and my fellow long-time critics of the official party line on UFO information should hold no great expectations over rumored or actual revelations by the UFOlogical policymakers in the Executive Branch. And I can understand why our pleas to congressmen to remedy the status quo generally have fallen not on deaf ears but on deft ears—the deftness that tells a senator or representative that the only controversial issues (s)he should support are those that will assure his/her reelection. What congressman in his right political mind is willing to avow that the UFO problem remains the world's latent Public Issue No. 1?

But what I can't understand is why your garden-variety citizen—who's interested not so much in UFOs as in the orderly processes of government (and who therefore expects to receive straight answers to straight questions)—must settle for the same kind of response that your crusading, undaunted UFO critic accepts as routine.

When I sought the records comprising this compilation, I had held the faint hope of being mistaken—that the director of the White House Military Office would've had the courtesy of assuring that each UFO-related inquiry would receive individual attention and point-by-point reply. Again, since my hope was rightly faint, I was only slightly disappointed. For, as the records plainly show, poor John Q. Public, the sincere and trusting American, has received nothing but lip service—or less in some cases.

But lest I turn these prefatory remarks into a time-wasting polemic, let me launch right into those records, so that you might decide for yourself whether the federal government has leveled and is leveling with us about its decades of allegedly passive involvement in the UFO controversy.

The letters represent a cross-section of American citizenry: students and house-wives, professionals and non-professionals, political liberals and conservatives, religious fundamentalists and liberalists, visionaries and pragmatists, con artists and kooks, commercializers and cultists. Some of the letters have a spur-of-the-moment, letters-to-the-editor flavor; others reveal careful planning and construction as either dialectic or a literary spoof. As a whole, they represent a valuable reservoir of contemporary Americana, ready to be savored (if not exploited) by sociologists, psychologists, theologians, and, of course, political scientists.

As for the president's replies—produced by the Presidential Inquiries Office of the secretary of the Air Force—they rarely show any deviation from the stereotype reproduced below. For this reason, I'm omitting them or am excerpting only the more original parts.

The nine-month gestation period of this correspondence confirms that a number of citizens can and do write the president serious letters of inquiry or concern about UFOs. The offspring of that period offers a memorable testimonial to one way we Americans choose to address public issues, and weigh the government's response to them. If from my choice of nuggets and nudges from several hundred letters you can gain some hope for reform in the way officialdom treats the UFO subject, then I will have achieved my purpose in presenting them.

Now, then, let's proceed with our short, sometimes somber, sometimes frolicsome journey through the wonderworld of presidential UFO correspondence, beginning with my letter of Feb, 6, 1977:

Arlington, Virginia

Dear Sir:

By now, you've probably received a number of letters urging you to fulfill your campaign promise to release to the public all heretofore unreleased files, reports, and other data on the federal government's role in the investigation of sightings of Unidentified Flying Objects. And probably all those letters routinely have been referred by your office to Headquarters, Department of the Air Force, for direct reply—despite the fact that the Air Force disavows its continued, formal involvement in the collection, evaluation, and dissemination of UFO-sighting reports; and despite the fact that, back in the days of its UFO public-relations instrument known as Project Blue Book, it persistently denied to newsmen and to other private citizens that the Blue Book managers were arbitrarily and systematically withholding reports from public scrutiny—reports that we now know were marked CONFIDENTIAL and SECRET and that now, in their final resting place at the U. S. National Archives, serve as ample evidence of the official conspiracy to deny public access to them back at the height of the UFO controversy in the 1950s and early 1960s.

Of course, there are some UFO-sighting reports that apparently have never made it into the Blue Book files, wherever those files be stored.

Here are two of them:

• A daylight sighting of a hovering discoid on October 11, 1952, by a Ground Observer Corps (GOC) spotter in Newport News, Va., who relayed the observation to the Richmond, Va., GOC Filter Center, which in turn notified Langley Air Force Base, which dispatched jet interceptors to the scene for what turned out to be an unsuccessful interception. The spotter subsequently was interviewed by a LAFB-based sergeant and told not to discuss the encounter with unauthorized persons, that this was one of the most substantiated flying-saucer sightings on record.

• The night-time encounter with a bizarre object on September 19, 1976, by two Iranian Air Force jets dispatched to intercept and identify the object, which subsequently caused a momentary instrument failure aboard the jets, and which was seen to discharge a spin-off object into an apparent landing trajectory. Knowledge of this classified report was leaked to one or more private UFO-research organizations.

Assuming there are numerous other such hard-core UFO cases as these languishing behind the closed doors of some specially commissioned agency, committee, or project, what use is there in referring this letter to the Department of the Air Force for reply—unless that Department be in charge of that function? Instead, why not examine for yourself the roles of the U. S. National Security Council, National Security Agency, Central Intelligence Agency, Defense Intelligence Agency, and Federal Bureau of Investigation in the continued intelligence analysis of UFO encounters? As a long-time critic of the "politics of UFOlogy," I'm hoping that your examination of those roles would culminate in a formal report of your findings to the public, in the course of which you undoubtedly will have fulfilled your campaign promise to disclose all UFO data now being kept secret by the federal government.

Yours very truly,
LARRY W. BRYANT

P. S.—I'm sending a copy of this letter to a local newspaper, to be published in its letters-to-the-Editor column as "An Open Letter to President Carter."
P.P.S.—If you need additional evidence of the sustained input of UFO-sighting reports into official reporting channels, I suggest that you make a personal check into the number of such reports received during the past 12 months, particularly those dispatched under terms of Joint Army-Navy-

Air Publication 146 (Canadian-United States Communications Instructions for Reporting Vital Intelligence Sightings).

The Air Force reply is dated February 16th.

Dear Larry [sic]:

On behalf of President Carter, this is in reply to your recent letter concerning unidentified flying objects (UFOs).

You should be aware that with the termination of Project Blue Book, the Air Force regulation establishing and controlling the program for investigation and analyzing UFOs was rescinded. Project Blue Book documents have been selected for inclusion in the National Archives in Washington, D. C., and are readily available to any interested parties.

In this regard, the Air Force has no information which is being withheld from the public nor is any additional information available. Since the termination of Project Blue Book, no evidence has been presented to indicate that further investigation of UFOs by the Air Force is warranted. Further, in view of the present constraints on available resources, there is little likelihood of renewed Air Force involvement in this matter.

Hopefully, the foregoing information will clarify the Air Force position on this matter.

Sincerely,
L. E. SEMINARE, JR.
Colonel, USAF

Part One:

The Critics Challenge

An Excursion into UFOrensics

Chapter 1

More UFO Letters to Jimmy Carter

As later published in New York City's Village Voice for October 3, 1977, the following telegram received no reply. Hence, its sender decided to dispatch the accompanying follow-up mailgram, which did receive the standard Air Force "kiss off" reply on August 16. As if to protest too much, Colonel Seminare made a point of addressing one item with a custom-made disclaimer: "Further, the United States military has no record of any military aircraft ever engaging in combat with a so-called UFO."

1-1.

Dear President Carter:
My name is Larry McCann, and I'm the producer of a new television show in New York called "UFO Update." My audience would like to know more about your campaign promise to divulge everything you know about UFOs and your own personal sightings, and we are anxiously awaiting your reply.

1-2.

July 26, 1977
Dear Mr. President:
I've yet to receive any reply to my telegram sent to you regarding your campaign pledge of full disclosure in the area of UFOs and their military connection. I have a vast audience on my television program, "UFO Update," shown in New York over WTVG/TV (Channel 68), and they have the right to know if our military forces have ever engaged in combat with a UFO. Air Force General Benjamin Chiclaw has revealed in the new book published by Doubleday, Situation Red, that the Air Force has lost many men and aircraft pursuing UFOs. I would appreciate a speedy reply to this telegram since the volume of mail from my viewers regarding this matter has been overwhelming and they would like to have an answer.

1-3.

Dear Mr. President:

Congratulations on your appointment to office. I'm kind of proud because I voted for you. I know it's going to take time to do all the things you said you were going to do, but I have a request to make of you. For the last five years I have been reading a lot of articles about UFO sightings in different parts of the United States, and how, when respected citizens report sightings to the Government or Air Force, they are made to feel so silly that they hate they ever made the report in the first place. As taxpaying, United States citizens these people deserve a better shake than they are getting; most of them come forward because they feel it is their duty as good citizens to do so. Another point I would like to make is this: if these objects are controlled craft, and they are surveying our planet, I think we are playing right into their hands by making the public reluctant to report their movements around our cities and towns.

Excuse me right here for second-guessing your reply, but I think you might say that people who sight these objects should report them to NICAP or some similar organization; but many people aren't into reading about UFOs or the organizations that report and follow their movements. When they see something unusual in the sky near their property the first place they call is their local police department, where they usually get (kindly) laughed at and brushed off on the Air Force, who has readymade answers for all UFO sightings; they are either conventional aircraft, a flock of birds reflecting some light, swamp gas (HA' HA'), or the planet Venus. For most people who don't know what they are dealing with, any one of the above answers from an Air Force officer is good enough for them. I think, and I'm sure many other Americans feel this way also, if there is any substantial evidence that any of the sightings can be attributed to objects either intra- or interplanetary, the Air Force should reveal it to us. It is man's nature to be curious about that which goes on about him. It is also man's nature to fear the unknown. In a way, the Air Force is just like the parents who tell their children that storks bring babies, to protect their innocent little minds; but deep down inside they know they can only tell them this for so long, and eventually they are going to have to tell the youngsters the truth. It is high time for the Government agencies concerned to cease suppressing any hard evidence relating to such phenomena and discontinue its policy of attempting to discredit the testimony of reliable witnesses.

Your predecessor, ex-President Gerald R. Ford, while he has a congressman, openly protested the swamp-gas answers the Air Force was giving the public, and stated that the American people are entitled to better explanations. Many people don't know that Capital newsman [AF-deleted] after a lengthy investigation, asserted that the Air Force was withholding facts from the public while at the same time it was publishing incorrect explanations.

I'm quite aware that things have changed somewhat with the special documentary programs that have been on television lately: "UFOs—Do you Believe?" and one more I can't recall the title of. These attempts are merely breaking the ice somewhat, but they are still not the official word that people want to hear from the Air Force.

To recall one last incident, our own astronauts have sighted objects, even though they know a lot more than they are able to tell the police. I believe they saw a lot more than craters on the moon, too. A few more prominent people who have seen or believe in the existence of these objects are people like U.S. Senator [Barry Goldwater], who stated: "I can't believe that in this never-ending universe our planet is the only one with intelligent life. I'm not convinced, after having been around 65 years, that human beings are the smartest creatures in the universe." Being a top-notch pilot with 44 years' experience, he rejects claims that UFOs are imaginary or natural phenomena. "I've doubted stories from many witnesses, but when qualified pilots and other experts tell me they've seen strange, unexplained flying objects, I have to put faith in their reports."

Mr. President, I know you are an honest man, and you don't want the people of our country to continue to be treated like little children who have to be protected by being ridiculed and made to feel guilty when they try to know the truth. I really think we are old enough to handle it in a responsible manner.

Thank You and Good Luck, Mr. President.

Chapter 2

The Theme of
Jimmy Carter's UFOmail

"In a free society, the government's trust in the people has less importance than the people's trust in government."—Larry W. Bryant (2/23/01). *That sentiment happens to run through the entire contents of this compilation.*

1-4.

Dear President Carter:

Some time ago I read in the *National Enquirer* that if you became president you would release all information to the public. I do know that the National Enquirer is not always dependable, but I sincerely hope that this time it is.

I have read several books on UFOs, and I am convinced beyond any doubt that they are not mere figments of the imagination, but actually alien spacecraft from other worlds. My own sightings convinced me even more. I have read (in that same article) that you have seen a UFO yourself.

When I first became interested in UFOs I was very much a skeptic. But now I am completely the opposite.

In these books I have read about government cover-ups, especially Air Force. I have read and I am convinced that both the government and the Air Force do in fact know that most UFOs are alien spacecraft. Of course, I am aware there have been many hoaxes. I have read that the Air Force has even threatened people who have had sightings with good evidence not to talk to the press or anybody about their sightings. This should stop immediately! Why should good, decent citizens be intimidated when they have the right to know the truth?! I am sure that by now you know the truth about UFOs. Of course, I have heard theories that there would be widespread panic, but I believe this is terribly underestimating the common sense of the American people. I believe if the government released, for publication, all UFO information over the course of the next few years it would not come as such a shock. After all, in a recent nationwide poll, 15 million Americans say they have seen a UFO.

I realize UFOs are not a major national concern, so I can't expect you to do anything about it right away. I strongly believe that releasing all information on UFOs is something you can't put off. I have seen that in just your first month in office you are a man of action, and not afraid to do things differently. For this reason I believe if you don't do it, nobody will for a long, long time.

An admirer.

P.S. I think it would be a wise move for the government to help fund the work of independent UFO investigative organizations such as NICAP, MUFON, etc.

1-5.

February 15, 1977

Dear Mr. President:

What are your ideas about resumption of Air Force investigations into UFO reports? Project Bluebook, ended in 1969, approached the entire study with a generally negative attitude. I'd like to see a positive Air Force and university investigative organization that would approach reports with a more openminded attitude.

I feel that if even the possibility of contact with a more technologically advanced civilization exists, we are in debt to facilitate that contact for all mankind.

P.S. Congrats on 1-month in the White House!

1-6.

March 24, 1977

Dear Sir:

Because I am convinced of your sincerity, I am asking you if UFOs are "visitors from outer space"?

I think most of us Americans are capable of dealing with the facts. It is the not knowing that bothers most of us, I think.

1-7.

April 15, 1977 (Reno, Nevada)

Dear Mr. President:

I doubt if you'll ever read this letter because it will be "one" in a thousand. But I will address this letter to you anyway.

I am writing you on a matter I consider very important. And that is UFOs (Unidentified Flying Objects) and the government's secrecy surrounding them so far. I remember your campaign promise concerning UFOs and hope it will be one you will keep.

I do believe the time has come to lift the lid off and release all the information the government has. Does the government in fact have an intact alien spacecraft hidden at Wright-Patterson A.F.B. along with its frozen occupants? As it stands now there is enough eyewitness testimony to say that something is or was hidden at the base.

I realize this information would have to be released slowly because of the effect it would have on some people. But it would be a great step in bringing back an open government—not one shrouded in secrecy.

Reply wanted, please.

Thank you.

1-8.

Dear Mr. President:

I am very glad that you are bringing the government closer to the public.

I have some questions that I hope you will be able to answer.

Since 1973 the subject of "Unidentified Flying Objects (UFOs)" or "Flying Saucers" has been getting more and more into the minds of the American people.

The 1973 Gallup Poll showed that 51% of the population of the United States believe in UFOs.

Since the U.S.A.F. closed "Project Bluebook" back in 1969, questions have been asked whether "Project Bluebook" was really organized.

The famous "Condon Report," costing the American taxpayer $300,000.00, ended saying that UFOs don't exist.

The report has been rejected by the American Institute of Astronautics and Aeronautics (AIAA) and The American Association for the Advancement of Science (AAAS). Many scientists said that the report was poorly done.

It is believed by a lot of people and scientists that the U.S. government is hiding a lot more than what they are telling to the American public.

Now that you are making the government to be closer to the American people, I would like to know if:

1) Are you going to release all or most of classified government reports on UFOs?

2) Will there be a new government investigation into the UFO mystery?

Only this time it should be under a civilian operated plan rather than a military plan (military plan is U.S.A.F. Project Blue Book).

I hope that you will be able to answer my questions.

1-9.

March 14, 1977

Dear Mr. President:

I was among the millions of Americans who had a question for you during your recent correspondence with the American people by telephone.

My question is not related to economic problems that face our country, but one I think needs a sincere scientific surveillance. As you may recall, in 1968 the Armed Services Committee of the Senate accepted the Condon Committee Report on unidentified flying objects and closed Project Blue Book. The Condon Committee's findings are not widely accepted by the scientific community. Project Blue Book was the Air Force's investigative committee which dealt with the UFO phenomenon for over 25 years. Many scientists today are convinced there is a need for a further scientific investigation into the subject. It is my understanding that you, Mr. President, sighted a UFO personally. Was this sighting reported to an authority who explained your report in a satisfactory manner and in a scientific way?

I teach astronomy and am Director of a Planetarium and an Observatory and consider myself a scientist. I do realize that UFOs have tremendous popular appeal and, unfortunately, "sell well." I am not interested in this aspect of it at all. At present, these phenomena exist only as reports which are frequently observed by very responsible people throughout the world. It is my objective to see that someday, somehow, we might find answers to these reports in the same way we have solved many previous scientific mysteries over the decades.

May I please call your attention to a very active organization engaged in scientific research in an attempt to solve these phenomena—the Center for UFO Studies, P. O. Box 11, Northfield, Illinois, under the directorship of [J. Allen Hynek], Astrophysicist, at Northwestern University. Dr. Hynek was the Air Force's chief consultant for Project Blue Book for 25 years. A member of Stanford University Department of Physics and Astronomy recently polled members of the American Astronomical Society, and the consensus is that there is a need for a solution to the UFO problem.

France is presently leading the world in UFO investigation. Their group, sponsored by the French government, is engaged in full research in the UFO field. As an example, Dr. [AF-deleted], Chief of Research for the French National Center for Scientific Research, and his colleagues are experimenting with magneto-hydrodynamic aerodyne systems which may someday help explain the motions of crafts within the confines of an atmosphere without sounds or sonic booms.

As a scientist, I am sure that you agree there is a need for us to find out more about the natural world in which we live and the space beyond.

Will you consider recommending to Congress that they at least look into the problem again in a sincere way and consider the possibility of re-opening Project Blue Book or preferably something even more progressive that would again put the United States as a leader in another active field of scientific research? Private funding is simply inadequate in accomplishing these goals.

I appreciate the opportunity of corresponding with you and I look forward to your reply.

Chapter 3

Know Thyself!

Poet-novelist Erica Jong once noted: "The common theme that runs through all of my work is the quest for self-knowledge." She added, "My work seems to be about using life as the learning process." As I re-read the 20-year-old manuscript for this book, I realize that Jong's observation resonates with both me and the book's co-contributors (the letter writers themselves). So this chapter continues the book's primary theme (how to cope with the official coverup of the UFO experience) and introduces its secondary theme: the quest for self-discovery, open communication, and mutual understanding between those who know (and share) the Ultimate Secret and those who do not.

1-10.

> Dear Mr. President:
> In the past decade there has been a rash of UFO sightings. The past administrations have disclaimed or ignored these sightings. I would like to know just what stand your administration will take. I personally feel that there are just too many unanswered questions in these sightings to totally ignore the question of their validity. Also, there is the fact that the Air Force refuses to answer several important questions about sightings and the reported presence of UFO on their bases. What is your opinion?

1-11.

> *Evening Tribune*, P. O. Box 191, San Diego, CA 92112
> 23 March 1977

> Dear Mr. President:
> During your campaign for election you promised to release information the government has on Unidentified Flying Objects.
> Could you please advise me of the status of the report.
> Thank you.

1-12.

March 6, 1977

Dear President Carter:

According to an article entitled "EXCLUSIVE—Jimmy Carter: The Night I Saw a UFO," in the June 8, 1976, issue of the *National Enquirer,* you witnessed a UFO in Thomaston, Ga., in 1973. According to the article, you and about 20 people watched it for ten minutes. I have been interested in the mystery of UFOs for a number of years. I have not seen one and do not necessarily believe that they represent extraterrestrial spacecraft. I do believe that there is serious work being done by scientists and reputable civilian UFO study groups in the U.S. and the world.

My question is, Mr. President, do you believe that the government should fund future UFO investigation projects somewhat like the Condon Committee, which studied the problem at the University of Colorado for the Air Force in 1968—69? My feeling is that the Condon Report, released by the Air Force in early 1969, did not satisfactorily get to the bottom of the UFO mystery. The article in the Enquirer stated that you are "convinced that UFOs exist because I have seen one." I would take that to mean that you believe UFOs exist as a rightful phenomenon unexplainable in terms of contemporary physics and does not fall within the scope of misidentification of natural objects.

If you could find time, I would appreciate it if you could tell me if the government has any plans which could be directed in the future to solving this problem once and for all. I might remind you that UFO reports are made nearly every day to various newspapers in the country, to police authorities in local communities, and to various civilian UFO study groups—for example, the Center for UFO Studies headed by Dr. J. Allen Hynek, former civilian consultant to the Air Force's Project Blue Book (which studied UFOs from 1947—1969). The UFO problem is a persistent and continuously intriguing one for the citizens of the United States and those handfuls of scientists who are taking their own time and money to look into the phenomenon.

Thanks for your time.

Chapter 4

Carter's Little UFOletters

Our 39th president—physicist, statesman, humanitarian, and avowed UFO witness— recently has added another milestone to his success: a best-seller memoir titled An Hour Before Daylight: Memories of My Rural Boyhood *(Simon & Schuster). Perhaps the book's popularity will induce him to write a sequel. If so, I doubt you'll find much there about his sighting or its aftermath. Word has it that on a few public occasions he has declined to discuss his UFO legacy. The Jimmy Carter UFO persona: suburban legend, or political liability? Let these letters help you decide.*

1-13.

Dear Mr. President:

During your campaign you made a commitment on several occasions to release much of the government's information on Unidentified Flying Objects. With this in mind I am asking two questions: first, do you intend to fulfill this commitment and, if so, when? Second, do you or defense department officials feel it is in the best interests of this country from a national security standpoint to keep such information from public scrutiny as has been standard procedure in the past?

Having an avid interest in this area and having completed extensive research on aerial phenomena while in college, I can assure you that such occurrences can no longer be confined to the realm of backroom mysticism but rather demand increased scientific study and research. In recent surveys the existence of UFOs is considered a matter of fact by the majority of Americans, and I am confident these people, as well as their critics, are intellectually and spiritually strong enough to be told the full story by their own government. Many people, both lay and scientific leaders, feel that UFOs have enjoyed the longest running cover-up of any happening in America's history. In this age of skyrocketing technological advancement it only follows that this government has a responsibility to let the full facts be known. We cannot any longer be led as sheep and be told nothing exists when the majority of us know there is every real possibility to the contrary.

I am hoping I came across as one intelligent human being to another, and it is my expressed desire that you act responsibly and with due speed in this matter. In the annals of "ufology" you are perhaps the only bright ray of hope we have had.

1-14.

February 1, 1977

Dear Mr. President:

I want to congratulate you on behalf of the North American UFO Organization, Inc., on your historical defeat of President Gerald Ford.

It was indeed an historical event…one that won't soon be forgotten.

I would like to take this opportunity to extend our full support, as a civic minded organization, toward conquering any and all of the crises now facing the nation; such as, energy, unemployment, economic conditions, taxes, trade, etc., as I know they require a great amount of courage and strength to face, even with a nation behind you.

While I know these problems require first and immediate attention, I feel our problem concerning UFOs should warrant your utmost consideration. The National Enquirer quotes you as saying: "and if I become President, I will release to the public all UFO data in the possession of the Government." The director of a leading UFO investigative group, Jack Acuff of the NICAP, Washington, D.C., told the Enquirer: "Material on UFOs is locked up in the National Archives that has never been made public." If a President were to have it released, it would be exciting news to the scientific community and of inestimable benefit to the public; and our organization feels the same way.

Therefore, Mr. President, we are appealing to your sense of fair play and honesty, of which you portrayed throughout your campaign for the President of the United States, in asking that you release all information the Government now has to our organization concerning UFOs.

1-15.

February 1, 1977

Dear Mr. President:

You once stated in an interview, and I quote, "If I become President, I'll make every piece of information this country has about UFO sightings available to the public and the scientists."

I have researched the UFO enigma for several years, and head a small research group conducting statistical studies, investigations, and serious research into this problem. Unfortunately, there are some individuals "studying" UFOs who couldn't tell Venus from the sun: the field attracts kooks like a magnet.

I certainly hope that your statement was not another "political promise." Apparently the government has deceived the American public regarding UFOs in the past (which is thoroughly documented). Now that you have been elected, I hope that this practice will end.

In the event that you need any further information on the UFO phenomenon in general, please contact me.

1-16.

February 4, 1977

Dear Mr. President:

It was reported in the *National Enquirer* that you stated, "If I become President, I'll make every piece of information this country has about UFO sightings available to the public and the scientists."

In your recent televised talk to the American public, you stated that you were going to honor all of your campaign promises. Mr. President, do you intend to honor the above promise?

Having researched the problem of Government documentation regarding UFOs, I am aware of quite a bit of such documentation currently being held by various Government agencies and departments. I would be more than willing to submit specific details of the existence of this documentation to you for any action you deem appropriate.

1-17.

Dear Mr. President:

Previously you told news reporters about your observations of an Unidentified Flying Object (UFO) you had seen over Thomaston, GA in 1973. The details were sketchy, however, offering little availability to determine what the object may have been.

If your sighting was to remain unidentified after close scrutiny, as it has been found that 20% of all investigated sightings do, then your sighting could be classified as an exceptional one from a source whose integrity could not be questioned (though this would not hold true with all ex-presidents, but I'll leave the names to your speculation!).

For this reason I have enclosed a sighting report form with this letter that I would like very much for you to complete if time is available during your hectic schedule. Many thanks.

1-18.

4 February 1977

Dear Mr. President:

During your recent "fireside" chat, you made it clear that you hope to have good communications with the citizenry of these United States. I would like at this time to ask you when we might expect you to carry out a promise made during your campaign last summer.

In its issue of June 8, 1976, the National Enquirer newspaper quoted you as saying "If I become President, I'll make every piece of information this country has about UFO sightings available to the public and the scientists."

Mr. Carter, I have followed the UFO mystery for over 25 years. In that time, I have seen USAF officers make comments about UFO sighters far worse than the comment Paul Rand Dixon made recently about Ralph Nader. I would hope that you will very quickly make "every piece of information" the government has about UFOs publicly available. I would hope that this would include information as to just who in the Federal Government is currently investigating them. Officially, or at least for public consumption, the USAF has been out of it since late 1969, but there are a great many people who feel that theirs was merely the overt investigation and that covertly another agency (a special branch of the CIA has been mentioned by some researchers) has both carried out investigations of UFO reports and harried sighters into not publicly reporting details of their observations/encounters with UFOs. Your assistance in piercing the "Silence Curtain" thrown up around UFO sightings for many years by the USAF and other agencies will be greatly appreciated.

I look forward to hearing from you in the near future.

1-19.

March 3, 1977

Dear Mr. President:

I read in a national newspaper that in an interview you had with Walter Cronkite before you were elected that if elected you promised to release all of the information the government had on unidentified flying objects (UFOs). Mr. President, do you still intend to do this?

I sincerely hope that you do because I feel that the government and the Air Force is keeping the real truth from the American people. I have never seen a UFO, but there have been so many reliable people reporting them, including astronauts, I believe that something must exist and that these people are not seeing things. Some people think that if the government were to say that the earth was being visited by extraterrestrials it would cause a worldwide panic, but I think this is pure nonsense! At any rate I hope you can fulfill this promise to the American people, and if you do I will then have more trust in our government. I am very patriotic, and I have great hopes for you and your administration. Good luck! P.S.: I had intended to ask you this on your forthcoming radio program, but since it is being held on a Saturday I will have to work and be unable to phone in.

1-20.

May 9, 1977

Dear President Carter:

I am writing to you this evening to ask you a favor. Would you please divulge to the public all the UFO information, evidence, and artifacts that our government possesses?

I ask this favor encouraged by a recent article in *U.S. News and World Report,* April 18, 1977. This article, in the "Washington Whispers" section, promises that the government will reverse its previous debunking policy on UFOs and give us, the public, the true story via CIA findings.

I ask you, Mr. President, to please let us know all the truth as soon as possible. Many of us private citizens have devoted many years to solving this "elusive phenomena."

Although you, personally, will probably never see this letter, I feel I can still write it knowing your administrative staff will at least give me an honest answer, which I know I never would have received before.

I thank you for taking the time to read my letter, and I hope to hear from you soon.

1-21.

April 13, 1977

Dear Mr. President:

I was surprised to learn about your intended action concerning UFOs.

The magazine *U.S. News & World Report* states that the President himself would disclose information on UFOs that will astound and surprise the American public. Is this information derived from the Project Blue Book or any other governmental projects? Or is this new information that has been kept from the public? As the magazine reports, Mr. President, you will disclose this information towards the end of the year. Is this a true statement?

I am concerned about UFO activity in the U.S. and their meaning of existence. I would appreciate a letter of reply. May I thank you for being concerned over this important matter. Thanking you in advance for a quick reply.

Chapter 5

The Carter Administration's UFO Evidence

This installment of the book as serialized upon the Internet provides us an intellectual time machine. It allows us to fast-forward to the near future when, finally, our government yields to the people's demand for immediate, full disclosure of UFO-E.T. reality. For a symbolic tracking of that disclosure process—expected to intensify during the next several months—visit the websites of http://www.paradigmclock.com *and* http://www.x-ppac.org

1-22.

Note: So far as can be determined, no Air Force reply was made to the following followup letter sent by a persistent correspondent to Colonel Seminare.

31 March 77

Dear Colonel Seminare:

Thank you very much for your letter of March 28th responding to my letter to President Carter concerning UFOs. Your letter raises some questions in my mind which I would hope, in view of the President's call for more openness between government and its citizens, you will answer fully.

1. In view of candidate Carter's campaign promise to "make every piece of information" about UFOs available to the public, has the USAF made a formal briefing to President Carter on the subject of UFOs? If so, when? Was this at his request or at the initiative of the USAF? If President Carter has not been briefed, has the USAF briefed any of his staff? Is so, when? If such a briefing was carried out, may I have a copy of the briefing materials? If not, why not? If there has not been a briefing, is one planned? If not, why not? And, who is the person in the White House charged with intercepting UFO letters such as mine and bucking them over to the USAF?

2. Although the USAF has officially been out of the "UFO business" since late 1969, has any ad hoc study been made of the UFO sighting re-

ported in 1973 by then Governor Carter? If so, what conclusion was reached as to the cause of this sighting, and when was this conclusion transmitted to Mr. Carter? If such a study has not been made, are there any plans now to make one?

3. What evidence would the USAF feel would have to be presented "to indicate that further investigation of UFOs by the Air Force is warranted"? Is the USAF aware of or interested in the recent survey of professional astronomers recently released by Professor Peter A. Sturrock? Please note that sixty-two of the respondents said they had seen OR "had made instrument recordings…which…might be related to the UFO phenomenon." Would such "instrument recordings" be the sort of evidence the USAF would consider in deciding if further study of the UFO phenomenon was warranted? If so, to whom should such recordings be sent?

4. Recently there were UFO reports from Southern California; witnesses included seven airmen from March AF Base, two L.A. sheriff's helicopter crewmen, and two California state highway patrolmen. A description of the objects seen by the USAF personnel was provided by Major Brian Daly, March AFB PIO. What action is being taken by the USAF in this case to determine if these reports do or do not constitute the evidence the USAF and/or DOD might require to reopen full-scale UFO investigations?

5. In view of the fact that the USAF is still charged with the air defense of the United States and in view of the further fact that responsible and often highly trained persons in and out of the military are still observing UFOs in the skies, over this country (and elsewhere), is not the USAF abdicating a portion of its responsibility by ignoring citizen reports of UFOs? And what action is taken on UFO reports made by military personnel to their superiors? Surely there must be some sort of an investigation made of reports such as those last week from March AFB, or of reports made by pilots, radar operators, etc.

I look forward to hearing from you in the near future.

1-23.

Dear Mr. President:

As a writer with some ten years' experience with magazines and newspapers, I am now working on a book involving unidentified flying objects. I am primarily interested in sightings involving indisputable sources such as yourself but with the focus on what is being done by individuals and organizations to locate and identify UFOs. I am a member of the National Press Woman's Association and have just been awarded the Margaret McDonald Journalism award by the Louisiana Press Woman's Association.

I am interested in the statement you made to the press during your campaign to release all UFO material to the public. Shortly following this statement the Blue Book material was opened to the public. Were you unaware at the time that the material was to be released or has all pertinent material been released so far as you know? I would also like to talk with you about any plans you might have or of which you might be aware for further investigation by a government-sponsored agency into UFO activity. And of course I would like a brief first-hand account of your own UFO sighting.

Would it be possible to set a time and date for a telephone interview?

I am well aware of your intense schedule and will keep questions as brief as possible if such an interview is possible.

I have already received the co-operation of such notables in the UFO field as Dr. J. Allen Hynek, the Center for UFO Studies, and Dennis Hauck of the International UFO Center.

I look forward to hearing from you in the near future.

1-24.

24 September 1977

Honorable Sir:

I am writing concerning an area of science that has been given cavalier treatment most of the time, but one with much potential value to the country and the future. It concerns Unidentified Flying Objects.

As a matter of introduction I am an aerospace project manager, dealing with state-of-the-art problems on a regular basis. I work quite closely with others in the same field, many that are quite well known, that share my concern about UFOs. We realize the magnitude of the emotions surrounding this subject, ranging from cults of true believers to cults of debunkers. However, in casting those polarized positions aside we find there is a core of interesting unexplained events that could provide an impetus to our technological future. This possibility, based on an accumulation of facts, is too great to ignore.

It appears that we have much to gain and little to lose if we approach the problem in the same way we do with other aerospace problems. That is, to work it like any other technological evolution—airplane design, spacecraft design, missile technology, etc. The past methods of using the military to take the abuse, or a university group to take a casual look, have all failed. On the other hand the projects that have been used by engineers, technicians, scientists, and others as a team have had great success.

My recommendation is to do a technology assessment and from that define specific projects, each with a positive goal of accomplishment, to strive for and expect success.

I am offering my service as an individual or through my employer, should he become involved, to this area of science.

1-25.

April 5, 1977

Dear Mr. President:

As a member of the Commonwealth (of Puerto Rico) House of Representatives, I wish to make you aware of a matter of some importance to the United States, to Puerto Rico, and to the rest of the world as well.

I refer to the controversial sightings of UFOs around the world. As a presidential candidate you told the *National Enquirer* (June 8, 1976), "If I become President, I'll make every piece of information this country has about UFO sightings available to the public and the scientists" because "I am convinced that UFOs exist, because I have seen one."

"One thing is for sure," the *Enquirer* quoted you as saying, "I'll never make fun of people who say they've seen unidentified objects in the sky!"

Inspired by your views on this interesting matter, four young members of our House of Representatives, Hon. Antonio Fas Alaamora, Hon. Roberto Rodriguez, Hon. Freddy Valentin, and myself, introduced a resolution—H.R. 151—whose sole purpose is to create a House special committee to gather statements from citizens who may have evidence on the existence of this type of scientific phenomena.

Our resolution has stirred controversy from several sectors in our community, as well as serious response. The former, probably because the whole UFO affair has been derided by those who make fun of any reports on UFO sightings.

Although there are other important problems to which we devote our time in search for permanent solutions, we feel H.R. 151 covers important ground. An opinion from you on the matter could help to enlighten those among our citizens who have declined to treat the subject with the seriousness it deserves.

With my best wishes for success in your highly important commitment to America's future, I remain,

Very truly yours,

LMA/dpl

Enclosure *[photocopy of the resolution, in Spanish, as depicted below]:*

ESTADO LIBRE ASOCIADO DE PUERTO RICO Sva. Asamblea la. Sesion Legislative Ordinaria CAMARA DE REPRESENTANTES R. de la C. 151 17 de marzo de 1977—

Presentada por los Representantes Fas Alzamora, Mudoz Arjona y Valentin Acevedo

Referida a la Comisio'n de Asuntos Internos—

RESOLUCION

Para crear una Comisio'n Especial que investigue las alegadas apariciones de "OVNIS," objetos voladores no identificados sobre Puerto Rico y todo lo relacionado con este asunto.

EXPOSICION DE MOTIVOS

Durante los pasados aBos ha salido a la luz publica una serie de informaciones sobre supuestas apariciones de "OVNIS," objetos voladores no identificados sobre Puerto Rico. Si bien es cierto que se iniciaron algunas investigaciones privadas sobre este hecho, no es menos cierto que al pueblo de Puerto Rico nunca se le ha dado conocimiento final y concreto de si las alegadas apariciones de los "OVNIS" son meros rumores o realidad.

El pueblo de Puerto Rico tiene derecho a conocer a fondo sobre este particular. Tiene por lo tanto, la C`mara de Representantes de Puerto Rico la^ obligacion de hacerse eco del clamor de la diudadanta y de investigar todo lo relacionado sobre los "OVNIS" sobre Puerto Rico que tanta inquietud ha causado en nuestra "Isla del Encanto."

RESUELVESE POR LA CAMARA DE REPRESENTANTES DE PUERTO RICO:

Seccion 1.- Se crea una Comision Especial de siete (7) representantes, cuatro (4) de ellos pertenecientes al partido de mayorta y tres (3) de ellos partenecientes al partido de minoria, para que investigue las alegadas apariciones de "OVNIS," objetos voladores no identificados sobre Puerto Rico y todo lo relacionado con este asunto.

Seccion 2.- La Comision debera rendir a este cuerpo un informe contentivo de sus conclusiones y recomendaciones a la mayor brevedad posible.

Chapter 6

Carter Hears More
From the UFO Vox Populi

The Carter UFO-disclosure promise reverberated across the seas, drawing favorable response from all walks of life and across all cultural boundaries. As you can see from Letter No. 1-25, some of that response originated from unexpected quarters. Today, we know that Puerto Rico has become a hot spot for UFO activity—and that its legislators have a renewed opportunity to take the lead in demanding greater access to the U.S. government's Pandora's box of hardcore UFO data.

1-26.

Dear Mr. President-Elect:

My name is *[deleted]*. My father is *[deleted]*, who was one of your best campaign workers in , New Hampshire. He convinced me that you were the candidate to vote for.

I am an engineer with *[deleted]*, a division of *[deleted]*. I'm also a volunteer field investigator for the Aerial Phenomena Research Organization, Inc. (APRO). I have never seen a UFO myself. However, I have interviewed many people who I feel have seen one.

It is my understanding that you have seen one and believe that they exist. Also, you have indicated that you would make any government knowledge about them public information. NASA has already taken some steps toward doing this by releasing some photos. Some of these photos have been interpreted by NASA to be of unidentifiable objects.

APRO is a scientific, objective organization which has been investigating this phenomena for some twenty-four years. It is APRO's premise that the UFO phenomenon is important enough to warrant an objective, scientific investigation. Enclosed is an introductory letter which explains APRO.

I realize that at present there are more important problems requiring immediate attention. However, I do hope that eventually you have the opportunity to look into this. I feel that the American public should be made aware of any knowledge which would substantiate the fact that they exist.

Your help in this matter would be greatly appreciated.

The above letter forwards the following introductory handout sheet:

"TO WHOMEVER THIS CONCERNS: *[deleted]* are Field Investigators for the Aerial Phenomena Research Organization (APRO). APRO was founded in 1952 and is the oldest objective organization involved in investigating sightings of unidentified flying objects, known as 'UFOs' or 'flying saucers.'

"Most sightings are misidentifications of aircraft and celestial phenomena. However, many sightings have been reported by sincere and reliable individuals and have been classified as unknown. These individuals have included engineers, scientists, airline and military pilots, military personnel, priests, police officers, factory workers, and U.S. astronauts. Unidentifiable objects were seen and photographed on the Gemini, Apollo, and Skylab space flights.

"It is the Premise of APRO that the UFO Phenomenon is important enough to warrant an objective, scientific investigation. It is hoped that continued investigation will provide more of an insight into this phenomenon.

"APRO is a civilian investigative organization. It is not a part of any government or military intelligence organization. All interviews will be kept confidential if the witness so wishes.

"*[deleted]* and myself would be interested in talking to you or anyone you know who has seen something which he or she feels may be an unidentifiable aerial object. This pertains to both current and past sightings. We may be contacted at the telephone listings below. Feel free to circulate this letter. However, we ask that you do not post this letter in a public place. We wish to only interview serious individuals."

Chapter 7

Jimmy Carter's
Naval (UFO) Intelligence

When it was posted upon the Internet, this chapter presaged a paradigm-shifting press conference held May 9, 2001, at the National Press Club Building in Washington, D.C.—subject: official evidence of UFO-E.T. reality, as disclosed by persons privy to that evidence. Some of the event's speakers formerly served with the Navy. (For a round-up of the ensuing media coverage, visit the website of researcher Paul Nahay: http://pnahay.home.sprynet.com/; click on "Paul's UFO Page.") Certain U.S. Navy agencies/officials have been up to their necks in managing and sustaining the UFO coverup—a fact probably not lost on former Navy officer Jimmy Carter.

1-27.

Dear Mr. President:

I am a 34-year-old NESEP (Naval Enlisted Scientific Education Program) Lieutenant in the U.S. Navy serving in the restricted line, 1610, (Cryptologic Officer) and am writing only as a private citizen. I was formerly an EM 1 (SS) in the Nuclear Power program and have served as an Assistant Weapons Officer on an SSBN. I proudly hail from Valdosta, Georgia.

For eight active years, plus six years of enthusiastic interest, I have followed the UFO phenomena as close as my duties have allowed. In that time, I have investigated a few minor cases; I have lectured in favor of more public awareness and understanding of the matter; I have listened to many different peoples' experiences with the phenomena and have actively corresponded with many of the creditable personalities presently working on a solution to this mystery.

I am aware of the article which appeared in the June 8th, 1976, *National Enquirer,* and I understand that it was probably one of the many low-key interviews conducted during your campaign. The article indicated that you had experienced the UFO phenomena and that you would release any and all information on UFOs which our Government holds, should you be elected. However, the only information the Air Force has ever publicly admitted it had has been released, and no other Department has ever let itself become associated with the matter, at least in the public eye.

There are many who have for years believed, and some still do, that the Air Force's Project Blue Book was a cover-up for some other Air Force project, studies being conducted by the National Science Foundation, NASA, or some other Government-supported agency. There are others who are beginning to see that this was and is probably not the case. This is in itself somewhat disappointing in that not looking into this phenomena may be as foolhardy as attempting to explain all such experiences away as figments of the imagination.

I have heard of sightings which were experienced aboard Navy ships, on board Naval Stations, and by Navy personnel on their off duty time. I have heard of cases where Air Force Officers would speak quite freely of UFOs over cocktails but would at the same time state that to mention such officially would probably jeopardize or end their career. These things happen but the information seldom reaches the people studying UFOs.

In May of 1976, two young French scientists, in search of an explanation as to why some of the reported UFOs could accelerate through or apparently travel faster than sound without a sonic boom, conceived a workable theory allowing for this observed phenomena, a proof that the marriage of science and UFO research can be viable and productive. With no support of such efforts in this country, we will find ourselves playing "catch-up" again in the future, as we did in the 60's with the space program.

I believe that our Government not only needs to make any and all UFO data available, but, further, that official statements should be brought forward declassifying all such data in all forms. Such statements extending to the point of lifting debriefing restrictions on all Department of Defense personnel and other Government Officials who have any knowledge of any data or experiences involved with UFOs or similar anomalies. Further, that any one having such information be invited to bring it forward, and should doubt exist as to the information's possible National Security impact, that they forward that information through their respective intelligence service, who would sanitize it for release to interested investigative bodies.

Such an official attitude would prevent ships' OOD's from saying "Let's not enter this mess in the deck log" and would help generate an acceptance of this phenomena such that much more than 10 percent of the experiences which occur would come forward for review and data base formulation. Such declarations would hopefully bring reams of new reports, which would be a monumental task to sort through, but would be welcome information to aid in the solution of this problem.

In my past duties, and in particular in my present duties, I have become fully aware of this Government's capability of maintaining the classification of information of a National Security nature. In any case I am aware that there may be valuable information concerning UFOs in official documents, logs, and messages that would probably not be released cursorily. Specifically, there are classified instructions within the Departments of Defense and other Departments which require holding back such information which might be found in U.S. Navy ships' deck logs, CIC logs, and/or other records of all classifications.

Through their own efforts, The Center for UFO Studies, of Evanston, Illinois, has made some inroads for "work load permitting" cooperation from some Government agencies. An effort which could be and should be widely expanded through Government action, allowing quick breakthroughs to Department of Defense levels, who could be most helpful, considering their assets.

I propose, in addition to releasing information, that some Department or agency, closely allied to the intelligence services, assign at least one person, with some knowledge of the UFO phenomena, to screening information which may come through the various agencies and further be tasked with reviewing those channels of communications which may produce UFO-related information. In addition, this office could become the liaison between the Government and the public, saving some embarrassment, when, as I feel it must, the public brings this subject back to official door steps.

Over the nearly thirty years of UFO history, the phenomena has remained highly and emotionally argued in the scientific community. Only a few parallels in history can compare with the controversy thus far evoked by this enigma. To present, our self-indulged task has moved very slowly forward due to the pressure of ridicule, official disclaim, and unsubstantiated fear, and, thus, so our future looks without some form of understanding, cooperation, and encouragement. We of the UFO community but ask for that understanding, cooperation, and encouragement.

Chapter 8

The Carter Administration's UFO Merry-Go-Round

If any letter deserves more than a casual glance from officialdom, then it should be this one. Its message—with its multi-signatory authority—remains undiluted with the passage of decades—all the more reason for readers to reproduce it as an e-mail message directed to: president@whitehouse.gov (especially in light of the UFO/E.T.-coverup disclosure process inaugurated at the National Press Club in Washington on May 9, 2001).

1-28.

August 5, 1977

Dear Mr. President:

As we understand it, in keeping with a campaign promise, you had your Science Advisor, Dr. Frank Press, query the Air Force and the CIA as to whether these agencies were withholding any data pertaining to Unidentified Flying Objects (UFOs). Apparently, both agencies responded to the effect they were not withholding any pertinent information on the subject.

Moreover, the CIA has released public statements to the effect that its only involvement in UFO research was the four-day Robertson panel inquiry in January of 1953. The CIA states that following the issuance of the Panel's report, it concluded that UFOs did not represent a threat to national security and therefore discontinued any interest or involvement in the subject.

The Air Force has publicly stated that they also concluded UFOs did not represent a threat to National Security, vis-a-vis their 22-year study of the phenomena and the recommendations of the Condon Committee report, and discontinued any interest or involvement in the subject following the disbandment of Air Force Project Blue Book in 1969. The Air Force also states that all the data it collected regarding UFOs now reposes in the National Archives, where it has been declassified and made available to the public.

Assuming that those statements are accurate, we hereby request that you, Mr. President, issue a statement allowing former military personnel and civilian government employees to speak publicly or privately about their government related UFO experiences, if they so wish, without fear of retribution or censure by the government, so long as they don't reveal non-related classified or proprietary information.

We make this request, sir, in order to satisfy our own research objectives, which include obtaining for study the details of all UFO sightings, photographs, films, and, if it exists, physical evidence. We have been approached by, and have approached, many former military personnel and civilian government employees who would otherwise give us their full and complete testimony, if they did not feel bound and restricted by oaths they took and caveats that were imposed upon them during their government employment.

Since no government agency claims to be currently engaged in UFO research, it seems that we—the civilian research groups—have the responsibility for studying all UFO sightings and attempting to identify them. We accept this task and hereby pledge to conduct a responsible investigation which seeks only the truth, but we strongly believe that a proclamation allowing military personnel and civilian government employees to give us their testimony is vitally necessary in order to reach that objective.

We would greatly appreciate your personal reply.

Respectfully,

The Undersigned UFO Researchers:

W. Todd Zechel (Technical Consultant for Scotia American Productions; New York, N.Y.); Dr. J. Allen Hynek (Former Scientific Consultant to Blue Book and Director of the Center for UFO Studies; Evanston, Ill.); L. J. Lorenzen (International Director of the Aerial Phenomena Research Organization; Tucson, Ariz.); William H. Spaulding (Director of Ground Saucer Watch; Phoenix, Ariz.); Walter H. Andrus, Jr. (International Director of the Mutual UFO Network; Seguin, Texas); Dr. James Harder (Director of Research for the Aerial Phenomena Research Organization; Berkeley, Calif.); James M. McCampbell (Director of Research for the Mutual UFO Network; Belmont, Calif.); Dr. Jacques Vallee (Computer Scientist; Palo Alto, Calif.); Dr. Bruce Maccabbee (Scientific Consultant to the National Investigations Committee on Aerial Phenomena; Silver Spring, Md.); Brad Sparks (Assistant to the Director of Research for the Aerial Phenomena Research Organization; Berkeley, Calif.); Larry W. Bryant (Member, Board of Directors for the International Fortean Organization, Inc.; College Park, Md.); Allan Hendry (Managing Editor for the International UFO Reporter; Evanston, Ill.); Stanton T. Friedman (Nuclear Physicist; Hayward, Calif.)

Chapter 9

Not All Silence Is Golden

Upon perusing this book's e-serialization, researcher Grant Cameron notified the author about his recent discovery at the Carter Library in Georgia. According to the staff there, they have no record of the current whereabouts of some 9,000 UFO-related letters that a few White House staffers had collected in canvass mail bags for a photo session in Washington. At least one of the librarians presumes the collection got destroyed. In his Internet-posted comment about this tragic loss, Cameron also decried the government's near-total lack of responsiveness to the few hundred letter writers whose missives somehow managed to escape destruction.

1-29.

February 7, 1977

Dear President Carter:

I fully realize that you have a great many problems of very high priority to deal with in your first months in office. Knowing this, I hesitate to write at this time. However, 1977 is the thirtieth year of a question, perhaps a problem, that goes unresolved—unidentified flying objects. I understand that you have had a personal UFO sighting and have expressed interest in the subject. I have had no personal observation but have been involved in the investigation of UFO events for several years.

I am an associate of the Center for UFO Studies, which is under the direction of Dr. J. Allen Hynek, Chairman of the Department of Astronomy at Northwestern University and former scientific consultant to the United States Air Force on UFOs. I have worked closely with Dr. Hynek in the study of UFO reports for the past ten years. During this time I have personally investigated over 450 UFO events.

It is a common belief that UFO reports involve only observations of distant lights in the night sky. This is far from the truth. Many of the reports involve very close encounters by several witnesses. Several thousand of these observations were made of objects on the ground.

For the past seven years I have conducted specialized research into cases in which the UFO not only lands, but also leaves a landing site, or traces. I have on file 1,018 physical-trace landing cases from fifty-three countries. On January 20, 1975, I presented a paper to the 13th Aerospace Sciences Convention (American Institute of Aeronautics and Astronautics) in Pasadena, California. The paper deals with high- quality trace landing reports that I have personally investigated. In July, 1975, the Center published a catalog of such cases that I compiled. I would be most happy to send the paper and catalog if you should be interested in seeing some of the "hard" data available on UFOs. The physical traces involve burnt, depressed, or dehydrated areas of soil or plant life. Imprints are found which appear to have been left by a landing gear. In some cases, footprints have been found. Many witnesses have also reported automobile engine failure while the UFO is on the ground or near it. Electrical interference and animal reaction has also been reported. Soil and plant samples have been sent to several laboratories; the results of this testing is on file. There is a wealth of "hard" data available for study.

For the past year I have been exchanging landing reports with Dr. Felix Zigel of the Moscow Aviation Institute in the Soviet Union. I have on file several close encounter reports from the Soviet Union, some involving pilots and scientists. Dr. Zigel has offered to test soil and plant life from landing sites that we have gathered in the United States and Canada. I have received many reports from countries around the world; the foreign activity seems to be quite intense.

I would briefly call your attention to the fact that a former astronaut and newly elected senator from New Mexico, Dr. Harrison Schmitt, has expressed his interest in UFOs. I would quote from a statement by Dr. Schmitt: "It's a viable part of the space program to find out if there's life on other worlds. If the government has any information on UFOs, it should be released to the public—barring anything that might affect national security. We ought to be involved in a search to find out if there's any good evidence that UFOs really are spacecraft that are being piloted by extraterrestrial beings."

That is my reason for this letter. There are many excellent reports in the files of investigators around the world. I would certainly hope that the United States would take the lead in a real objective study of UFOs.

I thank you very much for your time and trouble and wish you great success for the next four years and hopefully for the next eight years.

You have my continued support and best wishes.

Chapter 10

More from the Carter UFOrum

Short-story writer and poet Grace Paley once observed: "As a writer one of your jobs is to bring news of the world to the world." Of course, that insight applies to all writers of UFOletters to public officials. We write, not so much out of a drive for self-expression as out of a drive to communicate, to share concerns and solutions with a world often too preoccupied with other things. Hence, you have the following letters by which to observe the Paley charge in action.

1-30.

CENTER FOR UFO STUDIES
(924 Chicago Avenue, Evanston, Illinois 60202)
April 14, 1977

Dear President Carter:

Enclosed you will find past issues of a new publication, *The International UFO Reporter*. Knowing of your interest in the subject, I am taking the liberty of sending these on to you. Copies of these issues have also been sent to Dr. Frank Press, Director Designate, Office of Science and Technology Policy. I recently spoke with Dr. Press and am eagerly awaiting his comments on this publication. I would greatly appreciate any comments you may have.

JAH/ecp
encl: IUR.

Note: The Air Force's reaction to Dr. Hynek's letter, as entered on a correspondence control form (3 June 1977) was that "This UFO expert is asking for the President's comments regarding his (the 'expert's') monthly publication on UFOs. The AF can neither provide the President's personal views nor tell this expert anything he does not already know."

1-31.

February 5, 1977

Mr. President:

Recently our organization (Ground Saucer Watch of Phoenix, Arizona) has been hearing of your willingness to open a bonafide investigation into the vexing phenomena of unidentified flying objects (UFOs). Most of the previous efforts by the military/government establishment has, in our honest opinion, been anything but scientific or truthful.

Our organization, since its conception, has uncovered absolute proof of a government foul-up and cover-up. The usage of the FOIA (Freedom of Information Act) by our researchers has only substantiated these facts.

We stand ready at the present to supply to a duly appointed, objective research committee, sanctioned by your office, a high volume of data implicating the various intelligence offices of a deliberate UFO conspiracy.

If we can be of further service or supply you with additional data feel free to contact our organization. We are totally cognizant that there are more serious problems existing than the UFO phenomenon; however, we believe that it does need a final objective study to clarify and rectify the misconceptions and the atrocities against the unsuspecting UFO witness.

We hope your tenure as President can be fulfilling; best of luck to you in the future.

WHS/dsp Enc.

1-32.

AF Colonel Seminare's formula reply to the above GSW challenge prompted the following rejoinder from the organization's director.

February 26, 1977

Dear Colonel Seminare, Jr.:

I am in receipt of your letter dated February 16, 1977, and appreciate the speedy reply. Our organization is fully cognizant of the President's schedule, and therefore we did not expect a direct reply from him. The fact that the President has designated a White House liaison officer to answer inquiries and correspondence from the body politic is standard operating methodology for each administration. We also appreciate the careful consideration given to our request; however, with you acting as an intermediary, one question arises: was the President aware of our letter and your reply? Or are we to assume that the President is much too busy to be made aware of verbiage involving the study of UFOs?

Commencing with paragraph three of your letter, we realize that the Project Blue Book records have been relocated to NARS from their previous Maxwell AFB location, and that these same records are available to the public. However, not all the cases are in the NARS files! Obviously I will not take up your valuable tlme and give you a case-by-case list of "missing" evidence. Additionally, our organization can prove beyond any reasonable doubt that photographs, important to our research, have been removed and "lost" from the Air Force files. There is sufficient evidence to show that this important data is in the possession of certain intelligence agencies.

We are well aware of the Colorado Project results on the study of unidentified flying objects and its biased findings. For your information, the late Dr. Condon, who headed the project, spent the majority of his energies and the taxpayers' money on subjective, ridiculous abduction (contactee) cases and very little effort on the hard-data-type incidents.

There was extreme turmoil in the ranks of this project, which resulted in the firing of certain members of the study, prior to the conclusion of the same. You have listed three well-known conclusions by the Condon Committee, which are only opinions and not factual statements.

Realistically, how could an objective body of scientists reach the conclusions that UFOs categorized as "unidentified" (Unknown) are not extraterrestrial vehicles, when the project studied only ninety (90) cases and found close to fifty percent of them "unidentified"? These conclusions are well defined by the Colorado Project's voluminous writings. With reference to your letter statement that "No UFO reported, investigated, and evaluated by the Air Force has ever given any indication of threat to our national security," this surely must be an oversight on your part, as on December 24, 1959, the Inspector General of the Air Force released a directive to all commands, a warning to treat sightings of UFOs as "serious business" related to the nation's defense.

Additional data exists in the form of military/government documents, which state flatly that UFO sightings are related to the defense and security of the United States. Some of these include the Navy's MERINT document 94-P-3B and the Joint Chiefs of Staff document JANAP 146E.

In 1969, when Project Blue Book officially terminated its active phase of UFO investigation, one must assume that the UFO subject has been solved and there is no residuum to warrant a further investigation or to spend additional dollars on the subject. If the official position of the United States government is that UFOs do not exist, after two decades of study, why is information being suppressed?

Our organization is fully cognizant of your position, and it is not our intent to argue the Air Force's public relations policy on UFOs. However, we feel we have sufficient evidence to prove that the subject is not a dead one, that covert operations have transpired, outside the Air Force's investigation, and that the evidence is strong enough to warrant Congressional hearings on the subject.

As the fourth largest civilian UFO organization in the United States and with our twenty years of scientific investigation experience, we are well aware of the contents of Gale's Encyclopedia of Associations.

To be perfectly honest with you, we were expecting a better reply than we received, one that was devoid of all the PR and insincere grandiloquent rhetoric that we have been receiving during the past years. I hope you realize that your detailed reply, although appropriate for the body politic, does *not* begin to answer a multitude of unanswered UFO-oriented questions.

I hope you realize that our research efforts are serious, and we plan to continue with the same until all segments of the UFO enigma are made public. After all, if UFOs do not officially exist then what possible logic is there behind the continual data suppression tactics by all governmental agencies?

We appreciate your time and the information previously sent.

Chapter 11

The Carter White House: Habitat for UFOmystic Data?

A 17th-century German chemist, Johann Joachim Becher, noted: "The chemists are a strange class of mortals, impelled by an almost insane impulse to seek their pleasure among smoke and vapor, soot and flame, poisons and poverty; yet among all these evils I seem to live so sweetly, that may I die if I would change places with the Persian King." Ask Missouri UFOlogist Ted Phillips (author of Letter 1-29) if he agrees that what goes for chemistry, goes for UFOlogy! Might he trade places with, say, the president of the United States only if he could continue to practice UFOlogy?

1-33.

Note: To complete this round of fruitless dialectic, the following letter, written by a Washington. D.C., physicist, elicited the same response that Ground Saucer Watch's follow-up letter received from Colonel Seminare's office: silence.

April 19, 1977

Dear Colonel Seminare:

I have been sent a copy of your response to GSW, Inc. (your letter dated February 16, 1977). I am also aware of similar responses that you have sent to others who have written to the President in regard to his UFO statements during the campaign. I'm afraid your responses have not been very satisfactory to those of us who have studied and are well aware of the previous governmental research and of the present UFO situation with regard to the government.

As I understand it, the core of your answers to UFO queries is (a) the Air Force has turned over all of its documents to the National Archives and has therefore "come clean" vis-a-vis UFOs; and (b) the Air Force is no longer involved with UFOs. We are completely familiar with the statements which you have echoed that (1) no UFO reported, investigated, and evaluated by the A.F. has ever given any indication of threat to our national security; (2) there has been no evidence of technological developments or of scientific

principles beyond the present range of knowledge in any UFO reports evaluated as "unidentified"; and (3) there has been no evidence that the "uniden-
tifieds" are extraterrestrial vehicles. I note that you apparently are impressed
with the Colorado report and the fact that the reviewers from the National
Academy of Sciences "concurred with its scope, methodology, and findings." I am also well aware of the many UFO research groups that are listed
in public documents. I am also aware of several groups that consist of scientific personnel and that are not listed anywhere for fear of the peer ridicule
that was at least in part nurtured by the Air Force after 1953.

I submit that you yourself are not fully aware of the UFO situation.

For example, if the Air Force is no longer involved with UFOs, why
was it left to an Air Force officer (yourself) to respond to questions to the
President? Why was not a scientific advisor chosen to respond to queries
about a subject which, I think it is universally agreed, should be a scientific,
not an Air Force problem? By whose authority do you respond for the President? This question is deeper than just asking who is your superior officer; it really goes back to the "executive agency" referred to in your letter to
Mr. [AF-deleted]. Did said executive agency decide the Air Force should respond because of tradition or for some other, perhaps more suspicious,
reason (e.g., "cover up" of work going on in other agencies)?

With respect to (a) above (the A.F. has released all documents): I would
say that I tend to agree, although I certainly couldn't prove that the A.F. has
released all documents available to Project Blue Book (but not necessarily
to the A.F. higher commands) up through 1969. However, as I shall prove,
there are newer documents (I am enclosing a copy of one such)! I have been
to the Archives to see these released microfilm documents (have you?). It
becomes clear from these documents that the Air Force Office of Special
Investigations (AFOSI), the CIA, the FBI, the Office of Naval Intelligence,
have all been involved since the "inception" of UFOs in the late forties and
early fifties. UFO documents from these agencies (except for the AFOSI)
have not been released. In the A.F. documents that have been released one
can find evidence that tends to contradict conclusions (1) and (2) (above)
of Project Blue Book. (Conclusion (3) of PBB is more or less spurious, since
the only way to prove extraterrestriality would be to follow a UFO to an
extraterrestrial location; the failure to prove extraterrestriality does not
mean that there is no fundamentally unusual phenomenon or phenomena
occurring.) As an example of such evidence I am enclosing for your perusal a copy of a recent paper I have done on Project Blue Book Special Report No. 14 that was done under A.F. contract by the Battelle Institute during the time period 1952-54. The report was published (100 copies circulated
to Air Force bases and military and intelligence commands) in 1955. It has

since been cited by Project Blue Book as "proving" that UFO reports don't correspond to a unique type of phenomena. Since I fear that you may not be fully aware of the many aspects of UFO phenomena and the government interaction with it, I suggest you read this document as well as Ruppelt's book and Hynek's recent book. At the very least read the Addendum to my paper. I describe there a "covered up" UFO report made by five people, two of whom were aeronautical engineers from the Ames Research Laboratory.

With respect to (b) above (no continued A.F. involvement), I submit that you are wrong in the explicit sense of no A.F. involvement. I agree that there probably isn't, and probably won't be, an A.F. agency such as Project Blue Book that collects UFO reports from military and civilian sources alike. However, I know that documents that could be classified as UFO reports are still circulated via the A.F. to various A.F. commands and to various intelligence agencies. May I suggest you check up on the status of JANAP 146, related to Communications Instructions for Reporting Vital Intelligence Sightings (CIRVIS).

Perhaps you yourself are not aware of what the A.F. is doing. If so, you may choose to remain unaware. But, in the event that as part of this "open administration" feeling that is permeating the U.S. government (e.g., the Freedom of Information Act), you wish to find out for yourself what is going on, I am sending you a copy of a teletype sequence about a report made at Loring AFB, Maine, dated 31 October 1975. You might find it quite instructive to trace down the departments of the various agencies to which copies were sent. You may note immediately that several AFOSI offices got copies. Although the wording does not explicitly state "UFO'! anywhere, nevertheless the "identification" as an "unknown entity: unidentified aircraft sighted at low level . . ." suggests that in earlier times PBB would have gotten a copy. Note that this "aircraft" was not identified according to engine type or size, as one might expect from any ordinary aircraft that was under observation occasionally for about two hours. Also, one might ask what sort of aircraft would fly at 100-ft. altitude at night over a munitions storage area. In relation to this report, I would like to know whether or not any government agency did anything with it other than file it. Maybe you can find out. Or if not, maybe you can at least find out why you can't find out! Also, in relation to this report, I obtained it from an A.F. source which I consider credible. In other words, I don't believe the report is a hoax.

I am aware of other more recent reports circulated via teletype. One of the more interesting involved Iranian jets that sighted an object on the night of September 19, 1976.

I hope that this information I am supplying to you will be of use to you in doing your job. I realize that you probably cannot respond to inquiries in any way other than the A.F. "line," but you yourself may wish to know whether or not you are unwittingly partaking of a "cover-up." If you should find out anything from your own personal investigation I would very much like to know about it. As a scientist I am bothered by the thought that potentially useful data is just being filed somewhere and ignored. But somehow I just can't buy that. It seems to me that someone, somewhere in the government is still involved. But where? Who? . . .

In view of the possible delicacy of your position should you find out that the A.F. "line" is not necessarily straight, I will keep this letter to you confidential and look forward to your response. In your response you can inform me as to whether or not you wish to have this letter and your response circulated among interested parties (e.g., GSW, Dr. Hynek, other scientists).

Thank you for your time. I hope you have a chance to read my paper and . . . good hunting!

P.S.: *U.S. News & World Report* of April 18, 1977, pg. 11, has in its "Washington Whispers" column a statement concerning the possible release this year of CIA-related UFO information which will be "unsettling" and a "reversal of official policy."

Chapter 12

Carter's UFOtruth
or Consequences

In this final exchange for Part One, consider this White House comment unearthed by Grant Cameron:

"Whatever statement you saw concerning President Carter's view on UFOs was not exactly what he said. He had seen something that he thought was unexplainable that possibly might have been a UFO, and he will certainly disclose and describe any unusual phenomena he might see. He is committed to the fullest possible openness in government and would support full disclosure of material that was not defense-sensitive that might relate to UFOs. He did not, however, pledge to 'make every piece of information concerning the UFOs available to the public.' There might be some aspects of some sightings that would have defense implications that possibly should be safeguarded against immediate and full disclosure."—Walter Wurfel (Carter deputy press secretary); February 28, 1977

1-34.

   Note: On June 5, 1977, Canadian UFOlogist Harry Tokarz wrote direct to President Carter's Press Secretary, Jody Powell, seeking answers that Air Force spokesmen were ill-equipped (or disinclined) to provide in their formula response to UFO-oriented presidential inquiries. Tokarz's letter and the White House reply from Jim Purks (special assistant for media liaison) were published in the October 1977 issue of Saga magazine's "UFO Report." They are reproduced here along with Tokarz's letter of September 11, 1977, to Dr. Frank Press (head of the White House's Office of Science and Technology) and the latter's reply of September 22.

   Since this exchange of correspondence, the administrator of NASA publicly acknowledged receiving the formal tasking from Dr. Press to produce recommendations on which way the federal government should go from here as to a renewal of publicly funded UFO research.

June 5, 1977

Dear Mr. Powell:

I am writing to you regarding a matter of utmost importance, and I trust you will see fit to look into it and respond. As part of President Carter's campaign promises and victory speech, he stated implicitly that there would no longer be "cover-up" situations and that neither he nor his aides would knowingly lie to the public. As a Canadian citizen, I and many others are concerned because the U.S. policies on this delicate subject directly affect us here, since we are under NORAD's defence. I am referring to disclosures about UFOs. It was very disparaging to hear that Jim Purks was recently quoted as denying the contents of an article in U.S. News & World Report (April 18). I know that the statement made in this article came directly from you, so I consider the source authoritative and reliable. What gives? Are you people doing an "about-face" as so many administrations before you? The time for the truth is now, and I suspect that the CIA has put a "clamp" on this story that leaked out and that the President, regardless of his honesty, has succumbed to pressure in this matter and fallen down on his promises. May I remind you that in 1973, as governor of Georgia when he himself had a sighting he stated publicly that "if I become President I will release all information to the public on UFOs." The public can no longer be conned into thinking that all UFO data is now available for public scrutiny at the National Archives. Project Blue Book was nothing more than a public relations campaign, and you know it! Furthermore, UFO investigations and evaluations, as well as UFO policy has always (since 1953) been handled directly by the CIA and OSI. The public is entitled to the complete story on this global phenomenon, regardless of the consequences. Remember, the greatest possibility of panic will come from ignorance and not from education!

I am sure that if President Carter is given the complete story on UFOs by the CIA, he will make a public statement on the subject. After all, he has shown great candor in all other areas. However, many people suspect that the CIA is withholding this data even from him, and this calls into question who is really running the country. How many more years must unwitting people be traumatized by UFO encounters, simply because they were brainwashed into thinking they were fictitious, only to have a harrowing experience with them. The records show something on the order of 100,000 documented "close encounter" cases in the last 15 years, with 15 million Americans having witnessed a UFO (Gallup poll).

When we eliminate all the misinterpretations we still have an astronomical figure enough to prompt the President to make all the "unsettling disclosures" direct to the public. It seems that the Canadian government is awaiting Carter's decision on this matter and will probably follow suit as soon as a public statement is finally made by the White House or the Pentagon.

Thank you for your time. I hope the public is not disillusioned by this administration. I look forward to an honest reply.

Note: And, lo!—Mr. T's plea actually did elicit a response, as follows:

June 14, 1977

Dear Mr. Tokarz:

Thank you for sharing your concerns on information about Unidentified Flying Objects (UFOs) with Jody Powell, in your June 5th letter. You can be assured there has not been a "cover up," nor an attempt at one in the Carter Administration.

When President Carter took office he asked Science Adviser Frank Press to look into the UFO situation and determine if government information was being withheld. Dr. Press determined that government information on UFOs had been declassified and is now part of a 22-year compilation of reports that is public record and available for citizens to examine, or to purchase at a cost of $1,700 for the total record, at the National Archives.

Dr. Press also checked with the Central Intelligence Agency following the single, unattributed paragraph in the U.S. News & World Report issue, and the CIA said there are no further revelations to be made. I suggest you contact U.S. News & World Report directly concerning the accuracy of the unattributed paragraph. Also, as you know, the President appointed a man of the highest integrity, Admiral Stansfield Turner, in charge of the CIA and has great confidence in his work.

It might be helpful to review the overall situation. The CIA said it has not been involved with UFO reports for about 25 years. Over 20 years ago, the Air Force requested the agency to conduct a comprehensive study on UFO reports. A special group was formed at the CIA to determine if UFOs, or whatever they might be designated, constituted a hazard to the national security. This group issued a report, which is available to the public, stating there was no hazard to the national security. The U.S. Air Force disbanded a special unit in 1969, after a similar study determined there was no threat to the national security and UFOs were not a Defense Department matter.

Reports of UFO sightings are directed to local law-enforcement agencies, and this has been helpful. For example, a very recent report in Maryland was traced by the local authorities to some aerial advertising that was being done. I hope this information is helpful to you. As I said, the President is noted for his candor and, if he feels something is being covered up, he will speak out.

1-35.

September 11, 1977

Dear Dr. Press:

Enclosed please find some correspondence from Jim Purks with regards to my inquiries re the worldwide phenomenon of UFOs. Reading these replies may help you to establish how the entire "public information" issue on this highly important subject has been deliberately confused—and *directly* by none other than the CIA! I believe Mr. Purks, through Jody Powell, has honestly replied to these serious queries "to the best of his knowledge." However, as most of the informed public well knows, the CIA's reply is not only erroneous, but false and misleading. In my scientific quest for knowledge about UFOs, I have been directed to you for inquiries. Perhaps you may be more adequately advised on this topic, having dedicated your career to the sciences, a field that most certainly should not involve "cover-ups."

As a Canadian citizen, government suppression of UFO information concerns me because we are under NORAD's defense; therefore, the data should be made public through the U.S. Pentagon. The prominent Dr. J. Allen Hynek of Northwestern University has stated many times that "there are more sightings per capita in Canada than any country in the world"; and this situation has not only raised public consciousness in this country but has created quite a stir for answers—answers which have been closely guarded by the CIA for 30 years. Undoubtedly you have been advised of a most spectacular incident, yet not unique, that involved the scramble of two F-104 Jets from Selfridge AFB in Michigan to intercept a UFO over Ontario, Canada, in October of 1975. A more dramatic incident occurred in September of 1976 over Iran—this one involved direct hostility on the part of "another intelligence," not to mention the hostile attempts of the two pilots in the American jets involved. What should be of particular interest to a man of science in the latter case is the fact a "piece" of an unknown craft was obtained and is now under analysis at a U.S. Air Force Base in West Germany. This is documented, and there is not a shadow of a doubt about the so-called "reality" of this incident.

Perhaps you can enlighten me, after thirty years of government and civilian scientific investigation into UFOs, as to the *exact* reasons for the cover-up. Ignorance only breeds fear, and perhaps it's about time the CIA stopped being the "watchguards" of our "tender psyches." The evidence is overwhelming now with thousands of close encounter cases well investigated, as well as an abundant host of physical samples currently under analysis in various laboratories. The French government have now equipped all military as well as civilian police (gendarmie) with complete instruction manuals on how to properly investigate alleged UFO encounters…and publicly admit it! Sounds very progressive. Perhaps the White House is right now preparing an official announcement on this matter. I'm sure that many feel it's long overdue—particularly the millions who have claimed direct experiences with these mysterious craft of unknown origin.

I look forward to your sincere and educated reply.

Note: And, once again, Mr. T's persistence paid off:

September 22, 1977

Dear Mr. Tokarz:

I have your letter of September 11 related to your previous inquiries to Jim Purks, Special Assistant for Media Liaison at the White House, concerning the worldwide phenomenon of UFOs.

I appreciate your interest in and concern about this phenomenon. While our office has had a number of public inquiries on this matter since its reestablishment in 1976 we have not become involved in it in a scientific way. Therefore, I do not believe we can give you the kind of information you are seeking.

Both to establish a central place in the Federal Government to which the public can direct their questions on UFOs, and possibly to initiate a new program of serious scientific investigation on UFOs, we have recently recommended that the National Aeronautics and Space Administration become the lead agency for these activities. They have agreed to handle public inquiries, and at present also have under study a review of UFO activity during the past ten years. If, as a result of this preliminary review, they conclude that a new full-scale scientific investigation of the UFO phenomenon is warranted they will present the case for such a study. Their determination on this will probably not come before the end of the year, at which time their decision and any plans will be announced.

There is no doubt that a great deal of confusion and doubt has been generated by the handling of this matter over the years. We hope to begin to correct this in the months ahead. We hope you will bear with us while this matter is studied and a new approach is developed for dealing with it in ways that will satisfy both public needs and the requirements of a proper scientific investigation.

Part Two:

The Fanatics
Fan the Flames

Melodrama From the UFOlorn

Chapter 13

Disclosure Rationale and Strategy

As we begin Part Two of this serialized compilation of letters to the president on UFOs, perhaps you'll find pertinent this insight of novelist Tim O'Brien: "We give ourselves over to what is by nature mysterious, imagining the unknowable, and then miraculously knowing by virtue of what is imagined." He's of course referring to the craft of fiction, but he might just as well be considering poetry and other nonfiction—especially that prose which seeks to persuade others to help resolve a public mystery.

Back in the fifties/sixties/seventies, one such persuader-crusader, Dr. Leon Davidson of White Plains, New York, happened to emerge from the ranks of science. Armed with the (imaginative?) conviction that most of the reported UFO-encounter cases could be attributed to secret U.S. military-engineered craft, Davidson proceeded to badger a particular agency with his letters demanding confirmation of his conviction.

Curiously, that recipient of his persuasion—the U.S. Central Intelligence Agency (as revealed by CIA records freed-up via the Freedom of Information Act)—chose not to dismiss him out-of-hand but rather evinced some discomfort about his targeted tenacity. Whether the indefatigable Davidson ever bothered to include Carter on his list of correspondents remains to be determined.

2-1.

July 1, 1977 (Subject Matter: The UFO Situation)

Dear Mr. President:

I had nearly completed a treatise concerning the UFO subject, detailing its significance, aspects of its history, and current manifestation both national and worldwide, etc., in an attempt to present the subject clearly and precisely in the hope of justifying UFOs as a matter of sufficient importance to warrant serious attention by the President. However, a friend recently called to alert me to *U.S. News & World Report* magazine of April 18, 1977, in which there appears, on the "Washington Whispers" page, a headlined article which states that there may be official word coming on UFOs toward the end of this year and that data compiled by the C.I.A. will be presented. If I assume this information to be correct, there appears to be no need to burden you with a lengthy review of the subject since there is apparently both awareness and concern on your part.

In addition to this *U.S. News* piece, the June 8, 1976, edition of the National Enquirer carried a feature article which reported on your personal UFO sighting, quoting you as saying, "If I become President, I'll make every piece of information this country has about UFO sightings available to the public and the scientists," and, "I am convinced UFOs exist because I have seen one." This Enquirer article, along with the fact that you now have access to C.I.A. and other intelligence films on the subject (which I feel must exist) leads me to give additional credibility to the *U.S. News* piece and to go on the assumption that you have already ordered and received a detailed "Estimate of the Situation" type of report on UFOs from the intelligence community. Therefore, I will dispense with much of my original educationally oriented preliminary commentary and will simply attempt to zero in on the heart and essence of the matter I can only hope that my assumptions are correct.

At the outset, may I suggest that we not just make an announcement revealing the reality of UFOs to the American public and essentially leave it at that. The subject is too profound, the public interest both here and across the planet is too great, and the emotional reactions of the people to such a revelation are potentially too complex and disturbing to leave the subject with simply one set of remarks, however detailed in nature—if such is what is planned.

I predict that the public response will be large and that the questions which will be raised will be very numerous and fundamentally sound.

These questions will require answers which can be handled adequately only by individuals who have researched the subject in great depth and who are also aware of its potential psychological, social, religious, and philosophical impact on the public. Those of us who are in the social sciences are well aware of the nature of culture shock and the possible severity of its effect. In this particular instance relating to the UFO subject, the public has had a good deal of exposure and is partially prepared, but that preparation is still grossly inadequate, I feel, considering the enormous portent for mankind which the UFO subject holds.

Any statement coming from the top level of government is highly credible to the American people, especially now that your administration has begun to earn the widespread reputation of straightforwardness and honesty. With this in mind, a statement which reveals to the public that their country and their world is, and has been for some prolonged period of time, under surveillance by intelligent beings of highly superior capabilities, originating from some unknown point or points in outer space (or other dimensional space), operating in craft having fantastic performance characteristics, able to penetrate with impunity the air and military defenses of any nation, etc.,...will be emotional dynamite.

These will indeed be "unsettling disclosures," to quote U.S. News. Even if a qualifying statement is added, such as "these superior beings apparently are not hostile and do not appear to pose a threat to the security of the United States," the effect is still enormous.

I believe that the American people have the right to expect from their government something approaching an educational program emanating from a center established for this purpose and for the purpose of investigating the entire UFO subject. This would be a place to which they could direct their questions and expect to receive adequately researched answers in the form of periodic statements, bulletins, documentary films, and comprehensive evaluations. This is especially important, considering the fact that it is their own government which has created the present condition of ignorance and confusion by withholding UFO evidence for 30 years and by having allowed its military and intelligence agencies the liberty of issuing and promoting misleading and deceptive statements during this time.

Therefore, in addition to making an official announcement on UFOs to the American people, I am suggesting that we set up a Presidential Commission for UFO Research. This Commission would have as its duties the monitoring, investigation, and research of the entire spectrum of the UFO phenomenon, and the education of the American public concerning the significance of the UFO subject, especially as it relates to the possibility of contact with highly advanced extraterrestrial civilizations. This UFO office would also handle all mail concerning UFOs and prevent any additional burden being placed on the President's staff. I will provide more detail on this proposal later in this communication.

I am a psychologist who has been investigating the UFO subject for many years, have given numerous lectures on UFOs to the public, and have had many private discussions with persons whose occupations and professions range from astronomy and astrophysics to agriculture and law enforcement; and I find that the interest across the country is very great. Beyond this the quality of the questions which are being asked, some apprehensively and some with great anticipation, is indeed impressive. Other UFO researchers have experienced the same flood of excellent questions and expressions of legitimate concern by the American people, especially since the UFO phenomenon is now getting progressively bolder in our country and our government has to the present time remained ominously silent.

There is much that is happening now in the United States regarding UFO sightings which involve close encounters by Americans with UFO craft that are either close to the ground or which have actually landed. Contact with UFO crew members, the UFO entities themselves, is also occurring more frequently. Although these reports only seldom make the national press, they are clearly indicative of the fact that our country is being subjected to continuing and increasingly bold UFO activity. As an example of this, some of my most recent UFO investigation and research has centered in northern New Mexico, where UFO activity has been intense in recent months. I am working very closely with Police Chief Fernando Rivera of Taos, a competent law-enforcement official and graduate of the F.B.I. Law Enforcement Academy who is very concerned because this activity has centered in and around his town. It has involved, among many other events and other witnesses, one of his own police officers and a nearby state highway patrol officer (with four years' Air Force experience, Sergeant James Bustamante), who were involved in two separate, very close encounters with large cigar-shaped UFOs. Both officers were left badly shaken by their experiences. Perhaps even more important, I have just completed many months of work with a young couple who, with their four-month-old baby, apparently were abducted and taken aboard a huge disc-shaped UFO and subjected to a series of medical-type tests of a painful nature which left numerous vivid marks all over their bodies (the baby, too), yet were given some unusual and very significant experiences while on board the UFO which reveal a great deal about the basic character and disposition of the UFO entities.

Deep hypnosis was necessary to unlock a two-hour period of amnesia which the couple suffered for part of the experience. This case came to light because the young couple were deeply upset and sought help by calling the U.S. Air Force Academy and they, unable to help, directed them elsewhere. A brief mention of the case eventually made its way to Dr. Hynek, Department of Astronomy at Northwestern University, who telephoned me to see if I would possibly have time to investigate the case and help the young couple.

These interviews have been tape-recorded and are available at your request. But the main reason for bringing these cases to attention is to illustrate that there is much that is happening in our country at the present time regarding close and direct UFO encounters by our people rather than the usual more-or-less distant UFO sightings. These close encounters contain a great deal of information that our government is not receiving because the people have no office they may contact to report their experiences. Given the government's previous stance on the subject, which the public is quite well aware of (although they can't understand why such a position has been adopted), many witnesses are afraid to speak out because they fear ridicule.

The private UFO investigation groups in the country do what they can and manage to contact a few of these witnesses, but the existence of investigative groups is not well known to the public. These private groups also lack the finances to operate effectively, they frequently lack well-trained personnel, and, most important perhaps of all, the results of their investigations remain within their groups and do not become public knowledge.

The UFO witnesses themselves are frequently left highly traumatized by their encounters and often must seek help from the lingering psychological effects of their experiences. They, even more urgently than the general public, need answers to their questions.

Following is a short list of some of the major questions which the American citizen is now asking, now that 30 years have passed since the famous sighting by the pilot Kenneth Arnold in 1947, which introduced the general public to the existence of UFOs and to the term "flying Saucer." Similar questions, multiplied by the tens of thousands, can be expected to flood your office should you make a public statement on the subject:

• What is the motivation of the entities and the civilization(s) which are behind the UFO phenomenon? Why are they here?

• Why haven't they made contact on a governmental level?

• Why doesn't our government speak out on the subject?

• Are the UFO entities hostile or indifferent to our welfare?

• Do we have any defenses against them?

• Are they possibly benevolent?

• Is communication with them possible?

• Do they have societies anything like ours?

• Where do they come from?

• Is there a timetable to their activities here?

• Is that timetable discernible?

• What do they look like?

• Do they have thinking processes and emotions which we can understand? Can they understand us?

• Are UFOs coming to visit us because we ourselves are now, for the first time, venturing into outer space?

• Since they are obviously superior to us, how superior are they?

• Are we like animals to them? Do they hold us in disdain?

And always there arise questions which have to do with religion and UFOs: on whether UFO entities and the societies they represent have any religion at all, on whether they believe in God, love, justice, truth, freedom, compassion. Hesitantly, but frequently, the question is also asked whether the UFO entities know of one Jesus of Nazareth, who was called the Christ and who was crucified here, was transfigured, and was taken up into Heaven to be with his Father.

The American people in their straightforward honesty, realizing that many of their questions cannot be answered, still feel impelled to ask them; for they have a keen sense that if UFOs exist in the skies of our planet, then this is something which is very significant and which may well affect them directly.

Many more questions could be listed other than the sampling given. The public is shrewd and is asking all this and more and even now senses that if there is the possibility of culture contact with the advanced societies which lie behind the UFO phenomenon, then we, as Earth societies, have in the final analysis no control over how and when this potential large-scale contact will occur, that we have no defensive systems adequate to deal with UFOs, and that we are at the mercy of alien motives and programs which may be less than benign. The citizen's questions, their interests and their anxieties, must be adequately dealt with lest we do them more harm than good with our revelations.

My comments are not meant to imply that there will not also be a sense of impending drama, of excitement and anticipation among the people after an official statement informing them of the reality of the UFO phenomenon. This there will be, along with all of the other responses discussed. We live in the Space Age, or more correctly, in the dawning of it, and there has been nothing which has fired the imagination and interest of so many people across the entire planet as our own fledgling entry into outer space. UFOs are, significantly, part of this time and age, and the interest level is high.

A Proposal to Establish a Presidential Commission for UFO Research and Investigation:

For the foregoing reasons and others which I will delineate below, I am proposing that we establish a Presidential Commission which will monitor, investigate, and evaluate the UFO phenomenon in all of its aspects and which will report regularly to the President, the American people, and to the world public.

Such a Commission would be able to exercise many functions, among them to be a center to which the American people may address their questions on UFOs and related matters, to which they may submit reports of UFO sightings, and, more important, of any close encounters which they may have with either UFO craft or UFO entities. From this office they may expect to receive the best answers that are available at the time. I envision that, in an effort to keep costs down and better serve the public as well, only a few letters would be answered on an individual basis; most would be dealt with by incorporating answers to these inquiries into comprehensive bulletins, which, along with the Commission's research evaluations, would be carried by the media as items of public interest.

Other major aspects and functions of the proposed Commission are listed below:

• The Commission would expect to work closely with, and to have the full cooperation of, the government intelligence agencies and the military services in the matter of UFO information and reports. The Commission would be the central and primary agency which would receive, investigate, and evaluate all UFO information originating from any source.

• The Commission would quickly investigate those cases which warrant its attention in an effort to gather as much information as possible. A team of investigators would be maintained for this purpose.

• Certain very important UFO sightings and encounters and all major evaluations would, as I see it, be sent to the President first, when such information is of a very dramatic or potentially severely disturbing nature, and decisions would be made at that level if necessary as to proper timing of release of that material.

• To the extent that its funding would permit, the Commission would prepare documentary films on UFOs as public educational material for release to the media, public schools, universities, etc.

• Recognizing that there exist several large private UFO investigation groups in the U.S. which have done good pioneer work in the UFO field, the Commission would invite their participation.

• Other governments throughout the world would be invited to actively participate with the Presidential Commission in sharing information on the UFO situation in their respective countries. World patterns and a sense of "the large picture" could thus be developed at minimal cost. As a fringe benefit, but of importance, this international participation aspect of the proposed Commission on UFOs would alone, I think, be worth the rather modest cost of the project, for it would give many nations a sense of participation with us in a project of far-reaching and very dramatic significance. It is a project which overrides all national and regional considerations and which has the potential of bringing the family of man just a little closer together; for it is a problem common to all and there is in it a dramatic interest shared by all.

• With the level of world interest in UFOs being high because of the great number of UFO sightings across the globe, there are many foreign private UFO investigation groups which have done yeoman service in monitoring the phenomenon, publishing journals, and alerting their people and governments. These organizations would also be asked to be part of the Commission's world network.

• In addition to the above-listed activities, the proposed Commission would have another facet which, while not in the foreground as far as publicity is concerned (though not essentially secret), would be one of its primary commitments, perhaps its most important. This activity would be the endeavor to establish contact with the UFO entities themselves and the civilizations which they represent. Efforts would be made, as situations and knowledge permit, to accomplish this ultimate goal.

• The Commission would have for a staff highly qualified persons representing astronomy, physics, astrophysics, etc., and the social sciences, selected primarily from those persons who at the present time are dedicating a portion of their time to UFO research and investigation. Because of this selection factor, the greater portion of the staff would require little time to become familiar with the data.

In Conclusion: Additional Benefits to Be Expected from the Proposed Commission:

At this point, I would like to spend a few minutes to discuss some additional and far-reaching benefits to be gained by—

(1) An announcement of the reality of UFOs to the American people and the world.

(2) The establishment of the proposed Commission on UFOs.

If I have established here that announcing the reality of UFOs to the American public, in spite of being an open and honest approach to the subject and one which is very much needed and long overdue, will raise more questions than it answers and cause tremendous interest, but also raises the probability of creating considerable anxiety on a deep and very fundamental level, then I see the establishment of the Commission on UFOs as a necessary and beneficial follow-up to such an announcement.

This office would serve an educational function, gradually conditioning the American and world public to the realities of a complex outer universe which is presently intruding itself into the lives of the people on this planet. This is a good and necessary function, for if culture contact is possible with UFO Civilizations and is perhaps "imminent" from all indications, then the question of how we deal with and diminish the problems created by culture shock becomes increasingly important, especially today as the UFO phenomenon becomes more overt and sensational. The problem is very real for the UFO phenomenon, and what it portends carries connotations which strike at the very foundations of many institutions and old belief structures (while enhancing newer ones); and these belief structures, creating as they do a sense of confidence and implicit faith, are the very glue which holds the individual as well as society together. I submit that this office will be a factor serving to diminish the negative effects of culture shock through a process of education.

After spending many years in UFO research, I have come to the conclusion that the UFO entities who are behind the so-called UFO phenomenon are engaged in a strange (to us at least) but highly sophisticated form of culture contact which began in its present intense form a generation ago and which aims at conditioning mankind to its presence by various complex means, but means chiefly aimed at the emotional and intuitive level of mankind rather than simply at his conscious intellect.

While we ourselves are still not able to understand how to effectively reach certain levels of the unconscious mind, psychology nonetheless recognizes that this is the most effective avenue of altering perspective and widening conscious awareness. It appears that the UFO entities are engaged in a long-term process which is attempting to expand the consciousness of mankind to the point where he might be able to handle the fantastically advanced cultures which they represent. The attempt is being made, however, not by an appeal to man's intellect, which they could easily do by landing en masse and reading the "Outer Space Script" to us, but by giving us a tantalizing puzzle, complex and confusing, which incorporates portions of our myths and folklore and our dreams and hopes, as well as our most basic fears and haunting anxieties.

The puzzle itself is designed to provoke controversy and confusion, to be shocking yet intriguing, frightening yet beckoning; but it always allows us the option of ignoring the phenomenon for generations or picking at the pieces in the hope of finding what fits together so that we may finally see "the large picture."

It is a process which evolves the mind as it solves the problem, as all intricate problems are capable of doing. In this case, the process shows whether we can handle the UFO data and whether we are ready to look at what it portends.

The foregoing observations bring me to the basic conclusions outlined below:

• The UFO Societies are slowly conditioning the Earth Society to the fact of their presence and gauging their future actions from how well we handle the clues which they have given (and they DO leave clues, for it is evident that they could easily cover their tracks and do not; moreover, they frequently invite detection, especially lately).

• Our response to the clues they are leaving is a built-in part of their timetable.

• Occasional deliberate attempts are made by the UFO Societies to make the puzzle as confusing and complex as possible AND to deliberately mislead—this is part of their game plan.

• Our ability to separate the wheat from the chaff, the signal from the noise, is being used as a yardstick of our development and maturity.

• Their final goal is the widening of human consciousness in order that it may be able to handle, emotionally as well as intellectually, the fact of their reality, their presence, and their superiority in capability and accomplishment.

If these conclusions are valid, then your impending statement on UFOs, and the formation of the Commission on UFOs, is altogether very important; for not only would it serve to enlighten the people but also to indicate that we finally have decided to grow up and pull our heads out of the sand, so to speak, and publicly acknowledge and deal with what is happening. This is a very solid indication of the kind of maturity which indicates that we are at last ready to meet the UFO Societies face to face, or more properly, if not ready, that we are rapidly preparing to be so. This event, I firmly believe, will not be lost upon our UFO friends, and may well be a decisive factor in how they construct their timetable.

It is obvious that I take the position that at least some UFO groups are benign to outright benevolent and that establishing contact with them would be the summum bonum of all UFO research activity. I should say that the evidence also indicates that they are at the same time aloof, secretive, cautious, and eclectic. These latter characteristics are also understandable, I submit, given their apparent wide-ranging knowledge on the one hand and the general moral and ethical condition of mankind as reflected in much of his behavior on the other.

I strongly feel that there is sufficient evidence which clearly indicates that although the UFO entities remain mostly aloof and secretive, their behavior and intention are not hostile unless they are approached with hostility, but range from apparent indifference to a benign concern.

The UFO evidence suggests that some UFO groups are open to contact. The stakes for which we gamble in this contact endeavor are high, for it represents, I believe, one of the greatest opportunities ever available to the race of man. For the fact the UFOs exist is testimony that a great body of highly advanced knowledge must be behind the civilization which creates these amazing "artifacts." Perhaps we may share in this knowledge. Culture contact with highly advanced extraterrestrial civilizations could reap for us a harvest of benefits difficult to spell out without sounding like a fairy tale, and we cannot turn our backs on such a possibility.

This is the approximate size of the large picture which the UFO mystery represents. All parts of this picture certainly have not been filled in here, and perhaps even the perimeter of this picture is much larger than I have framed it. The entire issue of the psychic component of many UFO reports especially intrudes itself larger and larger during the past several years, and is one of the most interesting and increasingly well-documented aspects of the UFO picture, though it has not been mentioned earlier in this communication. The psychic aspect of the UFO subject, which was little seen in the earlier days of UFO manifestation, now is frequently a strong component of the reports; and given the psychic or E.S.P. potential in man, this is an exciting part of the picture.

The use of telepathy as the means of communication by UFO entities with Earth persons is now well reported worldwide. If these reports came to us merely from people who were either mentally unstable or romantic dreamers, we could easily discount them, but they do not. They come from a wide spectrum of people who, upon investigation, turn out to be mostly sound and solid citizens who had little if any previous familiarity with psychic matters; in fact, many of the witnesses do not even have a working vocabulary of E.S.P. terms but must fumble and search for words adequate to describe their experiences.

The reports of the use of psychic phenomena by UFO entities include widespread accounts of telepathy being the most common method by which UFO entities choose to communicate with Earth persons, which, along with the common use of a highly developed ability to read the thoughts of the witnesses in question, is enough to sometimes shock the witness into questioning his sanity.

Additionally, we have many reports of people being "drawn out of their bodies" to experience direct confrontation and communication with UFO entities. This splitting of the so-called astral body from the flesh body is a phenomenon now intriguing researchers from many disciplines, including medicine, psychiatry, and astrophysics, etc. Dr. Raymond Moody's book, "Life After Life," now a nationwide best seller, reports on the out-of-the-body experiences of many people who were pronounced clinically dead yet were able to see, hear, think, and to report upon the beautiful yet surprising experiences which they had (all of which persons give similar accounts) while out-of-the-body...a body which in all the cases had been pronounced dead. This book is indicative of what is happening in their field and of the tremendous surge of interest in the area of the psychic.

More aspects of what we call E.S.P. or psychic phenomena could be cited, but this short account is sufficient to indicate the complex nature of the UFO phenomenon.

We may speculate, however, that perhaps the UFO Civilization, having had a longer life cycle than mankind, has in the course of its development discovered the links between the material and the psychic (or other-dimensional) world and is able to make full use of each. The evidence points in this direction.

The UFO mystery splashes in and out of the psychic area, and it could be that we indeed have a lion by the tail here; for by solving the UFO mystery, we may gain knowledge of inestimable value in solving that even more profound mystery which is related to the very essence of man.

I feel that this Commission should be headed by a person who has a wide background in the social sciences and not by a person from the "hard" sciences. Hard-science specialists who have an interest in the UFO subject should, I feel, be a definite and necessary part of the staff but are not qualified to head this project because the problems are not primarily related to their disciplines. We are dealing with information retrieval from witnesses, with public education, with culture-shock problems, with individual and mass psychology in the face of possible interplanetary and interstellar contact between planetary societies of widely divergent backgrounds and levels of achievement. These are, I beg, not the problems or the meat of physics or astronomy.

Finally, I think that this Commission should be headed by a person who is intimately familiar with the subject matter and its broad implications rather than by a person selected primarily for his expertise in some other area. This will insure that the person selected does not have to spend most of his time trying to assimilate the great amount of reports and literature on the subject, which has accumulated over the past decades. Reading brief summaries in a crash briefing program will not do, since it allows the intervention of the editorial judgments of persons other than the director, and these editors may be quite unqualified to determine what should be included, especially since the UFO field is so new and unique that there are no yardsticks to use or models to relate to in making editorial judgments other than that which derives from a long-term study of the subject. Additionally, there must be time to digest the information and make sense of it—to see patterns and meanings and possible motives. These intellectual and subconscious processes cannot be expected to occur within a few months.

In Appreciation:

I would like to take a moment to tell you that I greatly respect the spirit of openness, unpretentiousness, and compassion which has characterized your leadership of our nation thus far. Not that these qualities have been displayed in the absence of a highly intelligent grasp of issues and problems—no, this quality too is very apparent, and that is as it ideally should be; but it is the former, more precious elements that I am here concerned with, for they radiate the Christ teachings of humility, service, and love.

I especially wish to commend your recent remarks on human rights, culminating in what I feel was a magnificent statement at the University of Notre Dame. You have brought to the Office of the Presidency that which has been lacking, the vision to see beyond constricting national interests to the needs and hopes and rights of all people everywhere...*and* the courage to act upon that vision.

You have acknowledged the fact that all people are spiritually interdependent. Beneath the Cross of Notre Dame we have heard you bear witness that we are "our brother's keeper" and that our brothers and sisters indeed include the great family of man.

Thank you, Mr. President, for your consideration of this proposal. I look forward to your reply.

RICHARD A. SIGISMUND
Psychologist/Social Scientist
1557 9th Street—No. 1
Boulder, CO 80302

Note: Despite the eloquence of the above letter writer's concluding remarks (or perhaps because of it), neither the Executive Office of the President nor the Office of the Secretary of the Air Force was moved to respond. Two months later, the suspense overwhelming him, he sent the following query addressed to "Mail Room, The White House." (It is not known whether he finally received a reply.)

September 3, 1977

Dear Sirs:

I am writing to inquire about a letter which I sent to President Carter two months ago. This letter was of considerable length and was concerned with the UFO subject. I have not received an acknowledgment of receipt of this letter by your office. Therefore, I would like to confirm that your office has received this letter and to learn of its progress.

Unfortunately, since I neglected to send the letter by registered mail I cannot be absolutely certain that it was in fact ever delivered to your office until I receive an acknowledgment of receipt.

Would you be so kind as to send me an acknowledgment and whatever information you may be able to obtain as to the present disposition of the communication in question. I would greatly appreciate hearing from you at the earliest possible moment. Thank you.

Chapter 14

Does the White House Have a UFO Hotline?

Poet Marvin Bell's words from one of his literary workshops can help us deal with the mind-set of certain UFO-research detractors: "About creative writing, there are some things to admit to our self. Curmudgeons cannot admit these things, and they will not want you to admit them either. They do not understand Kierkegaard's remark that laughter is a kind of prayer. They have no sense of humor. They do not want you to be freer than they are.... Like members of a closed guild, they do not want the truth to be known."

2-2.

ESTHETIC SCIENCES ORGANIZATION
(Certified 267235)
16 August 1977

Dear Mr. Shoob [of the White House]:

As you know from our many telecons over the past months and our letter to you of 11 February, instant, we have made a most concerted effort to reach President Carter in order to advise him of our research and investigative efforts concerning the cattle mutilations and UFOs, asking for his sanction and/or funding. This includes a 204-word telegram dispatched on 30 November 76 (which cannot be traced) and our Space Intelligence Committee (SIC) report which was sent to the President, "EYES ONLY," certified 24 January, instant, and which was never received by him, according to our records.

As you further know, a reply to the letter addressed to you was made by one Colonel Seminare, Jr., Office of the Secretary of the Air Force, under date of 4 March, instant, disclaiming any Air Force interest in UFOs, and enclosing, as an Attachment, the ESO subject SIC Report to President Carter. (We addressed the President, not the Air Force, or anyone else, in this matter).

Now then, since all of the aforementioned attempts have met with such a complete failure, please be advised of the following:

(1) The ESO is planning to release, on or about the 26th, instant, a News Announcement via AP Denver, advising the country that this organization will, over the Labor Day Weekend, give to the wire services a major Press Release and Story designed to advise the American people and the world of a portion of the results of our SIC Report, and

(2) To substantiate the validity of our research and desire to help those involved in the cattle mutilation and other UFO phenomena, we will also make public the U.S. Air Force's having full knowledge of the UFO situation by quoting from their Physics 370 textbook some of their hard-core UFO statistics, including after-effects from UFO landings on animals and humans, UFO technical information, and the government's speculation as to where in the universe they are coming from. (See attachment 3, herein.)

However, as one last effort, we are making you, once again, to bring these ESO efforts to the President's attention and to assure us of an official White House position reference our releasing the Labor Day Weekend story. We prefer a written response on appropriate letterhead from either President Carter, Press Secretary Jody Powell, or a responsible official of DOD or the CIA who either addresses the issue "squarely," giving official sanction for our release, or spells out specific areas and parameters within which they wish us to proceed.

Obviously, a response will be required by 25 August, instant, in order for us to work with the White House as we would prefer to do.

Perhaps, by making quite clear our intent, in line with our purpose and aims of bringing the truth to the American people, especially the ranchers and others who are the victims of this growing phenomenon, we will get a satisfactory response to this last attempt.

Thanking you once again for your time and cooperation in this serious matter.

JLH.jh

enc: Copy WU to President Carter, 30 November 76

Attachments: (1) ESO SIC Report; (2) Copy, L. E. Seminare, Jr., Colonel, USAF, Office of the Secretary; (3) COVER, Table of Contents, Pg. 456 of UFO chapter: SPACE PHYSICS—PHYSICS 370, USAFA

cy: Dan S. Hughes, Attorney at Law (ESO)

Note: The ESO's quasi-legal persistence succeeded in eliciting the following short-and-not-so-sweet reply from Colonel Seminare:

March 4, 1977

Dear *[AF-deleted]*:

This will respond to your February 11 letter to a Mr. Steven Shoob, the White House, concerning your work and interest in the so-called UFO phenomenon.

As you no doubt are aware, the Air Force was extensively involved for some 20 years in the investigation of reports of UFO sightings. That effort was concluded by the Air Force in 1969, and the results are well known. Apparently by reason of the Air Force's prior involvement, your letter was referred to this office for response directly to you.

Since the Air Force is no longer involved in investigating reports in this area, such as yours, it appears that my only recourse is to return to you the attachments to your letter. Also, I know of no Federal agency currently involved in investigating reports of UFO sightings.

Given these circumstances, I am unable to be of assistance to you.

Attachments

Note: Since they seem to have helped prolong the government's reaction to this particular correspondent, two of the "attachments" are reprinted below, beginning with the page excerpted from the Air Force Academy textbook

:

c. Flight characteristics (wobbling, fluttering, etc.)

d. Periodicity of sightings

e. Time duration

f. Curiosity or inquisitiveness

g. Avoidance

h. Hostility

Associated Effects:

a. Electromagnetic (compass, radio, ignition systems, etc.)

b. Radiation (burns, induced radioactivity, etc.)

c. Ground disturbance (dust stirred up, leaves moved, standing wave peaks on surface of water, etc.)

d. Sound (none, hissing, humming, roaring, thunderclaps, etc.)

e. Vibration (weak, strong, slow, fast)

f. Smell (ozone or other odor)

g. Flame (how much, where, when, color)

h. Smoke or cloud (amount, color, persistence)

i. Debris (type, amount, color, persistence)

j. Inhibition of voluntary motion by observers

k. Sighting of "creatures" or "beings"

After Effects:

a. Burned areas or animals

b. Depressed or flattened areas

c. Dead or missing animals

d. Mentally disturbed people

e. Missing items

—ESTHETIC SCIENCES ORGANIZATION—

THE SPACE INTELLIGENCE COMMITTEE (SIC) REPORT: As a result of the increase in the number of bizarre and unexplainable cattle mutilations sweeping the country, and because this organization felt strongly that there was significant scientific evidence to be gained linking an unknown technology with the phenomenon, a concentrated mobile research program was carried out covering a sixteen-month period beginning April, 1975, by the Esthetic Sciences Organization (ESO).

On-site evaluations utilizing certain electronics and magnetic sensitivities were employed, together with a comprehensive program of interrogation and interviews with the ranching community and law-enforcement personnel involved in those cases ESO researched. The results obtained and the conclusions drawn by the ESO are presented herewith.

EQUIPMENT USED—

UNIT: Mobile trailer unit; 16-foot Coachman Commander weighing 4,170 pounds loaded.

POWER: 12 do with several units in parallel (on site); Power inverted for 115 vat.

RADIO: CUB transceiver using—Urgency 9 standby and two working channels, AM rev/do.

TV: 12-inch Admiral B&W.

HARDWARE: Especially designed for use in the ETA quest and residual mutilation site readout. Radiation detection sensors; standard gamma, magnetic, and vibrational sensors; external systems especially designed for these tests and stimulation of the space-environment. ESO classified techniques and related circuitry.

INVESTIGATIVE DATA AND RESEARCH RESULTS—

CASE FC1: Approximately twelve miles south of Colorado Springs. Carcass oriented SE, head at the SE. Apparent urinary excretion preceded the animal's drop, which indicates a possible subjection to a high-intensity magnetic Gaussian field, causing shock to the nervous system and metabolism, resulting in a possible cardiac arrest. Further evidence of such a shock to the system is the fact that the urine excretions had become crystallized on the weeds it became in contact with. This gives some indication as to the effects of such an energy beam or plasma on the internal organs such as the bladder and/or kidneys. Two bodies of water were within several yards of the carcass. A 115 KV line from the Midway Substation paralleled the carcass. (Power has often been absorbed from high lines by UFOs. No such loss was indicated upon inquiry of the power engineer.)

CASE CC1: Approximately 28 miles NE of Colorado Springs. Two carcasses were found within a few yards of each other (actually 1,000 ft.). Adjacency of a body of water was evident in these cases and located between both animals. Line of direction between the two near to SE orientation. Disappearance phenomenon of headlights during at least three separate occasions near date of mutilation. TV reception suffered apparent loss of verticle-hold input signal voltage and later (several days) corrected itself with no cause found when examined by a technician. (This corresponding to CASE CC2 some miles adjacent to CC1, where that TV's horizontal-hold input signal voltage was reduced by sufficient millivolts to cause roll, only later to return to normal…two weeks later, without any need for repair.) Evidence indicated either plasma or energy manifestations capable of appearing and disappearing at will, in the cases of both disappearance phenomenon and the TV abnormalities. Certain audible intrusions at near 2:30 AM on one occasion at the same general time were sufficient to cause arousable sounds from a normal sleep pattern both of humans and animals at the residence of CC1.

CASE CC2: Approximately 23 miles east of Colorado Springs. TV signal input abnormalities began some several days prior to mutilation and described in CASE CC1. The entire screen went dead, and audio was lost, until after the event. Carcass orientation not determined. Carcass had patch of skin removed from neck, and a calf it was carrying had an identical patch removed from its neck (only smaller in proportion).

After-effects showed marine life abnormalities in a pond near the carcass, giving rise to the ESO conclusion that the school of fish in question were reacting to a residual magnetic Gaussian vertex no doubt caused by the craft used in the mutilation (much as how birds utilize the predominant magnetic field lines of the earth in order to migrate thousands of miles). In this case the fish were in a quasi-stupor and more or less looked [as if they'd gone] into a biological dipole at the moment of displacement incurred in their sensing mechanism. This left them swimming endlessly in circles a few hours after the mutilation.

CASE KC1: Approximately 46 miles NNE of Colorado Springs. This case is extremely significant for the following reasons:

1. Carcass was again lying in a SE orientation, head to the SE.

2. Residual effects assumed by the investigator (taken on by him), while invisible, nonodiferous and lacking in physiological effects upon same per-

son, still were sufficient to cause two German shepherd dogs, in turn, to immediately roll their eyes at the party, tuck their tail between their legs, and quickly retreat some six feet away, showing a display of fear, after touching his hand.

3. The sleep pattern of a white female, approximately 28 years of age, living in an isolated area 1 mile from the carcass was unusually sound, not waking to anything during the night of the mutilation; yet she had been restless and unable to sleep for two weeks prior. Nor did the two dogs become aroused. This is a common ETA technique (UFO) to induce sound sleep, both in humans and in animals, at will.

4. As in other cases, a low-level sound of an engine was repeatedly heard by this same respondent, and lights had been seen hovering silently.

5. Power failures in short, 1—2-second durations were observed by the respondent on several occasions at night, when there was no wind and no storms in the vicinity.

6. The ESO investigator also found a distinct magnetic polarization at the top three strands of a barbed-wire fence some 50 yards south of the carcass, giving evidence of an unusually strong magnetic plasma having been in the immediate area (carcass area) a few hours prior, sufficient to displace the dipole moment of the top three strands some 45 degrees from their norm.

7. A recording made by the investigator giving details of his testing procedures plainly yields a male voice exclaiming the single word "what?"

8. Another significant aspect of this case was the trail of cow dung evenly spaced about 6 feet between each dropping, giving indication of a shock inducement to the nervous system of the animal either for a continuous period, causing the animal's excretion over a 50-foot walking interval, or at precise intervals, causing bowel spasms to excrete, upon the energy (beam?) impact upon the living animal until it dropped from no doubt a cardiac failure. (This is why often a heart attack has seemed to be the cause of death, or lightning—they are practically one and the same in pure atmospheric physics or in the ETIUFO plasma physics of plasma energies).

9. A correlation significance is that a path several hundred yards long, in the same direction of the carcass orientation and the dung droppings was also evident in the form of grass depression about 6 inches in width. Evidently caused by pressure-simulation (mag beam path showing trajectory of vehicle used homing in on the animal prior to the mutilation or specimen gathering).

10. A depression of 3/4 inches in the soil about 4 feet behind the rear of the carcass was found, identical to that found at several other carcasses

and at several UFO landing areas. These were the shape of a heel about 4-by 5 inches. (Also found 12 miles east of Battle Creek, Michigan.)

This case embodied several very good examples of an ETA physics and technology. All of these things as well as the other cases given gave motivation for a special test set-up, which will be described, in general, as follows:

SPECIAL TEST CASE AND RESEARCH RUN/CASE BCl:

Mobile unit set up on a 2,700-acre ranch 35 miles NE of Pueblo, Colorado, on 21 September, 1975, where eight mutilations had occurred.

Object of the test run was to set up in isolation where microvolt readings could be obtained and magnetic Gaussian field strengths determined both from the norms at this latitude-longitude juncture, and in the presence of a UFO. This ranch field consisted of a 3-foot stand of growing corn, and the soil was baked hard. An adequate ground was established and certain extended circuitry was set up. A UFO was visually spotted about 9 PM for a short duration, lying NW at about 10 o'clock high and of extreme brilliance, pulsating orange; the investigator was alone at that time. At midnight the investigator was joined by the wife of a law-enforcement ESO associate and by another woman, all of whom are experienced UFO investigators in their own right. Certain testing was carried out and monitored by these two women between 1 and 1:30 AM, to which there was a like-response from the ETA proximity expressed in magnetic technology. A time loss was also experienced by all three from 4:30 to 6:00 AM. A physical mark was placed during this time upon the investigator's left middle finger, which has minimal evidence even at this report filing. Following many bizarre happenings experienced by the investigator the next day, he became ill and was taken from the unit at first darkness by the associate and his wife about 8 PM. Shortly after the unit was vacated with all systems turned off (but with exterior arrays attached) there ensued a profound ETA event. There appeared in the general area of the unit, and seen by several witnesses, three UFOs. Later, one vehicle directed a brilliant beam of light downward on the unit. It was found later through careful magnetic measurements that the polarization of the metallic structures of the lab were drastically displaced every 18 inches in vertical ascent and in a plane through the entire trailer. This displacement exists today. Also found was the fact that the beam had drained all battery systems in the unit, as well as having dropped that of the automobile to the trailer, even though it had been charged for 45 minutes that day. The most significant technological effect of this beam, however, was the closing of the relay in the larger recording unit and causing it to record. The beam's magnetic component was thusly recorded at an extremely maximum level and was found to be of a low frequency with a high frequency piggyback, as read from a scope. Further dissectioning of this signal will be carried out in laboratory procedures. A disquieting effect has been the causing of physical abnormalities in the molecular structuring or magnetic domains/moments of the unit, such that it causes extreme loss of hair of the head if it is occupied for any period of time. Permanent magnetic deflection of sensors is also a residual condition. (It has been proved to the investigators that the trailer was, in fact, marked in some way by the ETA UFO beam during this incident.)

Of interest is the fact that this same or another UFO appeared some ten nights later, putting the same type of beam on an old windmill that had been about 100 yards from the laboratory the night of the testing and initial beaming. No doubt looking for the unit and wondering if the windmill somehow was a part of the unit now not there. A complete report of this test site incident is now available from the ESO Director.

CONCLUSIONS—

There is a definite indication of the involvement of an entity which takes the form of a phenomenon seen as helicopters, autos, trucks (and other) or as lights, or not seen at all, by the normal optical sensors of the human body. Animals may see them when humans do not, or they may exhibit a sensing of the UFO or entity's presence through some other capability other than optical. (Dogs are used to ascertain the presence of an invisible entity such as UFOs.) Residual gamma count, background scatter audible signals such as found at UFO-frequented landing sites, together with a significant Gaussian energy field which is recordable, measurable, and sometimes displayed in other ways, constitute another such evidence of an ETA involvement. A serious study of the incisions (FC1 CASE) indicates a technique being used which can burn a circular incision in a progression around the desired specimen tissue desired, in such a precise manner that each 1/4-inch diameter hole is clean and precise beyond any known surgical capability. Residual effects at the carcass substantiate an ETA involvement—such as a lack of tracks, no disturbances to terrain and other facts such as gentle (or sometimes drastic) dropping of the carcass to the ground with no trace of the obvious gravitational attributes such as the mass-weight of the carcass, etc. However, from the standpoint of a physics which allows an ETA vehicle to utilize the magnetic domains of the earth in such a way that the resultant energy-craft-vector is evidenced as a SE trajectory, and when viewed from the relationship of magnetic to gravity, it can readily be seen that we have here a capability to move at extreme velocities (2,000 mph plus) and to either appear or not to.

Note: Of course. when you add a lawyer's name to any piece of correspondence (even if that lawyer be only remotely involved in past, present, or future activity of the correspondent), you can count on your communication's getting more than routine handling. In this case, the White House saw the light of exasperation at the end of the mail tube and demanded that the DOD's Special Assistant (John G. Kester) to the Secretary and the Deputy Secretary of Defense explain what was happening, or was going to happen, with ESO's latest missive. The result, courtesy of Colonel Seminare's office, was the following coup de grace:

FACT SHEET CONCERNING CORRESPONDENCE FROM "ESO"—
The Air Force is unable to provide any information regarding Mr. Harden's "Esthetic Sciences Organization" or the so-called SIC (Space Intelligence Committee) report he provides, except that we received Mr. Harden's February 11, 1977, letter addressed to Mr. Steven Shoob. We were directed to reply to Mr. Harden; a copy of that reply, which presents the Air Force position on the subject, is attached to his current letter.

Air Force Academy officials advise that Mr. Harden has been in frequent contact with the Academy's Office of Information. Apparently, that is his source of the book *Introductory Space Science*—Volume II, Physics 370; he attaches a copy of the cover, a Table of Contents page, and page 456. The volume has not been used in the Academy since at least 1972. The page 456 is taken out of context, apparently to infer that the course "proves" the Air Force is active in UFO investigations. The listing is in fact one of "Descriptors" in a system for cataloging reports of sightings. In fact, the chapter concludes that the investigation of UFOs does not lend itself to the employment of a scientific approach. As stated, the Academy no longer uses the volume, and the Physics Department does not offer a course in the investigation of UFO reports.

We understand also that there have in fact been several instances of cattle mutilations in the Colorado area in recent years. These events have had wide media coverage, some small part of which attributes the mutilations to UFOs. The matter is being looked into by the Colorado Bureau of Investigations and the Sheriffs Departments of several counties. The predominant belief is that the animal mutilations are the work of one or more religious or cultist groups; the investigations continue. Contact with Colorado officials will undoubtedly provide more detailed information in that regard.

Given the foregoing circumstances, together with Mr. Harden's "or else" attitude regarding a White House response to his demands, the prudent response would appear to be one of complete silence on the matter. A close reading of the "conclusions" of the so-called SIC Report will confirm the futility of any attempt to reason with the author.

Chapter 15

The White House As UFOlogy's *Bleak House*

When citizens' UFOletters first began trickling into the presidential mailroom (back during Truman's administration), who could've imagined that this flow of public concern would number in the thousands during the Carter years—and would continue flowing on into the twenty-first century? Well, perhaps Charles Dickens could've imagined it; for his novel Bleak House *revolves around a (fictional) lawsuit—"Jarndyce v. Jarndyce"—that went on for generations.*

2-3.

December 29, 1976

Dear President-Elect Carter:

During your presidential campaign, I sent you a letter dated July 10, 1976, and discussed with you the subject of Unidentified Flying Objects.

I outlined in the letter what the feelings were of President Ford at a time he was a congressman in 1969 and the fact that when he became President and had the great opportunity to relate the entire UFO information the government has to the American people, he failed to do so.

The *National Enquirer* newspaper of June 8, 1976, quoted you as saying: "If I become President, I'll make every piece of information this country has about UFO sightings available to the public, and the scientists." Now that's a good statement and a campaign promise. You were elected, and I trust you will stand by that statement and release this UFO information as soon as possible.

I do, however, know that *[AF-deleted]* met with you during your presidential campaign and gave you a full-scale intelligence briefing designed to prevent you from "making the wrong mistake." I feel that somewhere in this briefing the UFO subject was probably discussed. I likewise feel that there was a change of attitude at this point. I base this on a rather disturbing, but brief, letter I received from one *[AF-deleted]*, one of your Special Assistants during your campaign. In the letter sent me by *[AF-deleted]* and dated September 28, 1976, I was informed the following:

"It is true that Governor Carter has seen a U.F.O., but he has never said he would pursue this matter as President."

That smacks of the same old story that has for too many years played over and over like a worn-out l.p. recording; and as in past years of presidential candidates, many presidential promises have gone by the wayside once elected.

[AF-deleted]'s office, through his secretary, told me that President Ford would not comment on the UFO subject as this subject rightfully belongs to the Department of Defense. It seems that when a man reaches the highest office in this nation, that of President, he still is controlled as to what he can and cannot say.

One of my contact sources within intelligence circles informed me a few days ago that on December 18th you were told *not* to say anything relative to the UFO subject as far as the American public is concerned.

Is this true? Do you plan to release all the UFO information our government has to the public as you promised? I do not refer to the selected UFO cases in the Project Blue Book files. I have reference to ALL the UFO cases…some of which are locked up in government security files or similar files.

In closing…I have enclosed in this letter (the letter sent to Plains as I also sent a duplicate letter to your Georgia address in Atlanta) a photostat copy of the December 14, 1976, article that appeared in the National Enquirer on CBS News anchorman Walter Cronkite and the subject of UFOs about which he received this information from space scientists and high-level government officials.

One of the cases—the green-ray incident described in the enclosed article—was very interesting. I recently this year investigated an incident in Western Pennsylvania, along with a scientist friend of mine, of an apple tree that was zapped by a quick flash of a purple beam from a landed space craft. I removed burnt bark from the trunk of the tree.

…removed an apple from the tree. This apple was about the size of a tennis ball or a little larger. I placed the burnt tree bark and the apple in a container. I went to remove the apple and burnt bark from the container 34 days later for the purpose of filming it and using same in some of my UFO lectures. I couldn't find the apple. I removed the burnt bark and discovered the apple at the bottom of my container. It was *the size of a grape* and had totally dehydrated and petrified…it had turned to wood. My scientist friend informed me that apples that had fallen from the tree when it impacted on the ground did the same thing within a period of 14 to 45 days. But that is another story.

I sent Mr. *[AF-deleted]* a letter and complimented his article and went into discussion with him on a few UFO items. I received a letter from one *[AF-deleted]*, Administrative Assistant to [AF-deleted] at CBS News, and was told that Mr. *[AF-deleted]* "was not interviewed as reported in the article." She also said that *[AF-deleted]* "never said to anyone any of the things quoted in that article. He never heard of any of those incidents until he read them in the *Enquirer*. He never discussed the matter with *[AF-deleted]*." She closed by calling the article "false."

This is pretty hard for me to accept, and I base this on a personal experience I had with *National Enquirer* and how very strict they are in documenting everything they print. I checked your story out that appeared in the *Enquirer* and personally heard from the *Enquirer* president.

It appears to me that somewhere in this CBS News-*National Enquirer* incident something is not right. I am pursuing this matter further through CBS and the *National Enquirer* as well as through two of my major contact sources. Could you come up with any information?

Well, I've chatted by letter long enough. I thank you for taking the time to read this and consider its contents. I trust that you will keep your campaign promise by releasing all the UFO information to the public that the government has. As stated, I am very deeply involved in this field and would be most pleased to have the opportunity to discuss the UFO situation with you.

I plan to be in Washington from January 23rd to the 26th at the Hilton Hotel on Connecticut Avenue. The National Religious Broadcasters convention is being held there at that time, and I plan to see a few persons there. If it might be possible for us to get together, or someone within your cabinet or staff, kindly have someone contact me ahead of time and I will be most happy to bring along some very valuable information.

Incidentally, I still have that wooden apple, coupled with color-film slides and black-and-white prints of same. I personally talked with the gentleman that owns the property where this incident occurred in Western Pennsylvania during April, 1976. Also have some very interesting NASA pictures of what appears to be "constructional features" on the surface of Mars, as filmed on a fly-by mission. And there is much, much more.

Thank you for your time, and I trust that you will follow through with your promise. I await your reply. Incidentally, I sent a copy of my first letter to you to Mrs. Carter also, and I have likewise done the same with this as the UFO subject is truly a fascinating one. Thank Mrs. Carter for the nice letter of reply sent during your presidential campaign.

2-4.

February 22, 1977

Dear President Carter:

I am writing to you as a concerned person. What I am concerned about is the releasing of information in the government's files concerning UFOs.

I feel this area of space exploration and study has for too long been smothered out by a few people who are concerned only for themselves and their own wellbeing. And the truth of this precious information is never reaching the common public.

I have been made aware that in March of last year, during your spring primary campaign, you spoke with officials of the UFO Education Center.

In this meeting, a statement was made that you would release to the public all information in the government's files concerning UFOs.

I don't intend for this letter to sound like "Why haven't you taken any action toward this, as yet?" Rather, I want to let you know that I totally support your taking this action, when you feel the time is right, for all of humanity.

Actually, I am very impressed and happy with the situations you have confronted, and the decisions you have made, since you took the office.

Especially, the long-awaited decision of nuclear energy. No matter if these testings were for peaceful purposes (as for energy production), or for destructive reasons (the testing of nuclear bombs), the result of nuclear energy production is very destructive. The deadly byproduct, radioactivity, does not have an effective means for storage, and there is no fast way to destroy it. So, I am very pleased with your stand on nuclear weapons, and I hope that solar-energy will replace nuclear power plants in the very near future. This radioactivity from producing nuclear power is so very, very dangerous for the continuance of the planet. There is no safe means of storing the poison, and this means of energy production must be halted immediately.

I am very interested in the extraterrestrial space craft which are peacefully visiting our planet. They are indeed peaceful, human beings, coming only with peaceful motives. I know of Charlotte Blob, and the UFO Education Center, in Appleton, Wisconsin; and I know of their sincere efforts to make this precious information known to all interested individuals. So, you totally have my support, that I feel this information has to be released; and that it will be done, at the best possible time. For the benefit of all of Earth's peoples…

2-5.

Dear Mr. President:

I'm sending you a copy of this manuscript on UFOs, that's going to the *Enquirer* newspaper, because the Lord has instructed me to do so.

In an interview you gave, I believe, in March 1976, with the *Enquirer* people, they reported in their paper you promised to make available to the public anything concerning UFOs that the American people had a right to know.

This manuscript contains the correct answers on UFOs; it is Eternal Truth, revealed by God thru study and prayer, Matthew 21:22; and Mark 11:24.

I have been instructed to send you personally a copy, I trust this was not opened by an assistant. The original manuscript is going to the *Enquirer* newspaper. What the Lord has planned to do with the information thru you, as of this letter-writing time, I do not know. You are in tune with Jesus and you can find out from Him for yourself, your part in this; I'm obeying my instruction, following step at a time as the Lord leads me.

There is an awful lot more that I've not put in this work. There's more than enough in this work to convince any sincere seeking person; and it's been extremely hard to get this much down in the right wordage to convey the right and exact enough meanings so as to be informative, all the while being fought in the mind by Satan trying to stop me so as to keep the people in ignorance, so he (Satan) can have an easier time damning their souls to an Eternal Hell.

I have been praying daily for your life, for God to keep you alive, in good health; and asking God to keep you from being murdered, so you may complete your full term in office and be the instrument God needs in this country, and to fulfill His divine plan for the nations of earth.

I come to you, in letter, with the Rank and Position as an "Ambassador from Heaven" II Corinthians 5:20, and request of you to treat this manuscript with the utmost seriousness and priority; for it has an extreme importance, the Eternal Destiny of the immortal souls of the people of this United States of America which you have sworn on The Holy Eternal Word of God that you would guide and protect, when you voluntarily took the oath of office of Presidency of the United States of America.

Praying for you and yours, I am your faithful servant and fellow laborer in Christ Jesus, Our Lord and Soon-Coming King.

Yours in Christ Service.

Note: Apparently, the letter writer's one-page "manuscript" (reprinted below) is in response to the National Enquirer's *solicitation of proof that one or more reported UFOs originated from an extraterrestrial source—the "reward" being a cash sum to be paid via the* Enquirer's *panel of UFO analytical experts.*

Gentlemen:

I have more information (answers to what's going on?) than what is written here. Really, to a deep-thinking person you know how hard it is to put knowledge down on paper, in words that are able to convey the mind's thoughts, sufficient to be understood by people.

If you will but bow your head, very simply ask Jesus to open your mind to read and understand truth, you will know with deep conviction, you are doing just that: reading truth, Eternal Truth; and your minds and your senses will be made aware of Satan and his well-run society, his power to put thoughts in your minds, to cause you to doubt this material. Also, you will become aware of people who will come into the analyzation of this material with a very negative, mocking attitude. Satan thru people he controls will do everything possible to destroy this manuscript. If you will tune into your spiritual senses, you will feel a weird cold, chill around them. And I sincerely trust you will become vividly aware you are in possession of a knowledge more powerful than the knowledge of how to control the atom and build nuclear reactors.

One of the wisest things you could do would be to make more than one copy of this manuscript and put the original manuscript in a bank vault.

I'll be awaiting a response from you. And be praying for all involved in the analyzation of this material, that your minds may be open to the truth and God your creator. Isaiah 26:3 - II Corinthians 4:4 - II Corinthians 11:3 Philippians 4:7 - and I Timothy 6:5.

All of these things stated, has, is now, or shortly in the future will come to pass.

Please, please believe what you are going to read.

I have worked on this manuscript a long time, sending it in to you now just before the deadline in June of 1977, as stated in the reward notice offered in your paper.

The reward money will be used to preach this message to our United States, and maybe the world.

I'll assure you, it won't be wasted, but put to fruitful use, to benefit all people that will listen to the truth of what is going to come to pass.

2-6.

February 10, 1977

Dear Mr. President:

For more than 30 years I've had experiences first-hand with flying saucers or UFOs.

I know what's behind the mystery and would like to share it with you.

Since you have seen one and know that they exist, I felt that you would like to know more about them.

You stated in the *National Enquirer* that if you were elected President, you would make this information about them available to the public.

I feel certain that I can tell you more about this mystery than anyone else.

If I could be honored with a reply from your office or you directly, I'll send you information that will clarify this mystery to the point that you will want to look into it further.

May I hear from you concerning this matter?

Chapter 16

At Least Two Levels of Application

As you read (and re-read) the entries in this book, you may wonder how practical, in sum, they may be toward effecting the desired sociopolitical change: i.e., the full/prompt/verifiable official disclosure of the Ultimate Secret. Well, I submit that, on one level, they signify the conscience of the body politic, a conscience that rebukes and resists propagandistic erosion from the keepers of the Ultimate Secret. And, on another level of appreciation, they signify a bloc of perennial aid and comfort to all enemies of autocratic decisionmaking.

2-7.

February, 1977

Dear President Carter:

I realize that for your administration to be successful all Americans should ideally support you. Therefore, even though I sincerely wish President Ford were still our president, I support you and wish you continued good luck.

I also hope that as President of the United States, you will guide our nation in a new and expanded era of space exploration. I am sure you realize its importance.

I also would hope that as President you would release any secret documents (information) pertaining to UFOs.

America, as exemplified on January 20, 1977, is continuously growing and changing. But for our nation and our world the biggest change might come too late. If the subject of UFOs is not treated seriously and openly by all our leaders and people now, our ignorance could be our ultimate downfall. Maybe you think I'm crazy, but I hope you agree with me.

Have a nice day.

2-8.

April, 1977

Dear Mr. President:

When you were campaigning for the role of the President, you said that you would release all material to the public that the government has on

UFOs. I'm very interested in things of this manner. I would like to know if you could send me through the mail all the information that you have on UFOs (accounts, pictures, etc.).

2-9.

February, 1977

Dear President Carter:

Since you have said you are interested in UFOs, you may find the enclosed newspaper columns of mine of interest on the subject.

I have been a voluntary civilian UFO researcher, writer, lecturer for the past over 20 years, and much I write I base on personal experience that is my *proof* that something unusual is happening in our skies.

If you should be interested in discussing the matter any further I would be happy to be of service.

You said you still had two hours for reading each night!

May you be able to recognize God's Plan for us as it unfolds…and have the strength and understanding to follow through.

2-10.

February 12, 1977

Dear President Carter:

Last November I sent you a notice regarding the pilot research study which I was conducting with Mr. Ted Owens of Cape Charles, Virginia, as part of my Ph.D. research in parapsychology at the University of California, Berkeley.

At my request, Owens agreed to provide an objective demonstration to support his claim of being in regular telepathic contact with UFO intelligences by causing some of the following phenomena to appear, for a ninety-day period beginning November 7, 1976, within one hundred miles of San Francisco: |

(1) At least three major UFO appearances in front of police, scientists, or other reliable witnesses, and/or

(2) Reliable sightings of "alien life forms," and/or

(3) Electromagnetic anomalies such as radio interference, lightning, power failures, and power blackouts.

Owens stated that these phenomena would pose no threat to human life or security, provided that government officials made no attempt to interfere with the UFOs.

Owens has also requested that this experiment not be publicized outside of the relevant scientific and government communities. You are one of about seventy individuals to whom these notices have been sent. I trust you will use discretion in sharing this report.

During the ninety-day experimental period, I have received information regarding the three events mentioned in the enclosed newspaper clippings. I have not yet completed my analysis of the statistical frequencies with which these events are likely to occur.

I would very much appreciate any information which you may have regarding other events of relevance to this experiment. When these are collected and the analysis is complete, I shall be happy to send you a final report on this experiment, at your request.

P.S. The original notice sent to you as President-elect in Plains, Georgia.

2-11.

January 29, 1977

Dear President Jimmy Carter:

In news reports during the recent national Presidential campaign I noted that you had sighted an unidentified flying object in Georgia during the year 1973. You expressed vast interest in this subject, noting in news reports that you considered these unidentified flying objects as a very real phenomenon and seemed to feel that they possibly were intelligent machines from the planets of distant suns surveying our earth.

In news reports June 20, 1976, or around this time, during the campaign you promised that, if President, you would release all available secret information on UFOs held top secret in the Department of Defense and U.S. Air Force, as you felt something was being held back, and you wished all information that you possessed [were] available to the American public as part of the open new Administration, if elected. You also promised study of this tantalizing worldwide phenomenon that would bring answers. Especially I noted this report in the National Enquirer but also in other newspapers, I do believe. I am confident that you will do this.

Too many reliable persons in the last decades, and especially scientists, have witnessed the UFO phenomenon for such a manifestation to be denied. Possibly UFOs are a strange human psychological phenomenon, a yearning for human beings to be not alone in this universe and to find answers to the profound and elusive human problems of the world? Certainly in this consideration, for the most part ordinary phenomena and satellites could be responsible for these exciting UFO observations; however, a residue of UFO sightings, and a large residue at that, remains inexplicable and appears to be something staggeringly strange and hauntingly real, and possibly ominous for our world civilization if ignored.

Space may be the dark glorious womb of life evolving everywhere from atoms to molecules, to proteins, to amino acids, and to excited cells that settle upon distant worlds and upon our own green-blue world. The spirit of life is climbing over our minds into the inspiration of Infinity. Please act upon my suggestion, a matter of heart-pulsing interest to the citizens of America, and thus fulfill your observed campaign promise concerning information on UFOs.

2-12.

January 25, 1977

Dear President Carter:

This letter concerns your promise to make every piece of information this country has about UFO sightings available to the public, and the scientists, as reported in the National Enquirer, June 8th, 1976.

The previous administrations' "sweep it under the rug" policy concerning the subject of UFOs is both appalling and an insult to my intelligence. The Air Force's equally feeble attempts to cover up the real truth is unbelievable.

President Carter, may I suggest that material on UFOs, now locked in the National Archives and that has never been made public, be made into a movie and aired on prime-time T.V.

We the American people have placed our trust and confidence in you.

Your honest presentation of the UFO material will be significant in the years to come.

2-13

January 30, 1977

Dear President Carter:

I recently read that you had promised that, if you became President, you would release all the information on UFOs that the government possesses to the public. I would like to know when you will fulfill your promise and where I will be able to obtain a copy of the information.

I have also heard rumors that the Air Force has the body of an extra-terrestrial that they had found in the wreckage of a spaceship and they are keeping it at Andrews AFB. I know that if it were true and the general public was told it would cause panic. All I want to know is if this could be true. I would also like to know if you believe in extraterrestrials?

I *wish* you luck in the next four years.

Chapter 17

Jimmy Carter's Enduring Legacy of UFO Correspondence

For those readers oriented more to the latest in contemporary presidential history than to a rehash of the Carter UFOletters, I recommend that you peruse the proposed "Presidential Proclamation on UFO Freedom of Information and Accountability," which has gathered electronic signatures worldwide via its posting upon the website of http://www.petitionpetition.com. For a copy of the now-expired petition, you may contact me at the following e-mail address: overtci@cavtel.net. If you choose to write direct to the current president about the proposed proclamation, first consider reviewing the content of this book. That way, you'll better appreciate the depth of déja vù that awaits you.

2-14

March 9, 1977

Dear Mr. President:

I realize that you are quite busy and that your time is both valuable and limited; for these reasons I shall try to be as concise and direct as possible.

I am a married man in my middle twenties who has a limited education; by limited I mean high school diploma, some college spare-time studies, and mostly self-educated. And for the past fifteen years I have studied astrodynamics (advanced astrophysics or theoretical physics), radio-controlled rockets, and UFO (Unidentified Flying Objects).

My interest in UFOs came about not by choice but rather fate; for in the middle 60s prior to entering the Air Force I had quite a few encounters with flying discs and UFO occupants. However, as for proof of my encounters, I do not have any.

Mr. President, I have a most urgent matter which I would like to bring to your attention at this time. I have been researching into possible propulsion methods for UFOs or flying discs; and I believe I have discovered a method for propelling a saucer-type aircraft (lenticular aerodyne) by the use of an electromagnetic force field around such a craft.

Recently I submitted my hypothesis to the Air Force's Rocket Propulsion Lab at Edwards Air Force Base in California for review and possible contracting by the Government. Edwards replied that in their opinion my concept was not acceptable for their applications; however, they did not say my approach would not work.

My invention and hypothesis would have the advantages of being capable of high accelerations, sharp turns, sudden stops, banks, without any effects being felt by the passengers aboard the craft. Also, the ecological impact of my invention would also be just as rewarding; for it would be pollution-free, virtually silent in operation, and generate vast amounts of energy. This in turn in itself could lead us (society) into a new realm of energy conservation and utralization yet unimaginable. For the force which would propel this craft would be abundant throughout the Universe! Also, with advances in transportation one would expect advances equally as great in education, medicine, communications, etc.

Mr. President, I have not researched, engineered, drafted, and constructed my previous (solid-fueled) models to advocate warfare.

However, this electromagnetically propelled craft could lead toward an ultimate weapon for the U.S., thus securing a better status for national defense.

I am now working alone and on my own thru personal finances of a limited scale, no personnel, limited work area, and limited supplies. For this reason, Mr. President, I am now asking you for any personal and/or professional assistance which you may be able to supply me.

With just a few personnel to work with and perhaps a few hundred dollars (no more than a couple of thousand), I am convinced a highly practical and workable model of my craft can be properly constructed.

Mr. President, I have always been poor, but I believe that my ideas would help our Government immensely. Please look over my enclosed plans; I believe that you will find these quite interesting. Any assistance which you could provide me would be most deeply appreciated. If you can not be of assistance to me, perhaps you could forward my plans to the appropriate governmental agency.

I am sorry that I do not have a phone at this time by which I may be reached. However, if I can answer any inquiries, please do not hesitate to contact me at any time.

Thank you, Mr. President, for your valuable time and consideration.

Note: The Air Force also has a form-letter response for processing unsolicited proposals for research-and-development projects, as dispatched by Colonel Seminare to the above correspondent.

April 5, 1977

Dear Mr. *[AF-deleted]*:

On behalf of President Carter, this is in reply to your recent letter pertaining to your design for the JHF-X135 "Starcluster" spacecraft.

You will appreciate that as chief executive of our government, as well as Commander in Chief of the Armed Forces, the President cannot possibly respond personally to each communication addressed to him.

Consequently, the President has directed that each Executive agency designate an official as the White House liaison officer who is charged with the responsibility of giving correspondence such as yours the same careful consideration the President would, were he able to do so himself. This is my duty in the Air Force and the reason I am answering.

The Air Force is always receptive to new and novel ideas which will increase the operational effectiveness of our forces. Unfortunately, you did not provide sufficient information to permit a technical evaluation of your proposal. In order for Air Force officials to properly evaluate the potential of your ideas, you would be required to reveal technical data on design and performance and provide an estimate of the cost. The normal procedure for this evaluation would be for you to submit an unsolicited proposal to the appropriate Air Force agency. In this regard, I would suggest that you prepare a proposal in accordance with the attached guide and send it to the Air Force Rocket Propulsion Laboratory, Edwards Air Force Base, California 93523. Accordingly, I am returning your research data.

Hopefully, the foregoing information will be of assistance.

Note: True-believer inventors are a persistent lot. In this case, the would-be salesman of superpropulsion attempts to deny Colonel Seminare the last word:

May 15th, 1977

Dear Colonel Seminare:

Thank you for your correspondence of April 5th, 1977, which was in reply to a letter I sent President Carter concerning a concept I have for constructing a workable spacecraft using a new cosmic energy or gravity propulsion unit.

I am quite aware of the Air Force's policies governing such proposals which are to be put forward for scientific evaluation and research.

Also rest assured that I have already been to the appropriate parties concerning my proposals; among these parties has been the Rocket Propulsion Lab at Edwards A.F.B. in California. However, Edwards turned me down—because they said I had not provided ample data to properly evaluate my proposal. This may well have been. However, please consider that, as I have said, I do not currently have a patent on my concepts along these lines. Also, I believe you shall grant me that such a propulsion unit and craft would indeed have far-reaching effects, both socially and technologically, and would indeed provide the link for a new superior weapons system.

Mr. Rene Cousinet of France has constructed a "Lenticular Aerodyne" or saucer-shaped craft using a variable-angle, outer-turbine approach; this craft he intends to fly this coming summer (summer of '77). However, his craft is powered in horizontal flight by two jet-engine boosters on the lower surface. Yet this craft can not achieve spaceflight and outer atmospheric flights as would mine; nor could it match the velocities and maneuvers.

Under the circumstances, until I have received a patent on my concepts I can not release the essential data pertinent to its functions. I trust you understand my position? Also, I will say in all sincerity that the Air Force shall be hearing from me and want my concepts at a later date when they can then see for themselves just what my craft can achieve.

THANK YOU.

2-15.

May 26, 1977

Sir:

This letter is prompted by the "Perspectives" column in *Ufology*, published by the International UFO Registry, 175 Fifth Avenue, New York, NY 10010 (May 12, 1977, issue).

I ask that you find a means to release to the public the UFO information promised in your campaign. Any panic that might take place is caused by the lack of knowledge. This is a void that must be filled. No matter what form the "truth" might take, a gradual filtering of data to the world's population via talks, films, books, and various publications would help create an environment in which reason could come to replace unreasoning fear for the betterment of all. Thank you.

Note: And speaking of the International UFO Registry, a representative of that organization takes Colonel Seminare to task in the following rejoinder to the colonel's stock reply for presidential UFO mail:

July, 1977

To: Colonel Seminare, Jr.:

This is a letter on behalf of the people of the U.S. who have heard just enough propaganda on the UFO problem. Sure, there are no UFOs; that's why you put a fine of $10,000 and imprisonment to pilots if they reveal UFO information. Why so much concern over UFOs? And concerning Project Blue Book, who cares? It was just a lot of bull to keep the public quiet. All it was is a lot of half-cocked generals sitting together thinking of excuses why there are no UFOs while the public still sighted them. And sure, there are government-paid agencies covering up UFOs; one is the CIA and the AFSSO, and the biggest one's the Air Force. I am mad enough to shoot every plane I see; the ridiculousness of the whole thing is enough to make anyone laugh even more than the Russians.

I just hope the Air Force grows up enough to start to realize the problem without putting in James Bond-type tactics. No matter what you say or do UFOs are still going to be sighted and photographed. Whether you're doing this for national security or out of plain ignorance, UFOs still are going to remain a real problem.

And I hope the foregoing information will clarify the Air Force position as a cover-up agency on this matter.

2-16.

May 21, 1977

Dear Mr. President:

I have seen a Flying Saucer approx. 100 miles west of Houston, Texas, towards the end of May, 1952.

It was early in the morning when I noticed this bright object approx. 100 feet to the left of me. It traveled parallel with my car, then moved ahead approx. 100 feet. My car radio went dead, and I noticed that sparks on the pavement were surrounding my car and trailer.

The Saucer had created an energy field. The static electricity was being generated from the wheels of my car and trailer. The static electricity went up into the Saucer. The appearance of the Flying Saucer looked like a big round battery that was being charged. The portholes were rotating around the Saucer, giving out a sound which sounded like a cricket.

The Saucer traveled approx. 10 to 15 minutes until its energy cells appeared to be charged. When the Saucer broke contact with my car, the radio came back on. The Saucer made 3 half moons and took off instantly, looking like a blue ball of flame heading towards the South Pole.

I have worked with electricity for many years, and it is my opinion that the Flying Saucers are run by lightning, which is atmosphere and temperature.

The smell of carbon from the Saucer is the same as the smell of carbon from lightning. The only source of energy that can make a Saucer fly at that rate of speed is the harnessed energy of lightning. You use Positive to control the speed and use the Earth as Negative.

I believe that I can be of some help if anyone is interested in knowing more about the energy source of the Flying Saucer.

2-17.

February 24, 1977

Dear Mr. President:

Last night as I slept, I had an experience in which you came and sat down at my table where I was reading a book, which I gave you. I awoke with astonishment that I had failed in our personal encounter to mention the UFO subject, your interest in same being one of the four reasons that I have supported "Jimmy Carter for President" since learning that if you became President you would release to the public all UFO government information.

As a Born Again Christian, a scientist, and a UFO believer, you will serve God in a unique fashion as President to bring about the necessary correction of politics and government.

I feel that last night's experience was guidance nudging me to share with you the enclosed, which I am convinced is the true answer to the heretofore UFO mystery.

"God works in mysterious ways His wonders to perform."

Note: The title page of the enclosure to the above letter reads: "Five Hours with the Oligarchs of Venus."

2-18.

February 3, 1977

My dear President Carter:

I am writing you this letter because I desire very strongly to express an opinion of what I consider to be the fundamental challenge of our times. I am referring to the strong possibility of extraterrestrial life. Given the assumption that such intelligences exist on other worlds, I believe an immediate attempt should be made to contact these entities via a network of radio telescopes called "Cyclops" as well as by the use of interplanetary and interstellar probes.

Of course, the projects which I have mentioned would require a large amount of expenditures, but I believe the spin-off technology that would be derived from such ventures would in itself be sufficient compensation for these projects.

Therefore, I respectfully urge that you consider these space programs which I mentioned. I am sure that with your knowledge of pure and applied science, you will make the proper judgments.

I would also like to express my opinion on another very important scientific question. In this case I am referring to the most baffling mystery of all time. I am speaking, of course, of the UFO phenomenon.

Since you have actually seen such a craft, it appears to me that because of your scientific training you will approach the problem in a systematic manner. Therefore, I again urge you to initiate an extensive scientific investigation of this issue.

I sincerely hope that you will consider the suggestions I have discussed and use your scientific training and background to examine and resolve the serious matters I have mentioned.

I know your schedule is a busy one—especially at this time, Mr. President; however, if at any time in the near future you would care to comment on the subjects mentioned above, I would be very grateful if you would drop me a line expressing your viewpoints on these matters.

2-19.

March 29, 1977

Dear Mr. Carter:

I understand the problems you may encounter to keep your promise by revealing the secret information on the U.F.O.'s. But please know that we will help you keep this promise if you have any difficulties. We have encountered and conversed with the occupants of the U.F.O.'s beginning 24 years ago and have much experience with their intentions. We will be most willing to help you and collaborate with you to keep this promise. Believe me, we believe in your sincerity, and desire to help you. Call us, interrogate us; these higher intelligences desire to help humanity, but this help must be asked for. We would be the intermediaries of this help, as we have been trained by them to give you the best advice for contacting them, to explain to you the methodology they use to help us in our decisions.

Believe me, Jimmy Carter.

Fraternally.

2-20.

August 7, 1977

Dear Mr. President:

I know that you believe in UFOs, and so do I. I believe that they exist because I have seen them, and there are too many photographs and sightings of them for them to be false.

I would like to know what you are going to do on the subject because I think that we should not be hostile toward them, for many civilizations have been wiped out because of hostileness (Ex. Inca civilization).

I think that if they attack against us we should fight back, of course, but not be hostile until then.

I am thoroughly interested on this subject, so could you please write me back and tell me what you are going to do? Thank you.

2-21.

May 24, 1977

Dear President Carter:

I'm writing to you about a very interesting subject: Unidentified Flying Objects, otherwise known as UFOs. I look at it this way: you either believe or you don't. I am a believer because I have seen one before.

They tried to tell us it was just a spotlight, but there were too many coincidences; for instance: the telephone went dead, its fast disappearance, and when we finally did contact someone it was gone when they came. The next day in the paper there was about reportings of UFO landings. This is only one of many experiences that I've run across. My sister saw one while she was outside one night. It first looked as three separate planes and next it looked as one huge plane then back into three different ones. My cousins saw a strange, oval-shaped, red light, which they chased for over a quarter of a mile. Finally it just disappeared as if into thin air. It had to be going faster than the speed of light. A few of my other friends have seen them, too.

I would like to know if you believe in them or if you have seen any before. I watched a movie recently on UFOs, and it was very interesting. Do you think that some day we will live like *Star Trek* or *Space 1999*? I hope that it doesn't come to that. Please express your thoughts on this. I would greatly appreciate it.

Thank you very much.

Chapter 18

UFOmystic Meanderings
Beyond the White House Gates

If my above comment about the current WH occupant has moved the story too far forward for you, simply backtrack to the start of the Clinton administration. For this, I suggest that you begin with Chapter 32 ("Would Someone Please Tell the President?") of science writer Patrick Huyghe's Swamp Gas Times: My Two Decades on the UFO Beat (Paraview Press, New York).

2-22.

July 21, 1977

Dear Mr. President:

In *Time* magazine's issue of July 25, 1977, there is an article presumably giving the reasons for "Why the Lights Went Out" in New York City. They cite electrical bolts of lightning one after another and called the whole thing an Act of God. Imagine blaming four electrical hits one after another as being the cause for the massive failure: unbelievable.

If you will recall, during the blackout of November, 1965, the actor Stuart Whitman was contacted in his hotel room high above the streets by personalities in a flying saucer who told him then that they were responsible for the lights all going out. I'm sure that Stuart Whitman was considered quite off balance at the time, but there were many thousands of us who believed his story, which was printed in the newspapers from coast to coast.

Then, following the New York thing, the president of the El Paso Electric Company boasted that what had happened in New York could never happen in El Paso...so of course it did...almost immediately.

And there were no lightning storms, either. I lived in Alamogordo, New Mexico, at that time; and our town was affected also, as were other places in New Mexico and Texas. Friends of mine in El Paso phoned me to tell me that they were out in their backyard and saw the spaceship flying near the generator plant just seconds before their blackout.

Many thousands of us still wait for you to bring out the past-concealed records of the Air Force in regards to the UFO. Other countries recognize what has happened now all over the world, and it is estimated there are many millions who have not only seen this phenomenon of the End Time Bible Prophecies but have been in contact with these Brothers of other planets and Outer Space. What is the purpose of withholding facts on this subject now?

Remember: YOU promised.

God bless. . . .

Note: My e-publication of Letter 2-22 has prompted responses from the East Coast to the West. First, Timothy Beckley, a long-time researcher in New York City, writes:

Stuart Whitman told me several times of his experience while I was interviewing him for one of the tabloids. His story can be found in detail in my book *UFOs Among the Stars.* There were dozens of reports the night before and during the blackout that would indicate that UFOs were at least in the area. An employee of a church in Syracuse photographed a number of brightly lit objects, and they can be found in my *Strange Encounters* book. Most people laugh at the idea UFOs might have some way been involved in the '65 blackout…I didn't then—I don't now!

Next, California-based anthropologist C. Scott Littleton recalls:

Leaving aside the dubious "end-time" implications, the connection between the presence of one or more UFOs and the famous November 9, 1965, New York power blackout has long been suggested. See, for example, Richard M. Dolan's 2000 book *UFOs and the National Security State* (Keyhole Publishing Co., P. O. Box 92188, Rochester, NY 14692)—pp. 384-86. As Dolan points out, the blackout began in Syracuse at 5:15 p.m., at precisely the same time there was a multi-witness UFO sighting over the local New York Power Authority Substation. Other sightings in the Northeast, including NYC itself, soon followed. Despite the official finding that the failure of a Canadian relay station was the culprit, the presence of an electromagnetic interference—the kind of interference widely associated with the presence of UFOs—seems highly probable. Indeed, according to Dolan, shortly after the incident, both Con Edison and Bell Telephone quietly began shielding their equipment against electromagnetic effects.

Was the blackout simply an accident, a side-effect of their tapping into our power grid for their own purposes? It was neither the first nor the last time that UFOs have been spotted in the vicinity of electric power stations, although in most cases they didn't go off-line afterwards (however, cf. the El Paso case that you mention). Or was the NY episode, as well as other less publicized outages, a deliberate experiment on the part of the Alien Raj to see how we post-industrial 'natives' would react to such a situation?

One wonders...

2-23.

August 22, 1977

Dear Mr. Carter:

Since I cannot get into a press conference to speak to you about this subject, I can only write to you and hope that you might give an answer.

Even a short answer would be appreciated.

It is about this matter of UFOs. I have talked to people who believe that your statements regarding UFOs helped to get you elected. They claim that your sighting of a UFO as governor (which got a lot of media play), as well as your statement that you would release CIA documents relating to UFOs upon your election, gave you the edge over Ford. Some people believe that UFOs are becoming a political issue, and, if your campaign promise about releasing CIA documents is true, then this would seem to be the case.

From what I have read in the articles about your UFO sighting, it sounds like you are open-minded about the UFO phenomenon. What I would like to know is this: did you claim that you would release governmental UFO documents? If you did, have you changed your mind, or do you still intend to release certain information? I would imagine that your advisors would recommend that you do not do this, but that's my opinion.

I am a writer and researcher in the UFO field, and rather than write up something second-hand about your statements on this matter, I wanted to ask you myself.

Hope you can relax once in a while.

2-24.

Etna, Maine
June 12, 1977

Mr. President:

It is with the greatest respect that I am writing this letter to you, a man of great honor, a God-chosen Leader (so much needed) in this great country of ours, America. God bless you and our country, Sir!

My reason for this letter is a mixture of many things: astonishment, curiosity, and caution all put together in one.

Even knowing how busy you must be, I pray to God you will find time to read this. It gives me the confidence and strong assurance you will answer in honesty and truth.

On May the 12th, 1977, at 3:20 a.m. in the morning, on my way home from out of State, I saw a large, very speedy, moving, silvery, round object, not more than 6-7 feet above tree-tops crossing before me on Interstate Highway 95 in Maine. Imagine how I held my breath when not more than 1-2 minutes later another large object, same shape, form, and size, crossed before me in the same direction as the first. You could have never spotted them on any radar because they were flying very low.

Their movement was like a spinning force and extremely fast.

Although I am a woman I don't frighten too easily; my thoughts are settled because God is my Maker, Protector, and Guide—but, I must admit—a cold chill went down my hairline to my spine when I saw these two large silvery things so low, crossing the highway in front of me.

Only twenty minutes away from home, many thoughts ran through my mind. What to do? Whom to tell? Who would believe such a startling thing? Most folks would question one's sanity. You know, Sir, I heard from some articles in the papers about things called U.F.O.'s; but believe me, I never expected to see two of them so low and close in front of me.

I love America with all my heart and know what my duties are when I see something out of order, so I called the Highway Patrol and made a report. But you know, something like that does not ever leave your mind. You relive that over and over again, and in your mind you wonder: "What is it?! Where does it come from? Why is it, or are they not identifying themselves, or have they? What is the purpose of such visits? Why so secret?"

Nothing, or no-one, travels anywhere without a purpose or some intention. Whatever it is, it does not look like earth-powered to me.

To my logic, it appears that these beings (unless these things are satellite-powered) are of extreme intelligence and could be either very helpful or destructive to our planet earth. Often I wished to see another one again, only not so close; perhaps I could find some sort of hint or answer to this unbelievable thing.

There is a toll-free U.F.O. International Number, and I tried to notify them twice but only reached a recording asking for name, address, and phone number; never heard from anyone a thing. After contemplating about this thing again today, I prayed out of desperation; and the thought flashed to my mind to write an honest and open letter to YOU, Sir. I have faith in answers to prayers and also in YOU, Sir.

It seems to me that such powerful flying things should be identified, not only in the interest and safety of this country but also the entire world— by someone with good intent, is open, honest, straightforward, and does not sneak about in darkness or secrecy.

We are all in God's hands, a blessing for sure! BUT, God expects us to use wisdom in all things. A wise person never takes chances—only fools do.

Since God has entrusted this beautiful planet into our care and keeping, we should be concerned about its safety and welfare. Such strange things, coming and going so swift and easy without a calling card or some statement as to their business here, should get priority attention.

Else, someone might think nobody cares, and the world could be unpleasantly surprised. I pray to God that we will find the answer to this mystery soon; it sure puzzles me.

Mister President, forgive me for taking of your time, but this letter needed to be written or I would not be true to myself, God, or my country.

I pray to hear from you as openly as you heard from me. At least, as far as your conscience permits you to do.

In closing, may I speak from the heart and say: May God our Father the Almighty bless and keep you always, and continue to sharpen your spirit and mind in doing what you have been blessed and chosen to do. We are proud of your leadership and pledge our support to you as wholehearted Americans. God bless the President, YOU SIR, Jimmy Carter, and God bless AMERICA!

In Jesus Christ our Lord, Your Citizen.

2-25.

To President Carter:
For the past 30 years, the people of this country plus millions of persons abroad have been reporting strange craft, both in the sky and on the ground.

Sir, you said that if elected, you would have all data on U.F.O.'s made public. I think you are doing a good job so far, but some of the people of this nation are of the opinion that we are being led around by the nose, re: CIA cover-ups, Air Force warnings about national security, etc.

Mr. President, I think it's time someone listened to the people.

Sir, I think the people should be told what is going on. In fact, it is the right by law of our country to be told as much as possible if not all that is known about them.

I am sending this letter to the National Enquirer, as I don't think it would get to you through government channels. Plus, I have hopes others will see it and write their congressmen asking them to vote YES on it.

Some people will no doubt call me a kook. But who cares what they call me—I sure don't, because I think I am right in my convictions. After all, everyone is entitled to their opinion.

Sir, being a member of A.P.R.O., I am going to try to do my part to find some answers. I hope you can do your part to find some kind of a solution to this phenomenon, as it is getting out of hand.

Sir, it is the opinion of many that U.F.O. research should be a civilian project, and that the military and CIA be told to keep hands off.

As can be seen, they have failed to give the people of this country a logical explanation. Since when do our jets chase "SWAMP GAS"? Plus, they continue to withhold information from the public. After all, it's our money they are using. I say let the research groups have the information they need, and then maybe a solution could be found.

I could name several well-documented cases where U.F.O.'s were sighted. But for lack of space I will not include.

Sir, I wish you well, and may God be with you.

2-26.

Dear Mr. President:

I'm sure you've received a lot of letters about Unidentified Flying Objects (what is your stand on them, how do you feel about them?). I understand (at least I hope) that you do believe in them. First of all, I totally agree with you. There are people out there, and I think we should at least try to contact them, or at least show them we're peaceful enough to leave them alone.

There are a lot of inconsistencies—the Air Force has denied them for years, but yet there have been reports of fighter jets shooting at saucers, and even that there are *captured* saucers being held here by the FBI, the CIA, the Air Force, etc. They either always deny those reports, or say that we (Americans) would panic if we knew the truth. I think people are more tense now, because we're hiding the evidence, than we would be if we knew exactly what the aliens want (if anything).

I believe that you, the President, can and should push for an investigation on this subject, so we can know the answers to questions like *Where do they come from? Who are they? Why are they here?*

Please write and let me know how you feel about this idea.

Chapter 19

When UFO History
Speaks, Who Will Listen?

During your perusal of this collection of letters, you may have come to realize their in-nate historical and cultural value. And rightly so, since they do indeed rank with some of the more popular UFO-E.T. literature fervently sought by collectors.

Lately, a few such specialists in UFOana have been voicing concern that the score or more massive UFOlit collections now in private hands might suffer the fate of a frenzied spring house-cleaning by survivors of, say, an eccentric old aunt or uncle who couldn't bring her/himself to make adequate arrangements for the collection's longevity and wide public access.

Lest I fall into that tragic trap, I'm intensifying my own efforts to find a proper, practical, permanent, and public home for my own tons of UFOlit. My past attempts to find a willing institutional recipient for this proposed donation (and subsequent stewardship) have failed.

Readers having archival contacts with enough managerial clout to rule in favor of UFOlit preservation, rather than oblivion, can do me an immeasurable favor by re-ferring me to those contacts.

Let's learn from the Carter Administration/Library's mistake of letting several thousand UFOletters slip from the (albeit tenuous) grasp of scholarship, intellectual fellowship, and any related sociopolitical reform!

2-27.

February 7, 1977

Dear Sir:

I am one of America's leading experts on the unsolved enigma called Unidentified Flying Objects (UFOs). This monumental subject is one that our President has expressed interest in and vitally needs to learn about. So far as I know no other President has ever listened to any other source but the military-intelligence version of all this. Its ramifications reach beyond all the problems he now faces.

Will you please consider this request for a meeting under your "Visit the People" plan? I would bring with me *[AF-deleted]* and *[AF-deleted]*.

These are America's No. 1 and No. 2 researchers heading the nation's two major research organizations, with many years of experience.

Attached find several documents to illustrate what is presently going on in our precious country and the world.

Note: Apparently, the only "document" retained by the Air Force is the following tabulation of UFO statistics:

A SUMMARY OF UFO SIGHTINGS IN FIVE SOUTHEASTERN INDI-ANA COUNTIES AND ADJACENT AREAS DURING THE YEARS 1966 TO 1975

The total activity of these mysterious aeroforms is unknown because of the lack of a comprehensive reporting system and unseen visitation.

NUMBER OF SIGHTINGS: 325 individual witnesses in 75 incidents.

NUMBER OF UNIDENTIFIABLE OBJECTS SEEN: 102

TOTAL SIGHTINGS EACH COUNTY: Payette 155, Rush 69, Wayne 18, Franklin 17, Union 7, Strip-mines area 42, other areas 17. (Totals reflect effectiveness of reporting system, not true activity each county.)

LOCATION WHERE SEEN: Rural 262, residential 46, industrial, electrical transformer bank, Federal relay tower, NIKE Base area, 16. (Return visits made to these sites.)

TOTAL SIGHTINGS YEARLY: 1966-168 witnesses, 1967-51, 1968-18, 1969-2, 1970-0, 1971-6, 1972-8, 1973-64, 1974-8. Peak months were October 1966—98 witnesses and October 1973—64 witnesses.

TIME SEEN: Morning 6 a.m. to 12—5 objects, afternoon 12 to 6 p.m.—6, evening 6 p.m. to 12—67, night 12 to 6 a.m.—24.

SHAPE OF OBJECTS: Domed discs—16 objects (10 with a series of lights around rim), disc, saucer, cigar, or oval—40, round—16, unknown or other shapes—30.

SPEED: 23 objects sped out of sight from a standing start in 5 seconds or less.

SOUND: Silent—89 objects, whirling—4, buzzing—3, high-frequency sound—2, other sounds—4.

ACTION RELATIVE TO THE OBJECT: Hovered—41 objects, low overflight—39, landed or near-landing—7 incidents, number of occupants seen—7, projected beam—5 objects (In one instance the witnesses claimed what appeared to be a small car returned to craft in the light beam.) Paced autos—6 objects, jets chased 2 objects, photos taken—1.

PHYSICAL EFFECTS: Ground evidence—5 incidents, radio-TV interference—4 objects, burned circles in soybean fields—2, cone-shaped holes impressed in earth—1, red dust remained behind—1, mottled red-orange rocklike object remained behind—1, spewed-out greenish phosphorescent material—2, heel prints remained behind—1.

PHYSIOLOGICAL EFFECTS: Sulfur odor—2 incidents, personal fear created—16 persons, severe pain in lower chest—1, tingly and numb feeling—7 persons, animal panic—2 incidents.

2-28.

April 21, 1977

Dear Mr. President:

I must first apologize for taking your time, for I realize you are a busy man and have much more important things to attend to.

I am writing to you asking your opinion to the two following questions that have been on my mind for quite some time. I would truly appreciate it if you would send me a reply. Thank you very much.

(1) GOD forbid, will there be a WW III in the future?

(2) Are UFOs being taken seriously as being a threat to our country now, or maybe in the future?

Note: Thanks to the above concerned citizen, Colonel Seminare's staff probably felt relieved to have a chance to customize their formula response to UFO queries— as shown by this excerpt from the colonel's letter of June 10, 1977:

Your question whether there will be a World War III is, of course, foremost in the mind of the President and of our nation's military leaders. The mission of the Air Force, and the other services, is to protect the nation. The President is committed to a foreign policy that attempts to insure there will never be another world war. To the extent that the President and the military are successful in their missions, such a catastrophe may be avoided.

With regard to the question about unidentified flying objects (UFOs), as you may know, the Air Force has closed its research in this area and turned over all information to the National Archives. During the entire period that the Air Force was involved in this study, no evidence was developed to suggest that UFOs were extraterrestrial or posed a threat to the national security of the United States.

2-29.

January 27, 1977

Dear President Carter:

As America just celebrated her 200th anniversary July 4, 1976. With God's superintending, Providence has brought us you, President Carter, to lead our Nation during these troubled times. I was led to send you these following articles: "Nation Born to God in a Day"; "Who are These that Fly as Clouds?" I know you would be interested, as you study your Bible. The key that has unlocked the secrets of the vision given to Daniel has also supplied the meaning of world events and current happenings today. With much concern for the down disarmament of our nation, this was brought to my attention.

When the great air armada of Russia ascends for the coming invasion of the United States, for the attack, the security of the people dwelling in a country of unwalled villages. To plunder and loot, to turn their hands against our Nation, "practicing commerce and trade, and residing on the top of the earth," Ez. 38:8, 11, 12.

That the logical line of attack by Russia upon the United States would follow a course from Siberia to Alaska, south through to Canada, striking at the center of our country. Formerly, any contemplated foreign invasion of the United States had to be made from the sea, and would be directed against our coastal cities. Russia has no great sea power but has acquired a mighty air force, and we may yet see planes, furnished her by us, winging their way back loaded with explosives.

The conquest of the air has changed former methods of attack, and the most direct route for Russia to take in a move of aggression against us is over this very course.

Gog, of the land of Magog, the Chief Prince of Mechech (Moscow), describes great military preparation and the organization and regimentation of nations around her. Persia (Iran), Gomer (Germany).

Since you are interested in U.F.O.s, this little booklet is an eye-opener how God has provided to protect us as a Christian Nation.

May these Scriptures, foretold, bring about awakening to this peril.

President Carter, would you declare a defence to the North of our "America the Beautiful"? May God help you through this new year. God bless us and guide us through Jacob's trouble.

Note: Once again, a non-UFO-related issue affords Colonel Seminare's staff a chance to wax philosophic on a subject they obviously feel safe enough to emote upon:

February 7, 1977

Dear Mrs. *[AF-deleted]*:

On behalf of President Carter, I am replying to your January 27 letter regarding the northern defense of our United States.

I wish to thank you for taking the time to express your views on this issue.

You may be assured that the President and senior Air Force officials are vitally interested in a strong national defense and do not lightly make decisions which impact our armed forces' capabilities. They will continue to do everything possible to most effectively employ our national defense within our country.

The patriotic concern which prompted your correspondence is deeply appreciated.

Note: Some correspondents choose to put their messages on postcards:

2-30.

June, 1977

Dear President Carter:

Right now is the time to keep your promise to open up the government files on Unidentified Flying Objects.

Please don't make any excuses or allow your appointees to block this action.

Thanks.

2-31.

Mr. President:

It has recently come to my attention that you have, in fact, seen a U.F.O. I am most interested in this fact.

It has also come to my attention that certain other sightings have been reported, documented, and then dismissed! May I ask, why?

In all, there appear to be three types of U.F.O. sightings. These are known as: Class A, Class B, and Class C.

Class A is the mere viewing of a strange light or lights, either in the sky, on the ground, or in and around water, such as lakes, ponds, and oceans, including a section known as the "Devil's Triangle," off the coast of Florida.

Class B consists of a close-up view of a craft (?), or crafts, with or without sounds. These sightings usually occur, to the best of my knowledge, either early in the a.m. or early in the p.m. Occasionally there is damage either to the surrounding shrubbery or the viewer himself.

Class C is the most frightening of all sightings: actual physical contact with a U.F.O., or more likely, its occupants. Such is the case of the well-known "Pascagoula Kidnapping," where two men, Calvin Parker, age 19, and Charles Hickson, age 45, claim to have been kidnapped by a U.F.O. and its occupants while fishing from a deserted wharf in Pascagoula, Mississippi. Through hypnosis, it was positively concluded that the two men had indeed seen something. But our government (Air Force, F.B.I., C.I.A.) apparently "covered up" this find.

Mr. President, I feel it is the government's duty to report to the people what they have discovered about U.F.O.'s. Why has "Project Blue Book," which the Air Force undertook a few years back, not yet been revealed to the public?

I respectfully suggest that a committee be set up to document and file all reported sightings. A toll-free hotline should also be set up so people who should sight something strange could report it without fear of being called a crackpot. This committee should also be immune to any governmental hanky-panky.

I hope I have shed some light on this subject. Also, I would appreciate any details of your sighting. I would appreciate this very much. I am also including my telephone number, in case you would like to contact me.

2-32.

May 25, 1977

Dear Sir:

I am writing to you about a matter of great importance, or which I believe in. I read an article in the paper some time back that you had seen a flying saucer, and that you were trying to get information released on them.

I too have seen many U.F.O.'s: six at very close range; by that I mean less than a thousand yards. I have seen nine entries into our atmosphere, or burn-in's, as I call them, much like our space craft on re-entry. But that is not the reason I am writing to you. The method they use for silent flight at low altitudes and terrific speeds, paying no regard to the sound barrier or thermo barrier, seems to have our scientists and engineers completely baffled. Every article I read on U.F.O. sightings, the officials, upon being asked their opinion on the silent flights, all reply that they wish they knew. I too was curious; being mechanically inclined and somewhat of an inventor myself, I have come up with the only solution possible. It really is quite simple how they do it. I have spent several years researching and deep meditation on the matter of propulsion systems, and to my knowledge we have no such propulsion system. But I now believe that we have the material and technology to produce such a craft, as described above. I have this theory, partially worked out in my mind; and there are dozens of clues and facts that back my theory one-hundred percent. I am totally sincere in this statement that I have this information, but I have not known what to do with it. So I am writing this letter to you, hoping that you will advise as to what steps I should take. If my theory is true—and at this point I have no doubt that it is true—I believe it would have the importance of the atomic submarine or the Apollo programs. |

As for some of my background, I am 52 years old, and have been employed thirty-four years as a heavy-equipment operator, furnace operator, stationary engineer for Boeing Aircraft, and presently employed in the Automotive Body Refinishing, here in Morgan Co., Ky. I have tried to call you but was advised to write to you by your staff. Hoping to hear from you real soon.

2-33.

April 22, 1977

Dear Mr. President:

I feel the need to write to you. Not that I am going to say that you are doing a lousy job as President, but to ask you if you would help me and others on a problem concerning the UFO situation.

If you have read anything at all about UFOs, you will see that the number of sightings has grown greatly since 1947. (1947 is when Kenneth Arnold saw nine flying disks.) Along with this growth, there comes discouragement. People are constantly told, by the government, that their sighting was nothing more than the planet Venus, etc. This has caused many people to feel that if they report a sighting of a UFO, they will be put in the "nut house." I feel that this is the wrong attitude to take. I wish that people could see that the UFO problem is not one of these everyday problems that can be taken while sitting down.

In a UFO magazine, I read that you had a UFO sighting of your own. If this statement is true, then you can see why I am writing to you. I feel that it is about time that the American government unlocked their files and let the American people know what is happening. I can understand the feeling of not wanting to "stick the neck in the noose," but look at the scientists that have. There is Dr. J. Allen Hynek—former consultant to Project Blue Book. And there is Jacques Vallee, plus many more that feel that their names should not be publicly known. Why then is the American government afraid of telling the truth?

In their book *Beyond Earth: Man's Contact with UFOs*, Ralph and Judy Blum have stated that a recent Gallup poll revealed that fifteen million Americans have seen UFOs and that fifty-one percent of the population believes in UFOs. Yet, the government says that these people are wrong. Will you be willing to risk the chance on your presidency to help us out here and unlock the government files? I hope so. You are probably our only last chance.

What would the American public do if a UFO were to land in the U.S. today?

2-34.

January 1977

Dear Mr. President:

I don't know if this was said because of the heat of the campaign or that you promised to do it. You said you would open up all the UFO files, cases, and photographs and make them public. I would like to see this done. I don't think the Air Force should be allowed to swear their men to secrecy when they have contacts with UFOs. The Air Force says every sighting can be explained as natural phenomenon. I know of people (including myself) who have seen UFOs. Open up those files, and let's see the Air Force start explaining.

2-35.

February 5, 1977

Dear Sir:

Please read the enclosed movie ads and magazines. Please note the articles marked in the Tables of Contents.

These things (fourteen subjects) show that the American people know or suspect that we are not alone, even though the Federal Government is hushing up the truth for fear we will panic as people did at the broadcast of H. G. Wells' *War of the Worlds* in the 1930s.

2-36.

March 1977

Dear Mr. President:

I realize that you are a very busy man. I voted for you in the election, and I am glad you won. I tried calling you during your telephone conversation with the American people on Saturday, March 5, but found it impossible to get through. So I called the White House and gave them the message that I'm going to ask you now. During your campaign I read in the Enquirer newspaper that you said if you were elected president you would reveal to the American people all the government information on UFOs. I'm wondering, Mr. President, if you still intend to, and if so, when?

I don't know if this letter is ever going to reach you, but if it does I would appreciate it very much if you could answer me on this question.

Every time I read something on UFOs, it really intrigues me.

In closing, I just want to say that I think you are doing a good job and I like the way that you are communicating with the American public. I saw a movie years ago, "Yankee Doodle Dandy" with James Cagney (I believe I saw it about 10 times). And I liked when Mr. Cagney said to President Roosevelt something like "It's something, Mr. President, when someone can come off the street and talk to the top man!" You remind me of that, Mr. President. In closing, thank you again for your time.

2-37.

January 29, 1977

Dear Mr. President:

I read an article in the *Official UFO* magazine, March 1977 issue, that said you would make all pieces of information about U.F.O.'s available to the public. I would like to know if they are real or, if not, what they are. My family saw one (a U.F.O.) in 1973 in Owego, New York, and recently we have been seeing one of the same description as the U.F.O. you described in the article. The U.F.O. we saw would move slowly, speed up, and then stop in mid-air and then reverse its direction.

I had great confidence that you would make it to be President. We will keep praying that you will make out all right as President.

I would also like to know if you or someone else could find out if it would be all right for me to write to Mr. Richard Nixon to see if we might be related.

I would also like to find out if I could write to Mr. Nelson Rockefeller about the State Park he plans to build on Michigan Hill in Richford, New York.

I would write to them on my own, but I don't know their addresses and I was quite sure you would.

Thank you for your time and consideration; it is greatly appreciated.

2-38.

March 10, 1977

Dear Mr. President:

Ex-President Ford backed a U.F.O. investigation. Are you going to continue this investigation? Are you going to expand the investigation to other mysteries such as Bigfoot and the Loch Ness Monster?

Chapter 20

Cosmic Victims?

There are three kinds of people in Amerika: victims, former victims, and future victims. As regards the subculture of UFOlogy, we have three subsets: those "experiencers" victimized by certain UFO encounters; those citizens victimized by officialdom's entrenched UFO-secrecy policies and practices; and those researchers victimized by thoughtless/mean-spirited detractors bent on destroying the messenger. One needn't look far for representatives of that latter category of victimizers, who readily reveal a mind-set fueled by volitional ignorance and underlying fear.

You might say that the ultimate UFOlogical victim would be a young U. S. Marine diligently pulling guard duty at, say, Quantico, Virginia, only to find that he's being subjected to UFOsnatching from his base, where, the next day, he vows never again to trust the chain-of-command (for its out-of-hand dismissal of his harrowing experience); and where, a week or so later, the local county's all-news TV channel plays the Twilight Zone *theme as background music to introduce a canned putdown of the trooper's story.*

2-39.

April 26, 1977

Dear Mr. President:

Every American is aware of the economic and ecological problems facing our nation and our future generations. But there is a problem of a different nature that this American is aware of; and that problem is the oversight of past administrations to properly deal with the Unidentified Flying Object enigma.

The UFO phenomenon has long been a serious hobby of mine. In the past eleven years, although a writer by trade with a B.S. in Mass Communications, I have devoted much time to personally researching eyewitness UFO reports from Miami to Zurich. In my lectures and media appearances, I have had the opportunity to meet with the public and listen to their points of view on the subject. Because of my experiences in the field and open interest in the UFO as a learning avenue, a large portion of my listening audience has turned to me for the answers to this communicator's problem. Sadly enough, the public cannot get sufficient and truthful information from their government. One is led to believe this large network of scientists and military brass either don't have the answers, or are incapable of handling the public relations that goes with the territory.

The truth does not simply mean exposing the facts. No…instead we have something much more profound. We, as a people, must take an intelligent look into this enigma's physical, mental, and spiritual relationship to man and the surrounding universe. Our own history as well as our future may be reflected here.

Because of the world we live in, maintaining weapons power has become a necessity. So it is not surprising that the military has stamped a "No Trespassing" sign on UFO files and films. Surely the craft's speed potential and maneuverability out-class any of man's mechanical wonders. Do some of the echelon see a public display of information as a breakdown in military power? Man thinks of power in how much he can destroy. Perhaps the intelligence behind these craft don't have those concepts. Perhaps, to them, power is a state of knowledge.

I seek no fame in the unveiling of the facts. What I do seek is your involvement in the release of all UFO data. This was one of your pledges carried over the news wires. I will be glad to help in the organization of any plans, and would be honored to act as a communications liaison where needed. Yes, there definitely is a case for the modern UFO. Let's put an end to the Cosmic Watergate. The people are waiting.

2-40.

March 1, 1977

Dear President Carter:

I would like to know if you intend to make all government UFO information public knowledge. I think it's only fair that the American people should be allowed to know what is actually going on. All the presidents in the past have kept us in the dark on this subject, as well as other things. What the American people need and want now is a president who is willing to be completely honest and open with us, and let us know everything that is going on.

Frankly, I feel that making all U.F.O. knowledge public now will give the people time to accept and understand U.F.O.'s and alien beings from another world or universe, so that if and when they do land on earth and try to communicate with us, the public will be less likely to panic. A mass panic of this sort could prove fatal to us all. If they should land, and the people panic and start shooting at them and try to kill them because of fear and lack of understanding, they could wipe us out. After all, if they're intelligent and advanced enough to get here, they're surely capable of wiping us out or enslaving us, which would probably be a fate worse than death for the proud and free American people. I sincerely hope you are thinking of making this government knowledge public, and if not, I hope you will reconsider. I would sincerely appreciate a reply from you on your views of this matter.

May I also congratulate you for winning the election. I truly think you're just what the American people want and need now, a bright new face with sincerity and new ideas for the well being of our nation and her people.

2-41.

May 13, 1977

Dear Mr. President:
Recently I heard from a friend that the government is currently studying E.S.P. and telepathy. I was wondering if this is true and if so what have these studies found.

Also, I'd like to know if the Air Force or any other branch of the U.S.

Government has studied U.F.O.'s since the termination of Project Blue Book in December, 1969? And what have any of these studies turned up that wasn't determined by Project Blue Book? If possible, Mr. President, could you please tell me what you think of the U.F.O. phenomenon, and whether you think it warrants further investigation?

Thank you for your time.

2-42.

May 10, 1977

Dear President Carter:
Let me introduce myself. I am *[AF-deleted]*, a life-time resident of Cleveland.

The past few years I have become interested in information about U.F.O.'s, especially information withheld by our government. An organization I have been corresponding with informed me I should vote for you for President—the reason being their belief you would release this "confidential" information. I trust you will expedite this campaign promise as soon as possible.

Also—Good Luck at the National Level.

Yours in Christ

Note: Neither of the following two letters, written presumably by the same person, received a reply from the Air Force:

2-43.

February 3, 1977

My dear President Carter:

I am writing you this letter because I desire very strongly to express an opinion of what I consider to be the fundamental challenge of our times. I am referring to the strong possibility of extraterrestrial life. Given the assumption that such intelligences exist on other worlds, I believe an immediate attempt should be made to contact these entities via a network of radio telescopes called "Cyclops," as well as by the use of interplanetary and interstellar probes.

Of course, the projects which I have mentioned would require a large amount of expenditures, but I believe the spin-off technology that would be derived from such ventures would in itself be sufficient compensation for these projects.

Therefore, I respectfully urge that you consider these space programs which I mentioned. I am sure that with your knowledge of pure and applied science, you will make the proper judgments.

I would also like to express my opinion on another very important scientific question. In this case I am referring to the most baffling mystery of all time. I am speaking, of course, of the UFO phenomenon.

Since you have actually seen such a craft, it appears to me that because of your scientific training you will approach the problem in a systematic manner. Therefore, I again urge you to initiate an extensive scientific investigation of this issue.

I sincerely hope that you will consider the suggestions I have discussed and use your scientific training and background to examine and resolve the serious matters I have mentioned.

I know your schedule is a busy one—especially at this time, Mr. President; however, if at any time in the near future you would care to comment on the subjects mentioned above, I would be very grateful if you would drop me a line expressing your viewpoints on these matters.

2-44.

March 17, 1977

My dear President Carter:

As I have stated before in previous letters which I sent to you, I am a strong advocate of an advanced space program. In this letter I would like to relate to you my feelings concerning the possible colonization of extraterrestrial bodies by human civilization.

It is my belief that space colonization is a possible, if not practical, answer to some of mankind's most severe problems, such as overpopulation and diminishing energy resources. In my opinion, however, the primary reason for space colonization is the fact that it provides mankind with a new frontier in which to live, work, and finally develop into a more mature, universal society.

Because of the reasons I have just stated, it is now obvious to me that at no time in man's history on this planet has he so badly needed an avenue in which his most courageous and compassionate interests could be realized.

Therefore, I respectfully urge that your administration study and evaluate the space colonization project that has been developed by Dr. Gerald K. O'Neill of Princeton University.

I also respectfully urge you and your science advisors appraise the works of other space experts, who have developed concepts similar to Dr. O'Neill's.

In conclusion, I sincerely hope that you will consider the matters I have discussed, and I am sure that you will make judgments (concerning space colonization) that will be beneficial to the citizens of the United States as well as to all the peoples of the world.

Any comments you may have concerning the above-mentioned matters shall be deeply appreciated.

2-45.

March 17, 1977

Dear Mr. President:

I am writing with regard to the declassification of the government material contained in Project Blue Book. I would like to point out a couple of things that perhaps may have escaped your observation.

According to every survey (particularly Gallup Polls), more Americans believe in U.F.O.s and their occupancy by space intelligences than do not. Secondly, might I remind you that in a recent survey of over one thousand astronomers eighty percent indicated that there should be more interest and investigation in this area.

I also would like to point out that it was promised during your campaign for the Presidency that Blue Book would be made public along with its findings.

I personally have been involved in the research of phenomena for the past ten years, and find the public to be crying very loudly to deaf ears for this information to be made public. The only commonly held absurdity concerning this matter is the belief on the part of governmental officials that the public can be duped and lied to about the truth of this matter. I have yet to come across one American that doesn't openly laugh at the question "Do you accept or believe the government's explanation about U.F.O.'s?" THEY ALL AGREE SOMETHING, IF NOT EVERYTHING, IS BEING WITHHELD FROM THEM! For the government to think it is fooling anyone in this area is the most ridiculous position the government has ever taken on anything.

Had I the time, I could send to you hundreds, thousands, and even millions of signatures indicating the same position I am taking. Won't you PLEASE address this subject in ONE of your national addresses? I ask this in the name of honesty in government, common sense, obvious reality, and on behalf of millions and millions of Americans that do not take the time to write, as I have. P.S.: During your March "telephone-athon" I and my three children repeatedly dialed your number for hours, one right after the other, to try to get through to question you on this vital matter.

2-46.

January 8, 1977

Dear Mr. President:

In response to your request for ideas from the people that might help you, I have one idea in mind.

Mainly, it involves the "UFO CONTROVERSY, SECRECY HAZARDS, AIR FORCE, and CIA." Air Force regulation 11-30, withholding information "in the public interest," is admitted as official policy. In Air Force regulation 11-7, it is stated that sometimes information requested by Congress may not be furnished "even in confidence."

I'm interested in Aerial Phenomena as a hobby. After reading on the subject of UFOs, I'm disappointed in the way the government officials have handled this matter.

I have read: "The Central Intelligence Agency has used its power to guide and support the Air Force deception of Congress, the press, and the public. This is not an attempt to crucify the CIA, harsh as it may seem. Faced with a serious decision, it took the course it believed wisest for the nation, but regardless of motives the CIA and the Air Force now have put the country in a dangerous predicament. It could hardly be worse if they had deliberately planned it."

I have read these objects have the ability to neutralize gravity, by reversible electromagnetism, and they can overcome the forces of gravity.

One interesting case report happened on March 5, 1967, in Minot, North Dakota, where a circular metallic craft over 100-feet in diameter was heading for one of the Minutemen Grids. The object finally did depart, but the case is still unexplained.

Maybe we could consider the suggestion made by AIAA (American Institute of Astronautics and Aeronautics) urging a new full-scale, unbiased investigation, an objective examination of the best verified reports, with no censorship.

I have written to CBS's *60 Minutes* [and] to Congressman Harrington on this subject.

We should start explaining the evidence, instead of explaining it away as we have done in the past. Now that we have a President that works with the people, I'm optimistic of the future.

Thank you so much for taking the time to read my letter, which I hope has helped.

Note: In the UFO literature's ample quantity of spurious accounts and absurd theories, one story pops up with regularity: the unsupported (or undersupported) contention, hatched by writer Frank Scully in his 1950 book Behind the Flying Saucers, *that creatures from one or more disabled UFOs have been recovered bv government authorities and secretly pickled away at some military installation, there to undergo— what…prolonged study and experimentation? As You might expect, this story has several variations, one of which is presented to President Carter in the following letter:*

2-47.

March 10, 1977

Dear Mr. President:

This letter is a follow-up to a letter I sent to you in Plains by Special Delivery around the 15th of December. I don't know if you had a chance to read it. The subject I would like to bring to your attention is a U.F.O. report. I know you have stated that you yourself have seen one in 1973. It's nice to know we have a President that's not a skeptic when it comes to flying saucers.

This one particular subject has been kicking around for the last twelve or more years. It concerns a crashed U.F.O.

The story starts with a man named Baron Nicholas E. Von Poppen, a foreigner from Estonia, a small nation on the Baltic Sea. Von Poppen emigrated to the U.S. He took up with photography, concentrating on industrial photography. He developed a further specialty by applying photography to metallurgical analysis. In 1949 Von Poppen was contacted by the military intelligence agents. They threatened to deport him if he ever spoke of their meeting. They wanted him to accompany them on what they called an unusual photographic project utilizing his skills in photographing metals. He agreed, and they soon took off by a military plane.

They arrived at Los Alamos, the site of the first atomic bomb test. Von Poppen was taken by jeep to where a large, flat, circular object was resting on the ground. An Air Force captain described it as an authentic "flying saucer." Von Poppen was told to photograph close-up areas of the metal. In his two-day stay, he covered the whole ship in and out and described it as being thirty feet across. Inside were dead alien occupants. The largest was about four feet tall, weighing about thirty-five pounds; and the smallest about two feet in height. This information was passed on to a close friend named Dr. George C. Tyler, who passed on the information before his death. The downed craft was taken to Wright-Patterson Air Force Base. An unidentified lady was employed by the Signal Corps, working for the Army and the F.B.I. She worked the night shift on the teletype, and her duties included decoding messages and handling classified materials of many different sorts. She saw photographs of a crashed U.F.O. They were classified and carried top-security designation. No one under rank of major drove the truck that transported the craft to Wright-Patterson Air Force Base.

Now to my question. Is there any truth to this story, and does the Air Force have a flying saucer and its crew in deep freeze at Wright-Patterson? I think it's about time the American people should know the truth about the story.

2-48.

March 9, 1977

Dear Mr. President Carter:

I'm writing to you about a published magazine called *U.F.O.* It says you saw a flying saucer and you don't laugh when someone says that they have seen one. Well, I was stationed at March Field, California, in the Air Force in 1950 at Riverside, California. I was with the Air Police Squadron, and I was on patrol in a jeep at night when I was riding my zone patrol by myself. I looked up and saw eight saucers in formation, glowing and in formation like geese. The excitement caused me to turn my jeep over. Being that I was alone and no-one else saw this, I kept my mouth shut; and I was hospitalized and they called it a freak accident. I know that they are observing us; are you going to release the truth soon about them? Also, I heard the government holds captive a crashed saucer and its occupants. I know you are quite busy with all the world problems, but could you maybe get your secretary to send me a little data on this subject?

2-49.

April 1, 1977

My Dear Mr. President:

I was greatly impressed by your recent nationwide question-answer program aired over the radio. Speaking in all probity, it showed me you are a truly sincere man and care about the people, their gripes, comments, and questions. If this sounds as though I'm leading up to a question, I am. You see, for some time now I've read and heard about the government, or more specifically the Air Force, studying a captured U.F.O. This may sound a bit bizarre, yet I continue to hear the same story. I was wondering if this story were true; and if anyone could find out, you could, Mr. President.

2-50.

Mr. President:

I am taking this opportunity to write to you regarding a subject which I feel is critically important to our country, with the hope that you will either read this letter personally or perhaps receive a shorter, condensed version from your correspondence office, and possibly be influenced to the extent of taking some sort of action.

The subject is UFOs, or interplanetary (possibly interstellar) visitors to Earth, which have developed a scientific technology vastly superior to our own, and which have been investigated intensely by both military and civilian bureaus during the past few decades.

I have overcome my disinclination to appear presumptuous in submitting this letter to the executive branch of the government of the U.S.A. by convincing myself of the unique quality of an unusual experience which occurred in the fall of 1975 here in Seattle. In addition to the intellectual or academic qualifications associated with two advanced degrees in the scientific and mathematical fields of physics and astronomy at the University of Washington (which I attended from 1964 until 1973), I consider myself to be a highly intelligent and rational scientist, in spite of the unusual experience.

Briefly, the experience was as follows: I was in cell No. 641 of the Seattle city jail in late September and early October of 1975, when a so-called "alien," who supposedly was from some other planet, and who called himself a "preacher," was apprehended by the Seattle Police Department and confined temporarily in cell No. 643, only a few yards from my cell. I got a glimpse of him through the window of my cell; he looked incredibly unusual. I believe that he was about seven feet tall, weighed about 300 pounds, and had an extremely large, bald head. I do not remember many other details of his description, but I'm sure that the military personnel from Fort

Lewis (about fifteen or twenty miles south of Seattle) and the police officers on duty at the time remember much more.

Within ten or fifteen minutes, several of the people in the other one-
man cells on this block of the jail (from No. 641 to No. 649) began experiencing disturbing sensations which were apparently "projected" by "telepathy" from the mind of the "preacher." The officers from the police and
military (some of whom were young "AWOL-ers" from military bases in
King and Pierce Counties here in western Washington, or who used that
"cover") maintained a barrage of communication with "Preacher," as well
as those of us who were close enough to cell No. 643 to be under his mental influence, to try to find out what he wanted.

The first indication which I had that "Preacher" was influencing my
perception was a strange series of "twitches" which I felt in my mind.

I immediately kicked the door of my cell several times, and yelled to
the officers, "Help! Get me out of here! He's getting into my mind. Help!"

Several officers, including Officer Fagin and others who were on duty
at that time, moved me to the large "tank" or holding cell on the opposite
side of the building, temporarily; but as far as I know the half-dozen or so
other prisoners remained where they were. Several hours later, the police
returned me to the "isolation" areas (No. 641 to No. 649) to cell No. 641,
but the attempt at telepathic contact which had occurred did not recur.

But the others were not as fortunate. The prisoner in cell No. 645 apparently had his consciousness "invaded" by the personality of "Preacher,"
and he began speaking for him. "Preacher" repeated, over and over again,
the phrase "three PI R squared," which is nonsense to a mathematician (at
least in base ten). The correct equation is "four PI R squared," which is the
formula for the area of a sphere. We began talking to each other, with an
intermediary named "Richard" in No. 645 speaking for the "Preacher." I
told him that his formula was incorrect, and that a better formula than either of the two was, "four thirds PI R cubed," the integral of the first equation and the formula for the volume of a sphere in units cubed. "Preacher"
appeared to be amused by this, and we began a communication process on
a verbal level for several days. At one point, the "preacher" said, "We eat
people," and, "Remember this when you're thirty-two" (I'm about thirty
and one-fourth years old now: 10/19/1946).

Several days passed, and several incidents which are almost impossible to describe occurred. As truly as I can remember, the so-called "alien"
or "aliens" seemed to be able to teleport themselves to other parts of the
jail, and when they did, one of several prisoners who had "disappeared"
earlier returned to take their place. The Prisoner named "Richard," who
spoke for the mind or personality of "Preacher," lit his bed on fire with

matches, and the entire block was moved to the holding tank, where I had been taken earlier. There were eight or nine of us in the tank, where we were kept while the police officers put out the fire. But then something incredible happened: one by one, five or six of the people in the holding tank vanished, or "disappeared," until only three of us remained. The officers were unable to determine where they went.

The only door to the tank was locked, and was not opened.

When the smoke had been cleared, the three of us returned to the isolation block. We were stunned psychologically by the things which were happening around us, and we did not understand the situation which we were in—apparently at the mercy of humanoid beings which could invade and apparently take over human minds or personalities easily. "Richard" was put in the "hole" (a small metal room with sound-proof walls and no sink or toilet) as punishment for starting the fire. He was one of the three remaining.

But more "aliens" were brought into the isolation block. I did not see all of them, only the ones that were dragged by my cell's window by the officers.

The soldiers from Fort Lewis (according to them, they had been arrested for being AWOL) began to get excited and concerned by the activation of the military devices which they had somewhere (perhaps small electronic receivers). One of them yelled, "Sir! It's war! War has been declared!" We all expected to be vaporized by hydrogen bombs, because the police and National Guard officers were as frightened as we were. But several hours passed without anything happening but a lot of commotion on an extremely emotional level. I asked one of the officers, "How many cities did we save?" (I really believed that our country had undergone a nuclear attack.) The officer replied, "One! We only saved one." I thought that Seattle was the city that had not been bombed by the aliens, and that it was perhaps the only one left.

During the next few days, the police officers and the National Guard interrogated us continually in an attempt to determine the extent of the "alien's" ability to influence our perception or judgment. We were subjected to continual harassment of a painless but very unpleasant variety. Sometimes we were shifted from cell to cell in the middle of the night. We didn't get our meals regularly, and everyone was confused and exhausted.

Then, several police officers escorted me from cell No. 641 to the holding tank, where several people were being held since the jail was overcrowded, explaining that the prisoners were "disappearing" and that "You're the only one that can understand what's happening." They knew that I was a highly capable scientist, and that I knew what to do to control the alien's or aliens' influence.

As soon as I was in the holding tank with several other somewhat terrified people, several of those who had disappeared just as suddenly reappeared, and I don't know if they were returned as a consequence of my presence or if it was a coincidence. The officers appeared to believe that I somehow had influence over the situation. They said, "You're the only one who understands it!"

I went to court the following day, and was released by Judge Corrett; I returned home to the university district where I lived, unable to believe some of the memories of the preceding week. I had gone to jail on the charge of disturbing the peace, and was given credit for "time served."

But then, about two weeks later, I was arrested again for "destruction of property," having gotten involved in a fight in which the eyeglasses of Bill Ramey at the International House of Pancakes were broken. But I didn't want to return to the hellish conditions which I had experienced in the jail, so I resisted arrest. But I was arrested anyway, and taken back to jail. This time, even more inexplicable events took place; I was beaten senseless, and given an intravenous injection of what I believed to be "Thorazine" (Chlorpromazine). I thought I was dying, and maybe I was. But suddenly I found myself lying on the floor of cell No. 711, throwing up large amounts of water and what seemed to be raw eggs.

The lights were off since the cell was unoccupied other than by me, although it had enough room for over a dozen people. I began pounding on the door, and eventually an officer heard me and was perplexed about how I got into the cell. He took me back to isolation, where I had been before, but this time I was confined in cell No. 645, which had a window in the door that allowed me to look all the way down the corridor toward the holding tank and the sixth-floor desk.

But the desk was not there. Instead, an incredible conglomeration of panels and electronic displays, similar to something out of a science fiction movie, met my eyes. And that was not all. There were spheres of light, of many different colors, floating in the air around the equipment which was visible through the small window in the cell No. 645.

A small white sphere, brighter than the others but not as big, floated down the corridor toward me. I was apprehensive and a little frightened at first, when I realized that it was approaching. But I knew that I would be in danger only if I lost control of my emotions, so I began "sending" peaceful thoughts to the sphere of light. It moved to within a few feet of me, and then began to change size and color. At first, it was about a foot in diameter, but it began to grow in size as the color changed from white to yellow to orange to red. By that time, I was inside it, and could see only a deep reddish glow. After several minutes, during which I wondered whether my body was inside the light or whether the light was in my mind, the spheroid began receding and shrinking gradually.

I continued to experience the globes of light for several hours, at which time the air in the corridor became translucent and slightly opaque. And when the shimmering mist cleared, the officer's desk at the end of the corridor had replaced the undescribable, unimaginably futuristic consoles, and the spherical globes of light had disappeared.

Eventually my mind began to accept as real the events which I experienced, apparently. But now, more than a year later, I still spend a lot of time thinking about possible interpretations of these experiences which I have described so briefly in this letter. Perhaps the only definite conclusion that can be made is that "Reality is not only stranger than we imagine; very likely, it is stranger than we can imagine, forever..."

Mr. President, if you read this letter and are interested in receiving another letter from me in the near future, please respond by notifying me at the address which I have stated below, and I will send you a detailed response regarding my scientifically and mathematically plausible interpretations of some aspects of the technological processes which are, I believe, necessary and sufficient to explain logically how the situations and events which I have described in this letter could have been effectuated in reality.

Chapter 21

Harvesting the Fruits of UFOlogy

Two kinds of UFO researchers plow the fields of the unexplained: the descriptive *UFOl-ogist and the* prescriptive *UFOlogist. I tend to fall into the former category—partic-ularly in the context of this book's Part Two. To paraphrase descriptive linguist Lau-rence Urdang, I regard UFO research as a discipline yielding to my descriptive skills. Thus, it has become my self-assumed job to describe what I observe.*

For her part, the prescriptive UFOlogist concentrates on setting (and following) protocols for collecting data, analyzing cases, and disseminating her findings; in this capacity, she often may resort to issuing investigative instructions and to passing judg-ments upon data and researchers alike.

But it matters little whichever category appeals to you: if you choose to pursue UFOlogy long enough, you, too, will begin to succeed in cultivating the fields of the unexplained—and, in the process, to plant and fertilize the seeds of curiosity and con-viction for all who dare follow us.

2-51.

May 11, 1977

Dear Mr. President:

A news item I read in a national magazine and a NICAP report I received in the mail give me courage to write you. I can only hope and pray this let-ter reaches your eyes.

The news item mentioned a program of disclosure about UFOs. From 1972 to 1976 I received projected pictures (several hundred), on a screen, from an intelligence in another dimension. In 1974 I reported to the F.B.I. (Dir. C. Kelley) on them. The beings (three different types) wanted me to ask the U.S. Government to start a program of information on UFOs for the gen-eral public. This, to prevent the chaos and terror that seem to result when they present themselves. Also, for general economic consideration. When I inquired as to the reason for their visit, the answer was: it is the next step in the evolution of mankind. Inquiring as to how I could prove their presence, so as to make my story viable, they seem to think the U.S. Government has that proof. Since my background is not scientific, I asked them to get in touch with astronomers and scientists. I understand they did.

I made a trip to Washington, D.C., in November of 1975 to talk to the F.B.I. and U.S. Air Force. They were totally uninterested.

A top man from the extraterrestrials' particular constellation has arrived. The fact that they are from another time dimension does not preclude the fact that they are from another constellation, Cetus-particular star: Tau Ceti. And I have so informed scientists and the F.B.I. This is the same star involved in a signal experiment from Greenbank, West Virginia, and possibly from South America.

I have begun to doubt if presidents have been kept informed. I fully realize a president does not have time to give to investigation.

Therefore, I consider it vital that an official bureau, or some source of information be set up. That is, if sufficient proof exists.

Incidentally, they do not intend to reform us, but inform us. Certain information and technological data. On a separate sheet, enclosed, I give other information they gave me:

1. They apparently are able to convert and reconvert from the next dimension, which is why radar sometimes picks them up, and sometimes does not.

2. They were very interested in the presidential primaries. Also in the following: Lebanon, the meeting of oil interests in Panama City, Fla.; and gave me dates 1941-1945, which of course is WW II. It just may have something to do with the atomic blasts.

3. They have human emotions—humor and anger. They were quite disgusted with my inability to interpret their pictures (so was the F.B.I.). They know just what went on in the criminal areas.

4. I thought at first I was having visions—having nothing else to base the happenings on. In fact, I considered that perhaps all UFOs were projected pictures, but after reading all I could on other people's experiences, plus further inquiries on my own, I have come to a conclusion—they are real, and they are here.

5. They seem to borrow electricity, plus sound. They spoke my name early one morning, and I "saw" the sound.

6. One of them is a computer-type electrical man.

7. They have reported one man dead in a collision.

8. They are not around presently.

9. Showed me the Russian cosmonaut in space. I believe there were two in space, but they just projected one. I think in 1976.

10. They are concerned about crime.

11. I am not psychic. These images are from a UFO.

12. It is possible there is something interfering. I see only partial pictures recently. I have no material proof, but have a hunch there are renegades among them.

13. It is possible they arrived via the "Einstein-Rosen Bridges." This is not information they gave me. It is my own deduction.

2-52.

May 10, 1977

Mr. President:

Concerning the statement in the April 18th issue of *U.S. News & World Report* ("Washington Whispers"), what are the "unsettling disclosures based on CIA information about UFOs" that the Government, perhaps the President, will tell us before the year, 1977, is over?

To tell you the truth, as I am in my limited capacity able to discover, this news release makes the President look somewhat uninformed on this issue—for several reasons:

(1) The Department of Defense refuses comment on anything having to do with this subject, except as formerly released through the auspices of "Project Blue Book"—which is zilch! Senator Lloyd Bentsen just wrote me a letter received by him recently from the Department of Defense concerning same above.

(2) Almost 18 months ago, the Johnny Carson Show in Hollywood, California, had two guests, writers from Britain, saying that they had uncovered a plot between the U.S. and the Soviet Union to divide the world politically by saying that the world was under attack from "outer space folks."

Mr. Carter, as one Christian to another (at least you say that you are a born-again believer in the Lord), I would like to mention something to you that you may not be aware of yet as a fairly new Christian. In Revelation in the New Testament, it describes what perhaps is the invasion from outer space—but by satanic forces seven years before the Lord Jesus Christ returns in an attempt to rule the world before Jesus Christ returns.

The Devil is going to in-dwell a man in a similar fashion that the Father in-dwelt man in the form of Jesus, the Christ. This man will be what is called the anti-Christ and is actually the incarnation of Satan himself. This man's number is "666," and he will make an alliance with Israel for seven years—which he will break in the middle: after 3-1/2 years, declaring himself to be God in the rebuilt Jewish Temple.

The beast out of the sea, gentiles, is going to be a Western leader from a ten-nation renovated Roman Empire: which some believe is the Common Market. The second beast, the one out of the land (actually he is the number "666"), is going to be Jewish—or at least Hebrew in racial origin. I don't think that the Jews will have anything to do with him.

This information can also be gotten out of Daniel 9:27, in the Old Testament (Daniel 9:24-27).

I personally don't know a thing about when all of these events spoken of in the Bible will occur, but I do think that someone somewhere with the pull to get news releases made is trying to make the world scene look as if these things were going to happen soon—in order to gauge public reaction for some economic or political reason.

Well, Mr. President, is there really anything that the CIA or the Department of Defense has on this subject that the general public is not aware of; or have you lost your perspective on political ingenuity?

If there is anything new on this subject of "UFOs," then please tell us now so we can all share in what our Government is trying to do for us.

Also, possibly as number (3) Ms. Jean Dixon in the September 14, 1976, issue of the National Enquirer, with an interview with Paul Bannister, has frankly stated that she was taken up in a "UFO" and that they will land on Earth sometime this summer—but before August 1977, etc.

I personally consider this woman a cooke [sic], interesting, but a cooke, nevertheless.

Like I say, if you have this situation in hand, maybe you ought to let the rest of the public know about it so we will not consider that you are running the Government with the aid of clairvoyants and self-proclaimed seers.

Thank you for your consideration in this matter. Note: I heard your comments about seeing "UFOs" yourself while governor in Georgia—which I respect you personally for making; but if the CIA has otherwise, please fill us in now. Thanks again.

2-53.

March 17, 1977

Dear President Jimmy Carter:

I am sending you a carbon copy of my letter to the Department of Defense concerning the matter of Unidentified Flying Objects. You sighted a UFO in Georgia during the year 1973, along with many others in your company, according to news reports last year; and I would appreciate your comment to me or to the American people concerning this matter; and especially whether you are now willing to reveal the secret information that the Government has collected on UFOs throughout the years. Obviously, the recent Air Force answer to me that all Project Blue Book investigations of UFOs are open in the National Archives is suspect and cannot be believed.

I hope that you fulfill your campaign promise concerning this baffling and urgent matter to the American citizen.

Thank you for your kind consideration in this matter.

P.S. I was going to bring this UFO matter up during your National Telephon several weeks ago, as were many others; but since I could not contact you as at present I lack a telephone, I now present my question in writing.

Note: The above correspondent's letter to DOD is reprinted below:

March 17, 1977

Dear Secretary Harold Brown, Department of Defense:

In the newspapers I noted the arresting fact that President Jimmy Carter three years ago sighted a UFO (Unidentified Flying Object) in his state; and seemingly expressed his concept that the round glowing object that he sighted was very real, and a phenomenon that should be investigated.

Assistants in his Presidential campaign verified this particular news story, and columnists throughout the United States continually comment upon this vivid event in his life.

I do not hold the National Enquirer in high regard as a newspaper, but apparently he was interviewed by one of their reporters; and according to this newspaper, he expressed a belief that the UFO phenomenon is real and should be thoroughly investigated by the government if he were elected President, which he has been. Further, he expressed the idea, according to the Enquirer, that the government is holding back secret information about UFOs gathered throughout the years, and that he would release this information to the public as soon as possible when he became President.

The U.S. Air Force just wrote me and, as I know, say they have discontinued Project Blue Book and that all the Blue Book investigations are on open file in the National Archives. I do not believe this statement and suspect that the government is holding back information and covering up the real situation by pretending that everything is in the open and that they cannot afford to investigate further; as Jimmy Carter believed during his campaign, I would like a statement from Jimmy Carter that he was wrong in his campaign promise to open up the subject of UFOs to the U.S. public. Consider the situation in the CIA and other branches of government.

As I repeat, I have suspected, as have so many citizens of this country, that all has not been revealed about the UFO phenomenon, and possibly those sightings by so many reliable persons, including scientists and on U.S. defense radar with sightings at the same time, could be some kind of machines descending into our atmosphere from other worlds around other suns in other spiral nebulae; such is possible in theory, as the basic ingredients of life have been found in the Universe in gasses floating in space between the stars, as has just been reported by British astronomers today. Our scientists have been attempting to intercept messages from intelligent species in outer space for several years, and the government is supporting this program.

The Viking One and Two landings on Mars are a vivid illustration of Federal interest in probing for life forms in outer space.

Possibly the sightings of UFOs could be a strange psychological illusion that affects so many reliable persons, including our Defense officials, that certainly this matter should be studied very seriously.

I hope that President Carter will pursue the matter of UFOs vigorously, as he has promised in newspapers during his campaign, and reveal all that has been kept secret by the Department of Defense, as he asserts, in spite of Defense Department and Air Force statements to the contrary!

I would like to have President Carter comment directly to the American people on his feelings about the reality of UFOs and of the possibility of intelligent life in outer space, as well as his feelings about secrecy in Government, especially as the matter relates to UFOs. Please give me all the information that you have on UFOs currently, a newsworthy item indeed.

Thank you for your kind assistance.

2-54.

March, 1977

Dear Mr. President:

For more than thirty years, I've had experiences first-hand with flying saucers or UFOs.

I know what's behind the mystery, and would like to share it with you.

Since you have seen one and know that they exist, I felt that you would like to know more about them.

You stated in the *National Enquirer* that if you were elected President you would make this information about them available to the public.

I feel certain that I can tell you more about this mystery than anyone else. If I could be honored with a reply from your office or you directly, I'll send you information that will clarify this mystery to the point that you will want to look into it further.

May I hear from you concerning this matter?

Note: The above correspondent inclosed with his letter a flyer billing himself as "America's Most Authoritative Lecturer on the Most Mystifying Enigma of the Century—Endorsed by Leading Experts." Still another correspondent, below, registers his dissatisfaction with the Air Force's formula reply to UFO-oriented inquiries. There is no record of any reply made to this protest letter:

2-55.

May 24, 1977

Dear President Carter:

We recently sent you a letter in which we asked two very specific questions. Today we received an answer from the Department of the Air Force (copy enclosed). The letter does not in any way answer the questions we put to you.

The questions we had—and still have—are:

(1) Were the reports which came over the major news services last spring during your campaign correct when they quoted you as making a commitment to make all the government's UFO information public if you were elected?

(2) If you do have such a commitment—when will you be making some statement in regard to UFOs?

If the report was correct it seems to us it behooves you to honor a campaign promise and address the subject. If it wasn't true you should refute it.

You were very believable when you promised an open administration with mutual trust. We were disturbed by the "run around" answer to our letter, so we are writing again, hoping you will give us a straight answer to our questions.

With best regards and wishing you the strength and courage to carry on the program you have undertaken...

2-56.

May 8, 1976

Dear Mr. President:

It is my pleasure to enclose the second issue of *Good Morning, Mr. President* newsletter, with our warmest salutation on your first 100 days in office.

I have offered the columns of *Good Morning, Mr. President* to the President and all citizens prior to any other working program in this direction.

On January 20, 1977, the Premiere Inaugural Issue of *Good Morning, Mr. President* was on the desk of the Oval Office in the White House.

Still, we have not been mentioned; nor has any public statement of our modest, yet dignified, efforts to inform the public been made.

Consequently, by ignoring the newsletter, the public is ignorant of a matter of national concern.

Unfortunately, we are not backed by powerful corporations. We cannot reach public opinion nationally through the media. Although I foresee a slow road ahead, we are inspired and have decided to persevere and grow until this newsletter becomes a forum of American opinion.

As you will note, Mr. President, I am also the author and director of the World Telepathic Program "WELCOME, UFOs, TO EARTH."

Your willingness to promote these projects would show your readiness to do the unusual, but, let us not say, the impossible.

I remain fully confident that this one request be considered.

Respectfully yours,

GOOD MORNING, MR. PRESIDENT, INC.

Note: Issue No. 2 of the "ignored" newsletter, as forwarded to the President via the above letter, contains a copyrighted open letter to the President appealing for his endorsement of the correspondent's plan "to establish Telepathic Studies Centers; to study university courses in UFOlogy; to install Spatial Landing Gardens, everywhere." Also inclosed is an "excerpt from the MANIFESTO OF PEACE, serving as a preamble in the forthcoming book entitled UFOs Welcome to Earth.

Neither the following letter nor its followup (under the letterhead of the National Investigations Committee on Unidentified Flying Objects, Van Nuys, California) received a reply from the Air Force:

2-57.

24 January 1977

Dear Mr. Carter:

Warmest Christian greetings.

Please accept my personal pledge of support to you and to your administration as you rule this great nation, under God, for the next four years.

I am a minister of the Gospel and have also done considerable research and investigation into the subject of Unidentified Flying Objects!

If you feel that the day will ever come that the government would allow funds for an unbiased research into this mystery, I would be very happy to contribute of my thirty-one years of study on the subject.

I still lecture on UFOs before universities, colleges, and many church groups. Our newsletter goes into many nations.

In conclusion, please be assured of my prayers and those of the members of this ministerial association (International Evangelism Crusades, Inc.).

God bless you and your family, always.

Remaining, in His service...

2-58.

12 April 1977

Dear Mr. Carter:

Warmest Christian greetings.

According to the *U.S. News & World Report,* this week's issue, you are about to release certain information from the C.I.A. relative to the mystery of Unidentified Flying Objects.

In my former letters (from the International Evangelism Crusades, Inc.), I had informed you that my research into this subject started in 1945 while I was a student at Eastern Bible College (now Valley Forge) in Pennsylvania.

Mr. President, I would be very happy to cooperate with you to the fullest degree if you so desire.

My files, books, tapes, documentary films are all available to your office.

You have our one-hundred-percent full support. God bless you all.

2-59.

Mr. President:

I am a citizen and a good one. I obey all laws and am peaceful. But I would like to know why for a long period of time the book "Project Blue Book" (commercially produced excerpts from the National Archives files, compiled by Brad Steiger and published by Ballantine Books in 1976) was not released to the public (there is nothing in it that was not previously known), and why men in the military were told not to talk about UFO'S, and why the public should not see and hear the real truth about UFOs.

I myself have seen one and was not frightened, because I knew it would not hurt me. You may think I am a crazy nut. But please try to understand that I do not want to make myself look good. But what I want is for the suppression to stop. The people have a right to know.

THE TRUTH ABOUT UFOs

The truth about UFOs is that the military wants everybody to think that there is no such thing. There is! Also, the people in the military are hushed up when they talk about UFOs because the high brass knows something we don't. Maybe these people in the high brass don't want others to talk because they're afraid. Or maybe because they're aliens themselves. I have been investigating UFOs for quite a long time. I know how they travel, what technique they use, how they communicate, and why they are here. The military won't hush me up, because I know that I can have the freedom of speech and the press. Please, Mr.

President, why does this have to be? Let the people see what the military is really doing about UFOs.

2-60.

May, 1977

Mr. Carter:

At one time during your campaign you said that you would release the complete findings of the Military and all other government information on UFOs. Please, sir, keep your word. There are many people just like me who are (and could be literally) dying to know.

Also, as an experiment, I have sent letters to various government agencies asking for their complete records, if any, on me, my family, my friends, and any other information they may have on me. I appreciate any help you or your staff can give me in obtaining this information. I just want to know what the government knows about me. Thank you.

P.S. If you cannot divulge any information on UFOs to the general public, at least tell me. I promise not to tell anyone.

P.P.S. I am a Republican. Sorry about that.

2-61.

May 27, 1977

Mr. Mendoza:

My name is *[AF-deleted]*. My father's name is *[AF-deleted]*. You know him from Reed's drug store in D.C.

I've put this letter in care of you because I need a favor.

If you could, please forward this letter to Hugh Carter, asking him to in turn forward it to the President, Jimmy Carter.

Please, not one of his aides, but to HIM. It is very important that I get an answer from the President, not one of the "STAFF."

In deepest gratitude...

Note: And the inclosed letter (from the son of Reed?) reads:

May 27, 1977

Dear Mr. Carter:

My name is *[AF-deleted]*, and I am a UFO watcher, activist, fan etc....

In an issue of *Star* magazine you were quoted as saying, "If I become President, I will disclose any and all information pertaining to UFOs."

I wish for the sake of our nation, our country, and the world that you would make clear (publicly) once and for all the true facts about UFOs, extraterrestrial beings, etc., because myself and many others believe that this is a very *foremost* subject that deals with our nation's security.

I believe that this subject should take uppermost priority.

My question is, do you plan to do anything in the near future about this matter?

THANK YOU.

Chapter 22

Reaching out for Awareness, Understanding, and Action

Circa 1987, consummate communicator Isaac Asimov penned a 150-word "Meditation for Writers (Useful in Preventing Identity Crises and Existential Malaise)," the last part of which reads:

"And I know where I am—on the third planet of a solar system in the Milky Way galaxy in a huge universe. Intelligent beings may be one of the ways this universe becomes conscious of itself and able to create beauty and meaning.

"I am a living part of the universe but apart, because I'm self-aware.

I share this aloneness with all human beings, isolated within the three pounds of gray brain inside our skulls.

"But we can communicate.

"And I will do the best I can."

While these Carter correspondents rarely match the communicative skills of the late, great Asimov, they nevertheless probably share (and epitomize) the view that the mere act of communicating contributes to self-awareness—and, perhaps thereby, toward expanding our awareness of the mysteries, possibilities, and promises of the universe.

2-62.

April 4, 1977

Dear President Carter:

I'm waiting with baited [sic] breath for the scuttlebutt on those UFOs.

I'm a "true believer" and want to know what's up there. It's time the rest of us know what, if anything, the government knows.

P.S. You promised!

2-63.

January 7, 1977

Dear Mr. Carter:

Congratulations from a fellow American. Although I am registered a Republican, and voted for Gerald Ford, I wish you success in these trying times, and give you my support and prayers.

I realize it will take much guidance on your part, and I do not expect miracles to come about in a short time.

There is one thing you promised you would do: that is, to tell the American people the truth about UFOs. I hope you will be able to fulfill this promise soon.

I was a stewardess with American Airlines in 1947, and I became interested in what some pilots told me they saw. Since then I have been scanning the skies. One evening, in front of our house in Sarasota, Fla., my husband and I saw 3 silent flying objects come intermittently over the roof of a house across the street and turn to go down the street below the telephone wires and take off over the houses, again. Some time later the thought came to me: "look out the front window," and there was one of the same silent-type object flying over our house. I ran to the back of our house to look out our bedroom window. It came down for me to see in our back yard, becoming luminous and hovering for a second, then going up and away.

I am not afraid of them, and somehow I feel they are intelligent, spiritually minded beings not wanting to hurt us. I have read many books on the subject, and am extremely interested.

2-64.

Dear J. Carter:

I do recall your saying that if you became President in January that you would release all the government secrets about UFOs. I am a fond believer in UFOs and you. I would really like it if you would release.

Thank you.

P.S. I voted for you. And if you do decide not to release them, I would like it if you wrote me before you put them out, and what newspaper/magazine they will be in.

2-65.

Momence, Ill., April 2, 1977

Dear Mr. President Carter:

I wrote you a letter last month about those objects we see in the sky.

Last week, when my husband and I were in Shelby, Indiana, there were six of them up in the sky; and when we came home to Momence there were three up across the sky, and that large yellow object hovered just above my neighbor's roof. It kept coming down, and we don't know where it went.

Now, here is a picture of the object that was taken in Bradley. So see, I wish your AF fellow men to come to Momence and Indiana (Bradley) and find out if those things are coming from Russia.

Please, now you can see for yourself what is up in the sky. I see them from my bedroom window, and I have a large flashlight. I shine it on them, and then they turn the lights off for a while, then put the lights back on. As I told you in my other letter, Mr. *[AF-deleted]* has seen one come down in the field across the road where he lives; and where it landed the grass was all burnt. It isn't anything to laugh about as it is really real. And there is one straight up in the sky. One can barely see it, but it is there. As a rule, there are four or five up there. We'd say so long.

May God bless you in your fine work you are doing—also your family—and keep all in His care.

If you do have time, please answer.

2-66.

Marianna, Pennsylvania, March 16, 1977

Dear Mr. President:

I tried to call you to ask these two questions, but I couldn't get my call thru.

I read in an *Enquirer* magazine that you said if you became President you would let the American people know all the information that the government has on UFOs.

(1) Do you still intend to do this?

(2) Is there anything at all you can possibly do to see that the Black Lung Bill gets acted upon soon?

My husband is a miner and has pneumoconiosis very bad. It cost us $1,000.00 to hire a lawyer to try to get it for him. He has worked underground forty-five years and seven months, and I don't think he should have to pay an attorney; nor should he be given a hard time about this when his exrays show that he has it very badly.

Concerning the question about UFOs, I have had an occasion to see them several times, and am very interested in them; and I feel the people should be told that they are around. This way the people can be prepared in case they get involved in one. It may mean their life could be spared if they know how to deal with it and not approach one too closely.

Thank you, Mr. President, for reading my letter, and I'll look for an answer by mail.

2-67.

March 9, 1977

Dear Mr. President:

You promised us that there'll soon be a spiritual revival that will sweep this nation. You also promised to release all secret government information concerning UFOs. I as well as many other enlightened Americans sincerely feel that we can't have a truly great Christian revival until that secret UFO information, which is now still top secret, is released to the American public, for examination.

Mr. President, I was once a nonbeliever in God until I discovered that UFOs are for real. Millions of spiritually dead Americans need that truth! That truth, I feel, will dramatically turn our nation around in many ways.

When are you going to have that truth released? I and many others are getting very impatient. We can't tolerate the present atmosphere in this nation any longer.

2-68.

January 27, 1977

Dear President Carter:

According to recent publications, you stated something to the effect that if you became President the truth about UFOs (flying saucers) would be made public, etc.

If this is the case I might be of some assistance, since I have seen some of these mysterious aircraft up close on more than one occasion over the past thirty years.

I have also talked to and have had a number of personal experiences with people operating some of these aircraft.

I know of persons other than myself who have had close encounters with UFOs that may be persuaded to give you some assistance if you sincerely desire it; but our past bitter experiences with private UFO investigative groups, scientists, and various Federal agencies supposedly seeking the truth to the UFO mystery have left us frustrated and suspicious.

With the aid of UFO photographs and information pointed out to me by some UFO occupants and things I personally was allowed to observe, I can, I believe, help establish a basic starting point with which to duplicate one type of UFO propulsion system.

I was told by some UFO personnel to keep a low profile all these years, while at the same time I was to approach various aircraft companies, scientific personnel, and Federal agencies to convey the type of technical information to them mentioned herein if they showed any serious interest.

These things I tried to do at a great expense to myself and my family; however, because of the disastrous attitudes and official bungling of those mentioned above, my personal effort met with total failure.

I became interested in the UFO subject when I was in my teens, I am now almost fifty years old; and though I have a lot of experience and research time in the UFO field I know of no-one or agency, Federal or otherwise, that I can really trust any longer, and time is running out.

Some of the people involved in my cases have died and some do not have long to live. Those of us that have had valuable UFO contacts in the past are becoming fewer in number everyday; and another valuable source of information may be lost forever if some official doesn't start listening to those of us that have had personal UFO experiences.

We no longer recognize nor want anything else to do with civilian UFO groups such as A.R.R.O. or N.I.C.A.P. As far as we are concerned scientists like Dr. Hynek, Dr. Menzel, and several others are a joke.

I have reservations about writing this letter for a number of reasons.

One of them is because your new Secretary of Defense (Mr. Brown) was at one time Secretary of the Air Force, and his remarks, etc., pertaining to UFOs left a hell of a lot to be desired, to say the least.

Mr. President I tried to contact you personally a number of times by various means both at Plains and the White House, and if I receive no answer from you pertaining to the contents of this letter I will not try to contact you again.

With all due respect, I strongly urge that you carefully study the numerous enclosures accompanying this letter.

From my past personal experiences I have good reason to believe that with proper cooperation from you we can make personal contact with the same group of UFO personnel that I have encountered in the past. For the time being it seems to be their wish to maintain a low profile.

Therefore, I suggest that for the sake of your position publicly and my well-being personally we conduct any future business pertaining to the issues discussed herein in the strictest confidence. However, I am completely at your service and will cooperate with you to the fullest in any way you see fit. But time and attitude are of the utmost importance.

2-69.

May 30, 1977

Dear President:

I wanted to give you a little time in office before asking you about UFOs. You know, you promised in your speeches for President that you would let the public know all this country knows about UFOs. You can't leave this up to your aides or anyone else, including all those involved in the Blue Book. They just keep covering it up, and we want it from you only. Thanking you until I hear from you...

2-70.

May 1977

Dear Sir:

As you know, some of the letters you have got have probably come from the new shade-usco unit II; you have probably talked to some of my officers. Such as the one that wrote you only a few months ago. Well, I am writing to ask: well, I've read all about you in the UFO books and how you intended to do something about UFOs. But what do you intend to do about the Air Force and their great cover-up? There might be some things that you can do, but I don't think the Air Force would appreciate it. I will be waiting for an answer.

P.S. Yes, me and Bart are brothers!

2-71.

April 15, 1977

Dear Mr. President:

I have an interest in many hobbies. One of my hobbies is UFOs (Unidentified Flying Objects). I am interested because what is science fiction today may be a way of life in the future. I am a junior scientist in the United States Navy who is interested in the future of my country.

I would like to bring to your attention, Mr. President, a magazine article from Official UFO (March 1977 issue), stating that you once saw a UFO and that you would make information available to the public and the scientists.

I would like to request some information if the information is not classified.

The items I request are: information on a fallen UFO in Arizona in 1965, which included four alien bodies found with the spacecraft parts, with other information.

One of the government agents was from the National Aeronautics and Space Administration.

There have been other UFO crashes since 1965.

Being in the United States Navy, I was hoping I could get information on UFOs.

If you can send any information it would be appreciated.

Thank you, Mr. President, for your time.

Note: The Air Force, on June 22 1977, transferred the above letter to NASA for reply.

2-72.

January 27, 1977

Dear Mr. President:

In an interview with Mr. Malcolm Balfour, you said you'll make every piece of information available to the public and to the scientists about the UFOs. Do you still stand by your statement?

Mr. President, why are the *American people* to carry the burden of soaring prices? Why hasn't Big Business like the Oil Co's and Elec. Co's been helping pay their share?

Are these UFOs soaring prices?

P.S. Good luck with Congress.

2-73.

Dear Sir:

For twenty years I have been studying UFO and binding energy, and have some ideas that UFOs use broken binding energy to power their craft.

Because I think I have solved the way to break the bonds of atomic nuclei, I am writing this letter. I hope it interests you as much as it does me.

RELEASE OF BINDING ENERGY

Albert Einstein looked upon light as radiation energy and hence could not arrive at a conclusion on how to break the binding energy of the atomic nucleus. Most drawings of rays of light (as in Figure 1) look upon light as radiation.

Figure 1: Harold Urey put ultraviolet light together in a vacuum and provided me with a new picture of light rays:

, ;' . ~ + quantus '.~\ ' , ~ - quantus

Figure 2: A ray of ultraviolet is made up of quantus of both negative particles and positive particles. Therefore, light is quantum energy.

What Urey did in vacuum was collide ultraviolet light rays and interlock the particles. Rays held gravitationally in the beta around interlocked rays f/~1 particles interlocked

Figure 3: Infrared light has more positive quanta than negative quanta and makes up the light in positrons: ~ rays interlocked -~/~ L~ rays gravitationally balanced about interlocked rays in center POSITRON.

Figure 4: The neutrino is neutral outside the nucleus and is made up of both infrared and ultraviolet, half and half. The neutrino spins between beta and positron and is the binding particle: ~ ~' NEUTRINO.

Figure 5: There are more neutrinos in the atomic nucleus than formerly thought, because for every position and beta there is one neutrino spinning between them.

To break the binding of neutrinos, positions, and beta forces requires a powerfully energized ray of infrared in a laser effect, where one ray of energized light will start a chain reaction effect and will break thousands of positions. This will release thousands of electrons per ray. The result will be great amounts of electricity released. UFOs use this system to maintain antigravitational fields, and so can we. But more important, we no longer will have an energy crisis. Vast amounts of electricity can be generated from rocks, metal, or practically any solid. This is why Albert Einstein spent such a long time trying to formulate a theory for binding energy.

Note: Again, do you not get the feeling that Colonel Seminare's staff was relieved to be able to pass off the above letter to someone else for detailed reply—even if only to another HQ USAF office: "On behalf of President Carter, I am replying to your undated letter concerning a propulsion theory for unidentified flying objects. I wish to thank you for sharing your comments and am forwarding your letter to appropriate authorities in Air Force Headquarters for their review and information."

2-74.

May 1977

It's been a while now, and as far as I can tell you're doing a fairly good job.

I understand you can't do much changing until you get rid of all the useless red tape; after that then you can repair all the cracks in the liberty wall.

One thing—I know you're a busy man and can only do so much in this short a time, but I'm waiting for the UFO papers, tapes, and films to be declassified for the public. For years now I've been reading, collecting, and researching UFO reports. Most of mine were destroyed, but the Air Force has more information than I could ever gather. I just hope it will be open to the public soon.

Thank you for everything. I wasn't able to vote for you this time, but I will next time. Also, because I was behind you all the way I went around town handing out peanuts to people. Now that might not be much to most people, but this is all Goldwater country.

Oh, yes, if I'm not mistaken Mr. Goldwater said if you could balance the budget this term then he himself would nominate you for the second term.

I'm praying you do just to hear that loud-mouth bag of hot air nominate you for President.

Good luck—God bless.

2-75.

May 3, 1977

Dear Mr. President:

I recently read an article in a magazine about your sighting of a UFO.

The reason I am writing is I also saw one.

My husband, myself, and two friends were deer hunting at Chiliquin, Oregon, on October 1, 1974. We had gone out late in the afternoon, hunting. We were going up a steep mountain road. It had begun to get dark before we could find a place to turn around. I happened to look up in the sky, and just above a tall pine tree was this large object following us. We got to the end of the road and stopped. We thought at first it was a helicopter, but when we stopped it did too. No noise of any kind. It was sort of oval-shaped, had large bright lights all around, plus lights shining down like landing lights.

We sat there watching it; then we turned off the lights on our vehicle. The lights immediately went out on the object. We couldn't see it.

Then there was only a large vapor trail where it had turned off into the sky. The vapor trail was visible a long time after the object had disappeared.

It was a real scary experience. We didn't know whom to make a report at the time. So much for the UFO.

I want to congratulate you, Sir, on what a fine job you are doing as our President. The best of luck to you and your wonderful family.

You probably won't get to read my letter because I know how busy you are. But I just had to write to you.

My husband and I are both retired now. We keep busy hunting, fishing, and camping out, all of which we both enjoy.

2-76.

April 25, 1977

Dear President Carter:

As we are aware, we are living in a society of apathy, because we no longer know whom and what to believe in. Since you've become President, you've done plenty to restore faith in open government affairs.

For over thirty years I've studied and researched UFOs. Also, I've seen many and have gathered many items on then.

Enclosed are the NICAP "UFO Investigator" for February and March 1977 about your sighting and UFO affairs.

I'd like to suggest that when time comes for UFO information to come alive, please contact Dr. J. Allen Hynek, Center for UFO Studies, 924 Chicago Avenue, Evanston, Illinois 60202 (phone: 312-4911870), as he's the UFO expert. I've sent him many reports and items.

I'd also like to suggest that you obtain this book: Project Blue Book (price, $6.98), sold by Blue Book Coordinator, Dept. NE, 426-27 Milburn St., Bronxville, N.Y. 10708.

Many thanks for realizing UFOs merit concern, and are not a joke.

With best regards, and God bless you.

A Patriot

P.S. I'm very pleased someone in our government like you realizes it's time for America to stop being fuelish.

In my next letter to you I'll send some information on how we can save fuel and on a meeting I attended on energy, where only six persons attended.

It's a shame how apathy has been accepted by the public nowadays.

2-77.

April 1977

Dear Sir:

This letter comes as a formal request for a job investigating the UFO phenomenon under your administration.

With your scientific background, no-one should be more aware of the impact a successful investigation could have on the human race. It is my sincere belief this task can be accomplished by myself and five other individuals. Three of us are ex-Navy personnel: myself and one other trained in investigation; one man is a professional photographer and ex-weatherman. The fourth and most vital person is Dr. J. Allen Hynek.

Although I have not discussed this matter with him to date, Dr. Hynek has confided in me that this is one of his greatest ambitions. The remaining two people would be colleagues of Dr. Hynek.

If there is an interest by the United States to employ civilian personnel in this fashion, I would be most happy to discuss cost factors and details with anyone you appoint.

I am a male, Caucasian, 37 years of age and currently employed as a police officer for the city of Farrell, Mercer Co., Pa. I have been so employed for the past nine years.

Chapter 23

In These Electrifying Times

"If you would not be forgotten as soon as you are dead, either write things worth reading, or do things worth writing."—Benjamin Franklin.

As a sage who certainly followed his own advice, Uncle Ben might've dismissed much of the Carter UFOmail as unworthy of reading. But I suspect that he wouldn't have dismissed the spirit *of this correspondence: taxpayers' demanding their money's worth from a government from which they increasingly have become* alien*ated.*

Had Franklin been alive in the late 1970s, what would he have written to Carter about the UFO problem? Something on the order of a Poor Richard's Almanac *pun: "Are UFOreal, Mr. President?"*

2-78.

March 8, 1977

Dear Sirs:

This two-point question is what I would have asked our President in the "Help President Carter" project sponsored by Midnight:

(1) When campaigning, you allegedly stated that you, as President, would open up government files and reveal information on UFOs to the public.

It's time to open up.

(2) UFO occupants (or angels?) could have seeded this earth with white people, blacks, yellow, and reds, and instilled in us our origin as described in the Bible. However, the Adam and Eve mentioned could have originated on another planet, another galaxy. Considering the problems we create, maybe we are that galaxy's factory rejects that were "transplaneted."

2-79.

March 18, 1977

Dear President Carter:

On June 8, 1976, in the newspaper called the *National Enquirer,* there was an article about you saying that you had seen a UFO in 1973, one night in Thomaston, Georgia. It also stated that no-one really believed you.

Well, I saw one in 1963, March 30th, and no-one believed me then or now. I've always been bitter about no-one believing me when I say that I had seen a UFO once. My parents, relatives, and friends have laughed at me, leaving me feeling rather helpless.

That article quoted you as saying, "If I become the President, I'll make every piece of information this country has about UFO sightings available to the public, and the scientists."

To me, if you did this, you would be releasing a heavy burden from all people who have been laughed at and victimized who have claimed to have seen UFOs.

You could do this overnight if you really wished to, because you're head and chief of the military, who have this UFO data hidden away!

I know you can't do everything; you're not a miracle man, but this one thing I know you do have the power to do! When I voted for you, it was my wish and prayer that you would release all government data on UFOs because of your experience with a UFO. I'll never vote for you a 2nd time if you don't do this! Thank you.

2-80.

April 8, 1977

Honorable President Carter:

SUBJECT: Government UFO Disclosure Campaign Promise

You did promise in the campaign to divulge to the public any significant government information on UFOs, local newsmen reported.

Now is the time to fully open all government files, etc., to UFOlogists, to the press, to the public, to scientists at large.

A local ex-U.S. Air Force "Project Blue Book" investigator by the name of Mr. Richard Miller (c/o "The Solar Cross," P. O. box 215, Campbell, CA 95008) authenticatedly appears to be a "trance-medium" for "UFO" humans, who communicate by a form of telepathy which takes over the voice-box (larynx) of Mr. Miller approximately once/twice weekly. He has appeared on several San Francisco media channels/stations and has released cassette reels and printed transcriptions of these communications, whereby he makes no profit, apparently. These "space people" indicate a strong wish to assist earthman and a willingness or eagerness to particularly communicate with and assist, American leaders and scientists. Mr. Miller says he has relayed this to past Presidents and scientists, apparently with no response. Mr. Miller stated this on the *Ed Bosch Talk Show* on KLBR Radio, San Francisco, in 1976.

A partial catalog of his releases:

To Men of Earth (by Voctra); Spacecraft (by Kla-La); Magnetics and Spacecraft Elementary Magnetics (by Bellapian); A Solar Tour (by Mon-Ka).

A Galactic Tour (by Hatonn) (a descriptive tour of our near galaxy— the worlds, cultures, and activity that exist).

Methods of Communication (by Mon-ka).

Spacecraft (Kla-La answers some questions about spacecraft used by space people).

Symbols and Telepathy (by Korton and Soltec); Telekinesis and the Serial Universe (by Soltec); Telekinesis No. 2 and Telepathy No. 2.

The overall indication is that open communication and perhaps trade existed in man's remote prehistory in ancient advanced civilizations; and they indicate an eagerness to resume this, partly (largely) dependent on man's forsaking war, atomic weaponry, crime, poverty, and injustices. But they are eager to now talk with scientists and democratic leaders, Mr. Miller says. They indicate basically Earth is the only planet in this galaxy (out of countless inhabited ones) still having war, poverty, disease, etc., or extremes of suffering. We hope this assists and that you will publicly announce a date to release this government information—or will release it at once, as per your campaign promise.

2-81.

March 7, 1977

Mr. President:

I'm really proud having you as President. I ask the Lord to give you enough courage and energy to keep up the pace you started with.

I personally am interested in space science. I was so excited when in one of your campaign speeches you talked about UFOs and promised to reveal to the American people all the information available within the government.

I realize that you are very busy taking care of more important problems, but a little information for me will be satisfactory. And your answer will be very appreciated.

God bless you, and bless America.

2-82.

April 28, 1977

Dear President Carter:

I hope that you will keep your campaign promise to make available and throw open the records on unidentified flying objects, or UFOs. You promised, so keep your promise.

Don't fall into the trap that the American people are not ready for the information. Don't make up any other excuse. The person you appointed who is in charge of this information says he is not interested in UFOs.

He says he has other promises of yours to keep that are important.

Baloney! You promised, and any delay is a renege on your promise. It isn't going to cost the government much money to open the records.

Note: If the Guinness Book of World Records had a category for the most number of UFO sightings experienced by one person during a 3-year period, perhaps the former Air Force enlisted man who wrote the following letter should apply for the record:

2-83.

July 13, 1977

The President of the United States (Mr. Jimmy Carter);
Information: The Secretary of the Air Force;
The Chairman, Joint Chiefs of Staff (General G. S. Brown); The Director, Central Intelligence Agency (Admiral S. Turner);

Dear Mr. President:

This correspondence is written after lengthy consideration. Your open-mindedness reflected in your public statements on the subject of UFOs has encouraged me to originate this. I hope it will someday find its way through our government's paper-mill to your desk. Copies have been sent, as indicated, to enhance this end.

Since October, 1974, I, my family, and occasionally some friends have made approximately two hundred observations of extra/ultraterrestrial vehicles.

I recorded the sightings in a narrative format. Within the past forty-eight hours we observed a total of fifteen sightings here in the Sacramento area.

We are deeply affected by these encounters, and the subjective impressions which accompanied these latest sightings support this letter's generation.

If any agency is actively interested in this subject, please forward this material. I write in a spirit of cooperation and enthusiasm. I hope that any response will be of the same tenor. Attached are documents for identification and extracts of my notes.

I am convinced these UFOnauts intend to provide our government with a wealth of observational data. I would suggest informal verification of my statements by an appropriate official. If further interest develops, then high-level technology could be used to develop documentation of the various types of machines. This is most certainly a unique opportunity for an on-going operation versus the sporadic photos, etc., that are the usual. Such actions could lead to further developments, depending on the acceptance within your administration.

In closing, please realize that only personal experience can transmit the actuality of this profound and most serious subject.

October 13, 1974, 9:45-11:00 a.m., Fremont, California

Finished motorcycle ride—in backyard on a brilliantly clear day.

Thought occurred to look up. Saw strange filament of angel's hair descending—mostly vaporizing. (Some landed, and my daughter observed it under her microscope.) Disk appeared, going south to north (looking to the west, sun to rear). Observed it with binoculars—form indefinite—white glow about it; dark surfaces sometimes visible in the form. Disappeared to north. I went to drainage ditch at direction of definite thought. After ten minutes, just as ready to leave, again a direct thought to look one more time. Looked to the west at 45 degrees—disk again visible. Grew larger as it approached directly toward me (perspective change), till about the size of a nickel at arm's length.

Directly overhead, it turned 90 degrees to a northerly heading. Angel's hair fell about one hour more.

October 14, 1974, 8:00 p.m., Fremont, California

Observed lights (white with small red one) heading northeast under Jupiter. Two-thirds of the trajectory could have been an aircraft, but the final one-third showed tremendous acceleration as I thought, "This is probably an aircraft unless the trajectory changes somehow."

Observed with Liz—also binoculars for confirmation.

June 29, 1975—9:00-11:00 p.m., Clovis, New Mexico

Last day, this location. Adjacent to Cannon AFB. Five high-level overflights of UFOs. Observed with my daughter and Mr. D. K. of Clovis. Later, went to nearby field, alone, at 11:00 p.m. A single vehicle was almost stationary at limit of unaided visibility (observed with binoculars for confirmation). It had a slight velocity away from my position toward the north. Suddenly, another vehicle made a dramatic low-level overflight at my location. It was a golden, comet-like mass with a vapor trail—diffuse illumination. Within three minutes, a jet fighter peeled from the base's air traffic control pattern. Every light on the machine was blazing. It circled my location (180-degree turn) at very low speed. Altitude about eight hundred feet. Some minutes later the aircraft repeated the surveillance of the area, this time with only its navigational beacon on. A [illegible]—for what purpose—destruction?

August 14, 1975—10:00 p.m., west of Coyote, California

Dramatic encounter with another vehicle. It was blazing red to orange as it left a vapor trail. Its speed was very slow. The UFO followed our car as we proceeded north on McKern Road (58), about one-half to one mile to the west. It produced a luminous mist when the orange glow disappeared. Two of my friends accompanied me: Mr. *[AF-deleted]* of San Jose (a confirmed skeptic), and Mr. *[AF-deleted]* of Tokyo, Japan. Mr. _____ was more open-minded since he was an international airline pilot and had viewed the object clearly through binoculars. (See attached map.)

August 19, 1975—p.m., Fremont, California

Dramatic overflight of two UFOs in tandem traveling west to east.

Attempted time exposure but was unsuccessful.

August 21, 1975—p.m., Fremont, California

Moderately low overflight. Attempted time exposure at F1.4 with an ASA of 400. Followed with telepathic commentary. Two additional overflights then occurred—one high, one low at moderate apparent speed. Exposure of marginal quality, but track visible.

September 4, 1975—10:00 p.m., Fremont, California

Seven overflights. One was very low; blazing red and very fast. I viewed it toward the north as it traveled east to west.

September 5, 1975—10:00 p.p., Fremont, California

Two overflights. The second was the same as Coyote, California., on August 14, 1975. It was very low and very slow with an orange to red color as it left a trail of fumes/vapor. As it disappeared, a large luminous cloud formed southwest of our home.

November 25, 1975—1:15 a.m., Union City and Fremont, California

A very low approach of a UFO described by my wife—within one mile—as she returned from her friend's home (alone). It was a large vehicle, orange/white, and very bright. This was an emotional, passionate experience for her. (See attached map.)

[Drawing of a] DISK SIGHTED ON 10/13/74: Flight path—S.E.

Materialization (blue emission).

Dematerialization (blue emission).

Yellow emission; Indistinct form visible within gaseous shell.

30 degrees of tilt.

Point of observation: apartment patio north of object.

[Drawing of a] CLOUD-SHROUDED UFO

Distance from home estimated to be one-eighth mile.

Dark hole within luminous cloud.

Note: Here's Colonel Seminare's curious "kiss off" reply to the above letter.

Dear *[AF-deleted]*:

On behalf of President Carter, I am replying to your July 13 letter regarding your and members of your family's observations of extraterrestrial vehicles.

I must report that in the current circumstances, the Department of Defense is not likely to renew involvement in the study of unidentified flying objects.

As you may be aware, the considerable and fruitless Air Force commitment of resources in the past, and the extreme pressure on Department of Defense funds at this time, preclude such renewed effort.

I trust this information clarifies the Air Force position on this matter and extend best wishes in your endeavors.

2-84.

November 7, 1976

Dear President-elect Jimmy Carter:

Would you please send me and/or tell me how to find all information our government has on UFOs and flying saucers as you promised in your speech? Please, if necessary, I will pay for postage, copies, and other costs (please notify me in advance); or I will do a favor or work for you. I don't have much money, but I am strong, healthy, loving, educated, skilled, talented, and an excellent counselor and listener. I am a creator, and I will build a flying saucer. And I believe there may be information held by our government which I should examine before I build.

Good luck and love to you and your wife.

2-85.

July 1977

President Carter:

What do you think of the rising sightings of UFOs? I have seen one, and I'm no hoaxer or fanatic; but frankly I think that the few unexplained cases are probably someone visiting us from another planet.

Is there any new evidence about UFOs or that can prove all the cases?

What kind of signals were they picking up in Project Ozma when they focused on Tau Ceti?

P S. Have you ever seen a UFO or the movie *Star Wars?*

2-86.

February 4, 1977

Dear Mr. President Carter:

First of all, I want to thank you for working so hard to get to be our President. And I thank God that you won the job. And I strongly believe you see more than one term in office. I sure hope that will be your job for a long time to come.

Now, I am asking you if you can let all of the people know all about the UFO information that is at hand. I know that there are a lot of sightings and other news that the people would like to know about. I have seen seven UFOs myself, and one of them scared us very much. I don't think I would be afraid of one now. But I would sure like to know more about them. Thank you, and best of luck to you, always.

2-87.

February 19, 1977

Dear Mr. President:

While you were candidating, I recall you said if you were elected you would tell the people about the UFOs, as you had seen one. I would appreciate if you would explain this for me. We are praying for you that the Lord may bless you and yours, and that you may make a great President. Prov. 3: 5-6.

Thanking you.

2-88.

Marshall, Arkansas, February 4, 1977

Dear Mr. President:

Thank you for taking the time to acknowledge my letter to you in December.

We have just listened to your chat to the Nation on T.V. We were pleased and feel you are on the right track.

You have much to do—many problems to solve—and it's becoming a great concern to people, as to what the UFOs are doing here.

I am visiting in Marshall, Arkansas, an area that has frequent sightings of these lighted objects in the sky. I have seen two.

If you know what they are, you should tell us. They can frighten one.

I will enclose an article by a neighbor that has kept a record of her sightings; and our friends have strange stories to tell about what they have seen.

We pray for your safety and the health of all your loved ones.

May God bless and help you to make the right decisions, always.

2-89.

March 1977

Dear Mr. President:

During your recent campaign, you stated that you would do something about the UFO situation. I hope you were sincere. Since your inauguration nothing has been heard about your plans; the White House operator said she didn't know whom to refer me to, and suggested that I write.

Please inform me, If you have a committee established, who is the chairman? If you have not made plans for a committee chairman of UFO, or whatever title you might select, please consider me for the position.

I feel I would make a good chairman because I can organize and am interested in this subject.

2-90.

March 3, 1977

Dear Sir:

I request that *Midnight* ask President Carter to tell the world the real truth concerning UFOs and aliens from space.

I recently signed a motion pictures contract with a west coast producer that is to be shown on national television, entitled *The Contactees*. I signed the contract in the office of the *Dekalb News-Sun* in Decatur, Georgia, and the *Sun* ran a half-page article concerning the contract and my experiences with the aliens.

Since *Midnight* ran the cover story on me, I have been in constant contact with scientists and UFO experts all over the U.S.

What I have to show the general public at this moment concerning documented facts related to UFOs has never been examined by the experts.

After my terrifying second encounter with the aliens from space, I decided to send Jimmy Carter a package containing photos, and facts related to UFOs and aliens, etc. While he was Governor of Georgia, he carefully examined the facts and replied to a special request of mine related to the aliens.

The aliens changed my life, as they have others', including Jimmy Carter's. President Carter has a tremendous load of extremely important promises to fulfill to the American public.

What could be more important than for Jimmy to come right out and tell the world everything concerning UFOs? I thought, along with my fellow investigators, that it might be best to write a year or so before he tells everything. But because of recent developments, the sooner he tells all, the better off he will be.

Note: The above correspondent (presumably a former U.S. Coastguardsman named Norman Chastain) forwarded a copy of a newspaper clipping titled "Chastain's Confrontation Leaves No Doubt—'They're' Out There," by Dick Davis.

2-91.

February 1977

Dear Mr. Carter:

Mr. Carter, I was reading in a book that you saw a UFO. I believe there are UFOs. It says in the Bible there will be strange sightings in the sky. I believe you can make friends with the people in them.

Lots of people have seen them, so I believe in them; I don't seem to be scared of them. Have you heard about the two men fishing and that thing that took them up in it? If you were taken up in them, what would you do? Write me back if you can spare one minute from your new duties!

Thank you so much.

2-92.

March 18, 1977

Dear Mr. President:

It appears that the time is drawing near for information regarding flying saucers to be released to the public.

If and when flying saucers are put before the public, I think a tremendous amount of money could be amassed by the government and/or space program by letting individuals tour them. With the schools' having so much monetary difficulties, I wonder why a flying saucer could not be set down on each school premises and allow each student and each adult to view it for $1.00 or $2.00 apiece. Most people could afford that. Perhaps $1.00 per student and $2.00 per adult. Enough revenue could be taken in to pay off the national debt (or partly) or provide funding for various government programs. Perhaps a dab could be funneled back to each school to help in its athletic program or other deficient area in return for setting up and collecting monies for the tour.

I have always felt that flying saucers might be our next mode of transportation, and the time to put it on a "viewing" basis is while it is new and curious. No-one would be willing to pay to see it after it becomes "old hat" like the automobile is today.

If this worked in our country, perhaps it could be done in all countries and give them some operating capital.

A short tour-talk could be composed releasing harmless information, thereby introducing them to the public with a smooth blend rather than causing panic, as it is feared they might. Today's students will no doubt be piloting these vehicles, and something like this could psyche them up for the job.

This idea came to me while I was trying to come up with a fresh fund-raising idea in connection with our school's athletic and cheerleading financial problems. I think most fund-raising parents are crumbled out on cookie sales, sagging in the middle from cake bakes, have developed mental blocks on afghan raffles, have become stub-nosed from ticket sales, have turned beggars from donation drives, have spent so much time and work on rummage sales that their second hands are missing, feel like "pinup people" from button sales, and on and on with other paraphernalia.

This is by no means a letter of complaint; however, I have thought for many years that a flying saucer tour would be something new and different, and that many financial areas could benefit from it. As fast as they move, only one would be needed; and it could set down at every school ground across the nation in a short time—hence, instant revenue. I do not know what it costs to fly one, but it seems that I read where they fly on wind currents or magnetic flow from the atmosphere; so perhaps the cost would not be too great.

If this letter sounds too ridiculous to pay heed to, you need not bother to answer, but please don't order me "locked up," as I really am all right and it is only when I have to raise funds that I turn to the bizarre/bazaar. Anyhow, the Bible states that a woman's mind should have wings, and every once in a while mine does take flight.

Bless you and your family, and may all of you stay "in-tact" as you inch your way through the maze of problems and obstacles in running our nation.

I also urge that you pay "no never-mind" to the snide sweater remarks.

They look very comfortable and may help insulate you against the cold war and/or criticism that is bound to be yours in your present capacity.

I feel that you are sincere and will do your best to do what is right for our country and its inhabitants.

2-93.

Dear Jimmy:

Why don't we have any flying saucers in our Strategic Air Command? I don't believe they would be that hard to make, or that they'd be impossible.

I've never taken any physics or engineering, but it seems to me they could be designed and built.

These are very complicated and intricate machines. Enclosed is a single sketch of Basic Concepts of Flying Saucers.

If we could produce a flying saucer first, we would again have the upper hand in military superiority.

2-94.

April 21, 1977

Dear President Carter:

I am extremely excited to hear that you plan to release heretofore secret C.I.A. information concerning Unidentified Flying Objects. It is high time that we take our heads out of the proverbial sand and begin one of the most profound investigations humankind could ever undertake. I hope the United States assumes a position as vigorous leader in investigations into these crucial matters.

We are not alone.

2-95.

May 1977

Dear President Carter:

I read with eagerness your story of sighting a UFO in Georgia. As a firm believer in the existence of UFOs (not unidentified airplanes), I think it is great to also have a believer in the White House. Now, Mr. President, what are you going to do about investigations on UFOs? We need one badly—a good one, too. The civilian organizations cannot keep up with all the reports of UFOs. But, if the Government worked with them, they could do better. Mr. President, I am merely asking you to help the civilian organizations in their investigations. Start a donationally organized project to deeply investigate UFOs by the Government. UFOs may represent a definitive problem for mankind in the future if we do not find out about them.

For instance: what object flies at speeds up to 40,000 mph, turns 90-degree angles, and stops abruptly without any damage done to it?

Also, what conventional aircraft leaves behind radiation, indentations in the ground, and burn marks in fields? WHAT?"

You see, Mr. President, if we do not find out about UFOs, they could cause international warfare! And, it is time Americans stood up to be counted! The Russians already said UFOs are real, possibly extraterrestrial. Plus, Brazil had a government project devoted to UFOs. Our Air Force used to investigate (?) UFOs in the years 1948-1969, but they literally debunked them. I wrote Gerald Ford on the subject of UFOs earlier (1976), but a Colonel Seminare wrote me back and gave me the same "baloney" I've read all about in the past years (twenty-two, to be exact). Please consider the problem of UFOs at your next meeting, President Carter. And remember, you will be remembered for the great things you did in the White House. Let UFOs be one of them.

Thank you.

P.S. Please do not send this letter to the AF, because I already know what they will say and I do not care to read about it again. Also, tell President Carter good luck in 1980; I hope he wins if he runs again.

2-96.

Mt. Vernon, Illinois, April 28, 1977

Dear President Carter:

Since you don't have enough problems, I have to tell you mine; but they have to do with everyone of us, I'm afraid.

For three years, I've been contacted by beings from UFOs. They have been in my trailer. They control your mind, so therefore can make you let them in. They only let you remember what they want you to remember.

I work twemty-four miles away. I work for an answering service from 12:30 a.m. to 8:30 a.m., and I'm alone. They have landed all around there (it's in a private home). It has five acres of land, but they have landed in the front yard, out by where we park the cars, and out by the lady's garden and orchard.

The first time one landed, she came in the office and told me to look at the circle in the yard. I said, "That looks like where a UFO put down." Well, I saw right away it was the wrong thing to have said, so I never again mentioned it. I thought Mt. Vernon had lots of them, but they were thick over this town. All you had to do was glance up. They were there before I worked there.

No-one but my family and doctor knows about my experiences. The UFO clubs all want my information so some of them can write a book and get rich; and I refuse to give them the information. I contacted the National Enquirer in Florida with my story. So far, I haven't heard from them.

About six weeks ago, I was told to be good. I was going to be their leader. They turned something on the back of my head, and it stayed with me. The voice spoke in English. Believe me, I'm not one to lie.

I'm not to be anyone's leader unless I know what they are up to. It has scared me, I will say that. They have put things in use to monitor me by, and things in my ears to keep me, when they come over. Last week, they even put something on my car so they can keep me in the car. There were small tripod landing-leg holes in my yard. They set down right beside my car every night for a week. They don't intend to lose me. I work on Sundays; and in October I walked out to my car one evening to come home, and one was hovering about 100 feet to the side of my car, and not over 75 feet off the ground. In fact, it was hovering over a herd of cattle grazing. No sound or anything; the sun was just going down, and it was daytime. But it had its lights on; they were a beautiful blue. It had something hanging down with two lights on it. I watched it a few seconds, then got in my car and came home. It came along as I did, only stayed about three blocks away. Every Sunday afternoon, one would meet me on the way home. By that I mean they would come around in front of me to let me know they were there, usually with all red lights; they'd blink their lights, then turn them out.

Last summer, they did something bad that scared me so badly that I went to the doctor. Finding my blood pressure terribly high, he gave me some nerve medicine. I was able to get out on the road again. I can't remember anything happening at work that night, but the next day my blouse had dribbles of what looked like blood on it, and I was dirty. I had been outside, as I couldn't have got that dirty in the office. I put the blouse away, after showing it to the doctor, hoping to get it analyzed some day. The next day, while I was sleeping (this popped into my head), I sat up and started crying. I remember lifting some tiny little fingers; all I can remember is the frail little things I grabbed both with one hand, and they weren't much larger than a quarter.

Then I hid those tiny fingers; they were long but like a new-born baby's, just gristles. Maybe I thought it was going to choke me and that the only defense I had was sleep. But they let you remember it.

I also have footprints where they came up and off a creek by her house, and where one footprint was headed for the office door. I tried to get the footprints in the front yard when the deep snow was on, but they didn't turn out. The lady where I work doesn't know I took these pictures, and she's not aware of anything happening, because she doesn't read or keep up with what's going on in the world.

They have landed a small one about ten feet from the office window.

Seems like I can remember having been lifted by air to get into one.

Then I keep remembering these small men with funny looking jeans on; they had a v-shaped panel in the front, but only one talked—or that's all they let me remember. He had black hair and was sitting at a small round table. He spoke English, and whatever he said, I laughed. I think they were good to me.

I surely wish I knew of a capable doctor to do hypnosis, and had the money to find out what they have told me for three years. I think I have contacted several kinds. I can remember being asked, "What controls you?" I have a list of things I have remembered, but the things I can't remember are worrying me. I have several places on my body where I have been marked, one scar left after three days.

I forgot to tell you, I'm divorced and I'm 48 years old and have two grown sons, and they also have seen them around town for years. Please let me know if you have any ideas, as I'm desperate.

2-97.

January 22, 1977

Dear President Carter:

I hope this letter reaches you and not some secretary or computer. I know you are a busy man with your administration's making transition into the highest office in our land. And many problems arise over so many people. I hope you can help wheat prices for the farmer, because when the farmer does well, all of us do well.

I'm twenty-two years old, married, and I'm into a part-time business of my own.

I have four years of aviation power plants and airframes under my belt, and I've got a year of machinist time down, too. I'm a welder, and I make tanks full time for a tank company. I'm doing well, compared to many twemty-two-year-olds in this area.

I read this article in the *National Enquirer,* and this is the reason for this letter. I'm a common, ordinary man who believes in respect for elders, because of their knowledge, their wisdom, and the way to a successful life. They've been there and back. I believe in freedom of thought, speech, hard work, and religion. These are reasons for my success so far.

I have seen these strange lights. My grandfather, shortly before his death, told all his relations of Grandma's and Grandpa's experience with UFOs. I'll share the story.

My grand dad was sitting in his living room watching TV and thinking—normal for him—when he called Grandma outside. In a field to the east of the farm, three of the craft were hovering about 50 feet above the ground. Two of the craft started zipping around the field as if they were playing tag. Then the third one moved directly over Grandpa's house. Grandpa stood there and hollered out, "Come on down here where I can see you. Come and give me a ride."

Grandmother told Grand dad, if they have the ability to come there they could hear them and could smite the life from them. Grand dad shook his fist and swore at them, calling them cowards—to come down or give him a ride. This went on for over an hour. Grandpa was 86, and he was known for his word and truth. He was a sane man and very intelligent.

Grandma is the sweetest woman that walks this earth, and a true Christian. Their minds are not slipping, and she is not a liar. She lives one mile north of Nickerson, Kansas. Nickerson is ten miles west of Hutchison, Kansas. I wonder, there is a high-power line that runs from Great Bend to Hutchison. I wonder, that line runs parallel to my grand dad's land—fifty feet or so north of his fence line.

Recently, about three months ago, Ashland, Kansas, had a rage of four nights of UFOs, eight to ten miles west. I have a cousin who is the undersheriff of Clark County. Over TV the sheriff of Clark verified the sightings, and a big write-up hit the front pages of the Hutchison newspaper and the *Wichita Eagle Beacon*. My cousin told me that most of the people of Ashland saw the lights, including himself. How does anyone deny sightings and verifications like these with weather balloons, clouds, aircraft, satellites, etc.?

Mr. Carter, I don't believe in the lies and smoke screens our government has been feeding us common, ordinary men. I believe they are here, they are real, they have purpose and motives. I'm asking for the truth and more information on them. I'm not afraid of the unknown, but I'm afraid of the alternatives they may have for man. We are on the edge of space and atomic ages. Our people have advanced so quickly over the last twenty years that these beings may be observing us. But I wonder if we aren't seeds of their experiment for culture and advancement, maybe even our creation. My craving for knowledge is vast, and I won't settle for cons. Please answer my questions. Whatever answers I may receive I will share only with my wife, my parents, and my wife's parents. I trust these people to never speak to others.

I wish you luck with your new job. It's one I wouldn't want. I hope you bring prosperity and peace for our country. It's a hell of a job with no thanks, but it's one job that has to be done.

2-98.

May 1977

Dear President Carter:

God bless you and your family, Sir. We pray our Lord will guide you and yours, and keep you all safe. We love and respect you for what you are doing, and trying to do, for our America. I am sure we will never know just how hard and trying your job really is, but we are behind you all the way.

While you were campaigning for President, you said one of the things you would do was make known to the public all the information the government had kept hidden or locked up on UFOs. I don't think I have overlooked it in the papers. Could you tell me when you will do this—release information on UFOs, I mean. Thank you for listening to me, Mr. President, and may our Lord make you happy and prosperous.

2-99.

May 3, 1977

Dear Mr. President:

I would like to ask you a foolish but yet not so foolish question—even though I don't think that I'll get an answer (not yours, anyway).

My question is: if there are such things as UFOs, and if they were to try to make contact with the world, what would you do?

Their intelligence is very good, for they say that their aircraft fly very fast. If you were to order them shot down, you might be ordering the end of the world; for who knows if they have weapons greater than ours.

I myself have never seen a UFO, but it is possible. Earth is only one intelligent planet known—who knows that there is not any more?

This could be a very serious issue. I myself would be interested in making world contact. But I know I would be frightened of the matter, which I am sure everyone would be.

Mr. President, I know that this was a foolish question. But I guess that curiosity killed the cat. So, as you see, I am the cat, very curious on hearing your response.

Please write me an answer, so that my mind doesn't wonder.

Mr. President, I thank you very much for reading this letter (if you did).

You are doing a great job so far, and I'm sure you will do so all through your Presidency. Thank you.

Chapter 24

Beaton's Baton

Back in the eighties, Rodney T. Beaton, then attending the University of New Mexico, founded the first-ever (and only?) student-campus group devoted to helping resolve the UFO problem. He dubbed it "Students Against UFO Secrecy." It was a spin-off, of course, from the public-interest group Citizens Against UFO Secrecy (http://www.caus.org).

UFOpolitically ahead of his time, Beaton took delight in expressing a novel rationale for the UFO coverup. The feds, he said, simply abhor (and fear) the prospect that "we, the sheeple" might be induced to swing our allegiance from the United States of Advertising to some as-yet mysterious, powerful off-world federation unfit (or un-USA-approved) for human eyes, much less for human imagination. Hence, the alien beacon, theorized Beaton, must be beaten back by the bureaucrats—for our own welfare (and for that of generations to come.)

2-100.

April 12, 1977

Dear Mr. President:

I would like to tell you that your Presidency thus far gives me new hope in our government and the future. I, and my husband, voted for you and remain convinced we made the right choice. I like your stand on human rights, the decision not to pursue the fifty-dollar payment, and review of the water projects. Your energy proposals may hurt each of us, but I realize something must be done soon.

Before you were elected, there was an article in the *National Enquirer* that said you had seen a UFO and would tell the American people the truth about UFOs if elected and if in a position to know. I have never seen a UFO but have always been interested in them, and I wonder about the various reports that the Air Force has covered up the truth.

One man on a local radio station here said that the truth would panic the people. I realize one can't believe everything written in the Enquirer, but I would like to have your answer on the subject. One interesting book I have just read is *Aliens from Space,* by Donald E. Keyhoe (USMC, Ret.). Surely these reports of UFOs for so long and by reliable people must have substance.

I enjoyed "A Day with the President" tonight on NBC. I hope you always will remain close and open to the people, and I wish you God's love and guidance through these precarious times.

2-101.

January 20, 1977

Dear Mr. President:

I would first like to congratulate you on your hard-fought, well-deserved victory. I proudly displayed an "Elect Carter for President" pin.

My question to you is this: what will you do to promote the investigations looking into UFO findings? I remember reading in a newspaper that you stated if you were elected you would do your best to help that cause. The reason for this, the paper went on, was that you yourself had seen one.

As I close I wish you the best of luck in your next four years in office.

Sincerely a supporter,

P.S. I would appreciate a written reply. Thank you. In addition, I ask something more, as strange as it may seem; I would love to have an invitation to the inauguration. So if you have any extra, please send it to me. It would mean a great deal. Thank you again.

2-102.

May 10, 1977

Dear Mr. President:

During your Presidential campaign, you had made the commitment that you, Sir, would release to the American people all of the UFO secrecy now held in the Archives of the Federal Government, consisting of various agencies. Your article with this commitment appeared in the June 8, 1976 issue of the *National Enquirer* newspaper. I have voted for you, mainly for this reason. I do faithfully hope you will not disappoint me, as one of millions of citizens who has voted for you.

By now, Sir, you have no doubt received numerous letters pertaining to this urgency in order to fulfill this extreme campaign promise of vast importance. And I speak of the full release of those UFO documents and files and also many reports marked CONFIDENTIAL and SECRET.

I am fully aware of the ridiculous attitude of the U.S. Air Force—their long-ago closing officially the Project Blue Book and their previous investigative offices under other titles. I have deeply resented the U.S. Air Force attitude, to say the least—to the point of disgust with their absurdity.

At 3:00 a.m., Wednesday, March 30, 1955 (over twenty-two years ago), I had a close-up encounter with a UFO (flying saucer) near Benson, Arizona. I was on tour as a musician, playing one-nighter engagements. I have suffered and continue to suffer with my right elbow, which has a continued burning sensation twenty-four hours per day, every day, for the last twenty-two years. The best orthopedic doctors had concluded, to me, that I have a form of some type of radiation they know nothing about, to date, medically. And their final conclusion was that there is no cure for my condition. The X-rays show a black mark in the interior joint of my right elbow. Incidentally, I want to mention that the X-rays machines are torture to my elbow during photographing. I have now exhausted this medical procedure. Various doctors had in all practical sense assumed and determined that my elbow injury occurred while leaning on the open door of my car, in the window frame; and my elbow acted as a conductor on the metal of the car door window frame (driver's side) when the flying saucer turned on its side and hit me with a brilliant beam of light, engulfing me and my car as I stood there watching the flying saucer in amazement and fright.

They, the flying saucer, hit me with that terrible beam of light for a good twenty seconds or so and then turned it off. I felt as though my entire body were set afire, and was blinded for several seconds and barely managed to jump in the car, rev the motor (which was acting as though to stall out), and get away down the highway. My car had lost maximum power, and I was lucky, indeed, to escape, as the saucer didn't chase after me.

I am very glad to note you had seen a UFO yourself in Georgia. I am sure you were amazed, to say the least.

I do sincerely hope you will personally read this very important letter from me. I will be terribly upset if your secretary simply and in a routine manner views this letter with an attitude of acceptance but may, in the event, forward this letter to the U.S. Air Force for perusal and routine reply. I will be angered! I have had it with U.S. Air Force and their repeated lies and misinformation and misleading and the continued suppression of the truth about UFOs. I want a direct reply from you, Sir, Mr. President—and a reply from your office assuring me that you will keep and fulfill your campaign promise by releasing, now, the secret information, as described above, to the American public, on the UFO (flying saucer) phenomenon.

Thank you very much in advance, anxiously awaiting your significant reply. Very sincerely yours, in pain…

P.S. Enclosed are two articles published at different periods about my personal UFO (flying saucer) encounter, 3:00 a.m., Wednesday, March 30, 1955.

Note: One of the articles inclosed with the above letter is titled "UFO Attacks Eyewitness—Aliens Permanently Cripple Arizona Man" (Modern People, *October 27, 1974). The other article, from a UFOzine, is titled "Witness Still Suffers Side Effects 20 Years After UFO Encounter." Both articles identify the subject as Andy Florio, a band leader now residing in Los Angeles. California. Florio's self-fulfilling prophecy about the fate of his plea to President Carter culminated in the following "last word" response to Colonel Seminare's standard reply:*

June 3, 1977

Dear Colonel Seminare:

In view of the fact that you and I don't know each other personally, it is difficult for me to write you this letter-reply. You are obviously doing your job of correspondence as ordered. Writing to you is like writing to a ghost and/or someone who doesn't exist.

I have just returned from a trip to Las Vegas, Nevada, and found your dynamic-most-profound stock letter-reply, dated May 25, 1977, which you wrote me on behalf of President Jimmy Carter. It is indeed a stock-reply letter as this identically written letter to me also appears in the recent magazine issue of *UFO Report* (July 1977), addressed to: "Dear Larry."

Your stock-letter reply to me, received, is an insult to my intelligence and to my person. And it is not in any way a reply to my letter of May 10, 1977, sent to President Jimmy Carter; and I resent it deeply!

Your stock-letter reply to me is one of repetitious statements about "Project Blue Book," etc., which I am totally familiar with since 1969, including all the events and blunders of the Condon Committee on UFO investigation (1966 inclusive). What the hell has anything you say, in your letter of May 25, 1977, have to do with a reply to my letter to President Carter? Nothing!

As one of many victims of a UFO (flying saucer) close-up encounter, and suffering with an ailing right elbow, I am insisting with an appeal to President Jimmy Carter to be even a greater man and a greater President by living up to his one of many campaign commitments—revealing publicly to the American people all and any of the TOP SECRET UFO documents and knowledge, as he stated he would do so if he became President of the United States. I also mean that President Carter should, indeed, make a televised speech on the UFO secrets and his own personal experience of seeing one himself.

A copy of this letter-reply is being sent to President Jimmy Carter.

Also, copies of this communication and your stock-letter reply will be sent to my Congressman, and various Congressmen and Senators for their comments and perusal.

2-103.

June, 1977

Dear President Carter:

I have been waiting expectantly ever since the Presidential inauguration for you to announce to the world what the U.S. Government knows about Unidentified Flying Objects. Being a Christian and a Southern Baptist like I am, I believed you when you promised to lift the veil of secrecy from these so-called flying saucers. I have been very intrigued with these objects for more than 30 years, and have read untold books and magazines on this strange phenomenon. I have only seen one during all this period of time. My sister and I were driving in a car between Garland and Dallas, Texas, at night, when this purplish-blue light came into view on the left side and to the front of my car. The glow looked like the light from a welder's torch. As the light got directly in front of my car, it suddenly disappeared like someone had turned off a light switch. It was less than five hundred feet from my car, it seemed.

I have talked to several people who had very close sightings, both in the daytime and at night. All agreed it could not have been anything made on earth. Dorothy Kilgallen announced before her death that a high-ranking official in England had told her that their scientists and air force personnel had been on a captured disc-shaped object and that the pilots of it were about 3.5 feet tall.

General Douglas MacArthur told a West Point graduating class that he felt that the next great war America entered would be "interplanetary."

When Senator Goldwater was running for President, I paid $100.00 to attend a dinner to ask him about these objects. He is a firm believer that they are from another planet.

Dr. J. Allen Hynek is one of the foremost civilian authorities on this subject, and I went to see him in Denton, Texas. At the conclusion of his lecture, I asked him before TV news cameras whether he had ever considered the possibility these could be angels, demons, or some sort of Satanic activity. He said the fact that they could suddenly appear and just as suddenly disappear gave them an ethereal atmosphere.

Most Bible scholars believe they are Satanic. One leading theologian in Dallas thinks Satan is going to use "flying saucers" as his excuse to the world for the sudden disappearance of the Christians when the "Rapture" occurs.

I certainly believe the world should know the results of the many millions of dollars spent by the CIA, the NSA, the Air Force, the U.S. Navy in their study of UFOs. U.S. News & World Report stated that an announcement would be made this year from you or someone in authority with the Government to tell us ominous news. We are ready to hear.

Please tell us!

I made a trip to Wright-Patterson Air Force Base in Dayton, Ohio, and asked if I could come in and talk to someone about UFOs. The guard told me to come back one hundred years later and then they might let me in.

P.S. I am a deacon of First Baptist Church in Dallas.

2-104

January 17, 1977

Honorable Sir:

In some of the preelection newspaper articles you were quoted as saying you would make all UFO information available to all if you were elected.

I am writing to inquire when, where, and how this information will be released.

Specifically, I am interested in engineering-type information. I think much can be learned through the proper analysis and use of the data. As an engineer, I would expect to see an advance in the state of technology as a whole and particularly in the energy area.

Some specific items that would be helpful are—

a) Details of the malfunctions of F-4 systems in Teheran, Iran, during the UFO intercept on September 19, 1976.

b) Details of the UFO/missile clash over NATO exercises on September 20, 1976.

c) What caused the tank column in West Germany to stall out when the UFO was overhead?

d) Details of the Holloman AFB contact and landing incident, including release of the movie film of the incident, flight characteristics, and what happened to the prime players involved.

e) Comparison of the HF frequency data gathered on numerous occasions that would lead to a better understanding of the power and control systems.

f) Gun-camera films dating from 1947 to the recent intercept at Selfridge AFB, Michigan.

I am seriously interested in the ways this information can benefit our country, through technology advancement. I hope you will give it some attention in the busy days ahead.

2-105.

Redmond, Washington, February 2, 1977

Dear Mr. Carter:

I am a thirty-two-year-old father and husband. I would like a personal answer to this letter.

In your quest for the office of President, you promised that when you got in office you would—and I quote—"make every piece of information this country has about UFO sightings available to the public and the scientists."

I would like you to do this as soon as possible, if not sooner. I have read many books and reports on UFOs, over the years. I do believe strongly in UFOs. I do not believe that there would be any panic or fear from the release of this information.

In just about every book I've read, there is one strong piece of information that is very much the same, and that is the Government intervention in all major sightings. I have also written to various government offices and requested information under the new Freedom of Information Act. All I got was a run-around and blank, empty pages.

I would just once like to see our leaders give the average American a break and be one-hundred-percent honest with them.

Also, I've read that at Wright-Patterson AFB, Ohio, there is a building that has armed guards protecting it; and inside is the remains of a UFO.

I'm sorry, but I can't find the book I read this in, but to the best of my knowledge, this happened in the 1960s in New Mexico. If there is any basis for this, I believe this is very important.

I do hope that this is important enough to get a little of your attention. I realize you've very important and quite busy. But the future of all mankind could be in the truth of UFOs. There is but one God in the whole universe, and the pilots of the UFOs are Christian people and believe in God, as you and I do.

I'm enclosing a copy of a report I did for college. I would like it returned if possible. I would, if you want, be willing to work on a committee to make this information public. Granted, I'm not the most knowledgeable person on this subject—and not the best educated, as you can tell by the many spelling errors, but I believe the American people would more likely accept the truth from an average person than from a professional politician. I also wish you all the success in your job as President, and God be with you and guide you.

Here are three more postcards:

2-106.

January 6, 1977

Dear President Carter:

I know when you get your administration underway you will remember your promise to speak out about flying saucers and release govt. info about them. You are one pres. who could tell the people calmly what is happening should a mass sighting appear…which I feel from over twenty years' civil research is to happen as sightings increase (although not reported in big dailies, of course). There may be something we can learn from these space people…although you seem to be going along universal lines.

I can of course only release you to God.

Note: This one is a picture postcard published by the Amalgamated Flying Saucer Clubs of America. Inc. (Northridge, California), purporting to show, in full color, an "Extraterrestrial Spaceship" photographed by Paul Villa on June 16, 1963, near Albuquerque, New Mexico:

2-107.

March 3, 1977

President Carter:

Please fulfill your campaign promise to release to the public the UFO information the previous administrations have suppressed.

2-108.

February 24, 1977

Dear President Carter:

Please don't forget your promise to release information on flying saucers that is in government files.

Being one of an estimated fifteen million Americans (including Muhammad Ali, Arthur Godfrey, governors of Ohio and Florida, and many other well-known Americans) who have had sightings, you would have a personal interest in this.

And here are three telegrams:

2-109.

May 18, 1977

Mr. President, reference previous correspondence. Would feel grateful if you would kindly set me an appointment in Washington for a filmed interview regarding UFOs. Essential for my report, which already brought your attention. With thanks and deep respects.

2-110.

July 13, 1977

For the eyes of the President alone. One of your campaign promises was that you were going to completely reveal to the public, scientists, and world all information concerning UFOs, which you have seen yourself.

Hundreds of thousands of us voted for you because you were going to bring honesty of government on this subject. What about code name "Black Knight," a 2,000-foot-diameter mother ship that has been coming to the vicinity of Earth since 1947 with 36,000-MPH cruising speed, with smaller UFOs seen entering; and hundreds of military and civilian pilots' airport and police reports on others? How much is buried in Air Force, CIA, NSA, and FBI files?

Suggest appointing Dr. Allen Hynek, Jim Lorenzen, Major Donald Keyhoe, Frank Edwards, Alan Landsburg, Ion Hobana, and Senator Barry Goldwater and other members of Congress—not a Condon cover-up. I have terminal cancer, so hope truth is brought out soon.

2-111.

August 7, 1977

Please, Mr. President, tell the people the UFOs are man-made here on this earth. They are, and you know it.

The following correspondent chose to address his/her letter to Vice President Mondale.

2-112.

February 6, 1977

Dear Mr. Vice President:

On the assumption that the Carter Administration has no firm position on Unidentified Flying Objects, the attached position (Paper No. 6) is proposed.

Of course, it is possible that such a position will never be needed—but just in case. This is in the best tradition of government planning: I'm sure the Army has at least three contingency plans tucked away in numerous locations to deal with a possible invasion by San Marino.

The subject has been in my mind since I read (somewhere) during the campaign that if elected Carter would release all secret government information on UFOs. Of course, I realize he's been busy, but we are waiting the fulfillment of this most interesting campaign promise. If in fact he made it.

With every good wish…

P.S. Thanks for the acknowledgement, but it's not necessary.

POSITION PAPER NO. 6: UNIDENTIFIED FLYING OBJECTS

1. Several assumptions on UFOs.

a. Since they got here before we got there, a superior intelligence and technology may be assumed.

b. That a peaceful purpose is probable. Apparently, they have never really harmed anyone.

c. That they have a highly developed extrasensory perception; and, therefore, no language barrier should exist.

2. Our policy toward the personnel of UFOs, once contact has been made, should be:

a. That we welcome any advances in technology that they can give us, and any other intelligence that will enable this planet to bring some degree of order out of chaos.

b. Since it is obvious that vast areas of Earth have populations incapable of self-government, we should direct their attention to those areas needing the most help. To wit:

(1) The countries of Africa, South and Central America.

(2) Specific countries—such as Spain, Ireland, the Philippines, and the Arab oil areas.

(3) And last, but certainly not least, those states of our own almost enlightened land that voted for a continuation of the Nixon-Ford-Kissinger unenlightenment.

2-113.

April 8, 1977

Dear Jimmy Carter:

I read a few months ago in the *National Enquirer* that if elected President you would make public everything the U.S. Government knows about flying saucers.

I have been waiting to hear from you on this subject.

You are an excellent President and a man of your word. I just hope it's not a case of your finding out the truth was too frightening to tell.

2-114.

Dear Sir:

I believe that "he who governs least, governs best." I fear that much of our bureaucratic maze is born out of misdirected energy.

For example, the overclassification bungles that somehow wallow their way to the surface from time to time. I would guess that it's the monkey-side of human nature that makes us feel powerful and privileged to have a secret. Is this rampant in our government.

The variety and amount of withheld info is probably vast. For openers, I'd like to see a complete disclosure of the UFO file. Our taxes pay individuals, who in turn collect this information. Recently, something fell into a New Hampshire pond. The National Guard was called, I suppose to guard the "secret." Reporters were banned. Who gave this, and other similar orders, and why?

With swamp gas in my eyes…

2-115.

February, 1977

Honorable Sir:

Would you please send a confidential courier to Polson, Montana (Salish Hotel)—experienced in UFOs. I have information at the range of forty feet that would chill your blood.

2-116.

March 7, 1977

Hon. Mr. President Carter:

Thank you very much for your letter, and I am happy that so far it looks like everything will get better—including the weather.

I would like to know if our Government knows more about the UFO than it has made public.

Wish you the best…

2-117.

Akron, Ohio, August 15, 1977

TO: Director of Scheduling, the White House:

Enclosed you will find a sealed envelope containing my memorandum addressed to the President, just as you have encouraged me to do. I would deeply appreciate it if you can personally see to it that he receives it as soon as possible. It would be most unfortunate to see it get mixed in with his fan mail, etc., as someone else would open the letter. Please do what you can to prevent this from occurring, for the information is strictly confidential.

May I again take this opportunity to personally thank you for your most courteous efforts and replies, on my behalf, in endeavoring to schedule an appointment for me with the President. Perhaps at a later date this will become possible. Regardless of the outcome, I remain grateful for your help.

MEMORANDUM; TO: Jimmy Carter, President, United States of America; FROM: *[AF-deleted]*; DATE: August 15, 1977;

SUBJECT: UFOs

After several different requests, through the proper channels, for a scheduled meeting with you have been rather fruitless, I now wish to submit this memorandum for your personal and very serious examination.

In the two written requests sent to the attention of Midge Costanza and Fran Voorde respectively, I asked for a brief Presidential appointment in the near future, if at all possible. Although details and specific subject content were not included in my communications with your staff, general references to the realm of national security and defense were given in both letters (dated June 23, 1977, and July 9, 1977).

I now would like to elaborate, Mr. President, as concisely as I can, concerning a (if not the) most subtle, yet most potent threat to the United States of America. The danger involves not only this great nation, but the physical, psychological, and spiritual well-being of all people on the face of the whole earth! Sir, I refer emphatically to UFOs.

After approximately two years' study and analysis into the matter from many, many different and varied objective viewpoints, I must, without doubt or reservation whatsoever, conclude that UFOs definitely exist and the intelligent beings who occupy them are not Homo sapiens. Through much evaluation of the sightings, personal encounters, and other evidence submitted to various qualified UFO investigating committees and organizations, I have found that the very real "tie-ins" with the occult and psychic sciences are typical of the "phenomenon."

Yet, despite the hoaxes, frauds, and mistaken identifications, there remains the genuine proof of alien beings with material bodies along with their vehicles, which leave landing marks on the ground and are often detected on radar screens. Each year, more and more of the world's population are witnessing their appearance. In America alone, according to a 1973 Gallup Poll, fifteen million people claim to have seen a UFO and fifty-one percent of our population believes they are real! Compare this with a 1966 Gallup Poll in which only five million claim to have seen them. Increasingly, year by year, come reports from around the globe of reputable people in the military, law-enforcement agencies, government, business fields—

just about any and every background imaginable—who have either sighted or have been contacted by, in some way, a UFO.

By now, you are no doubt asking yourself, "If this is for real, and what you are saying is correct, what does it all mean?" This question has been the core of my studies and the basis of my desperate attempts to, in some way, warn you, Mr. President, of the dangers involved as the situation continues to develop.

First of all, I wish to inform you that, like you, I too am a born-again Christian, and that Jesus is my personal Savior and Lord. I believe the precious Word of God from cover to cover. Having studied very deeply and very intently end-time prophecy over the last four years, I am familiar with God's prophetic plan of the ages. The perfection there is indeed overwhelming and wonderful because it is all true. Not once has one single prophecy in the Bible failed, nor will it ever. Mr. President, you know and sense as well as I do, that Jesus is soon coming back for his own. Immediately after that, however, this world is going to be subjected to the most terrible seven years of tribulation it has ever seen or will see again. I firmly believe, Sir, that the UFO phenomenon is setting up the world right now for that. I am profoundly convinced that the UFO intelligences are fallen beings with supernatural powers and knowledge and are specifically referred to in Scripture in such passages as: Eph. 6:12, Eph. 2:2, Eph. 3:10, Colonel 1:16, Colonel 2:15, I. Pet. 3:22, Is. 24:21-22, and many others. In short, they are of the Satanic kingdom. I also believe that they will play a major part in deceiving the world to accept Antichrist during the tribulation.

Looking back on world history, I find that nearly every single civilized nation or primitive society that was idolatrous had ancient legends of "gods" coming down from the skies and teaching marvelous life philosophies and advanced technology. But none worshipped the true God. As one looks back through the history books and the Bible, he sees the abounding sin and perversion that became part of those societies. Each time, the result was, after numerous warnings, Divine judgment. Even the people of Israel, when they backslid, were no exception.

Idolatry again will abound during the tribulation and culminate with the worship of the Antichrist and his image (Rev. 13:14-15, Rev. 9:20-21, Is. 2:18-20).

Many individuals right now, who are in contact with UFOs, regard and worship these as "gods" today, much in the same ways that the early Greeks, Egyptians, and Babylonians did hundred of years ago.

My concern is this, Mr. President: recent reports from contacts with aliens say that they are now in the process of making contact with government officials throughout the world in preparing people to accept them.

By no means am I implying that everything they say or everything we hear is true; but let us, as Christians, carefully weigh these things in the light of God's Word and use the discernment of the Holy Spirit. In any event, Mr. President, if this country or any other country welcomes these fallen beings as "gods" or even as super intelligences from another planet come to save mankind from himself, woe unto that country! If any society receives counsel and instruction from them, woe unto that society; for judgment from God will surely follow!

In view of these insights, Sir, the most complex defense systems in the world are all useless against UFOs, simply because they, being of spirit composition, have the ability to materialize and dematerialize at will and also possess supernatural powers. The only sure defense against them is a people humbling themselves in prayer before God (II Cor. 10-3-5, Eph. 6:12-18, II Chron. 7:14).

It would be impossible for me to give all the results of my findings on a few sheets of paper. It would literally require a number of books!

However, I sincerely hope that you will not just take my word for it but search out the matter cautiously and prayerfully for yourself, Mr. President. Let the Bible be the final word, and ask the Lord to show you the truth of the matter. Should you want a scientific and professional opinion, may I suggest you contact Dr. J. Allen Hynek, C/O CUFOS, 924 Chicago Avenue, Evanston, IL 60202. He, for more than two decades, was an astronomical consultant to the U.S. Air Force's Project "Sign" and Project "Blue Book." Today, he is one of the world's most outstanding and respected researchers in the field of UFOs. Although his conclusions, no doubt, would differ from mine (I have no knowledge that he is a Christian), he nevertheless has facts and evidence which would be of interest to you, I'm sure.

If ever I can personally be of service to you, please do not hesitate to get in touch with me. Any questions you might have I will be more than happy to answer, if I can. I am praying for you and the important decisions which you are and will be making. God bless you and your family. Please acknowledge receipt of this memorandum. Thank you!

2-118.

June 10, 1977

Dear Human Person:

The enclosed letter is personal and confidential. It contains questions which only President Carter can answer. The answer that I hope to receive from our President will be treated as you treat his letter from me. If you do not treat it as "personal" and "confidential," his answer letter will not be treated "personal" and "confidential."

My reason for this is in the letter. Let President Carter be the one who allows my letter be known to you, if he chooses it to be. The only other person I would not mind reading the enclosed letter is Mrs. Carter, President Carter's wife.

Mrs. Carter is "One" with President Carter. Whatever he knows, she knows, because that is God's word.

Peace be with you.

Note: Portions of the above correspondent's letter to the President are illegible from the copy made available for this compilation.

Dear President Carter:

You are a born-again Christian and you have seen a UFO. I need your help. Please tell me of your experience with the UFO. I need to know—was it before or after you became born again? Was the one you saw one only of sight? Did the beings within speak to you in any way? Were they of God?

Now you see why this letter is meant to be "personal" and "confidential." These are questions only you can answer. I know you are a very busy man, but I voted for you...

All the others before us did not have Christ—or did they, too, know Christ? It would be interesting to learn if the other beings knew the Christ as we know Him. Or to learn that God chose this planet to be different from all His other great works before us.

The answers are in the Bible, but we are not open enough to see where they are. Jesus said it more beautifully than I just did when he said to the Pharisees in Matthews 19:8, "It was because you were so unteachable." We are still "unteachable."

You are in a position, right now, to open one more door, which many are pushing to have opened. We are ready to learn more of God's wondrous works. Will you, dear Christian Brother, open that door? or will you leave it shut?

If you have taken this letter and treated it as "personal" and "confidential," than I in return will treat your answer the same way—between you, me, and God. With your permission, I would like to share your answer with one friend; but only with one person, because she is like myself. If you request not even my friend, in the name of Jesus, my brother in God, ought not share your letter—it shall be as you request. Amen.

2-119.

February 19, 1977

Dear Mr. President:

First, may I thank you for the invitation to speak on subjects of special interest to me.

By way of introduction, I am a fifty-two-year-old Navy/Air Force veteran of World War II. Which leads to my second thought. After the war I was able, thanks to the G.I. Bill, to receive on-the-job training at a plane factory in the high-skill trade of piano tuning and repairing—a trade I have followed for the last thirty-one years. I say, Thanks, America! Related thought: G.I. Education Benefits have recently been discontinued. I think this act was a mistake! It seems to me to have been a very valuable investment to underwrite the education of service veterans.

Also, it was an inducement to prospective volunteers.

A matter of great interest to me, a Navy Air veteran, is the subject of the Aerial Phenomena (UFO) incidents occurring in or over our country and the world—especially since June of 1947. I think, and I hope you concur, the people have a right to information from their government in this matter. The fear or panic consideration is no longer a valid reason for secrecy, if indeed it ever was. I have found it difficult to obtain information on this subject for 30 years, and it is my opinion that the Air Force handled their investigations poorly, to say the least. What will this do to future credibility of the Air Force?

Please, Mr. President, end this veil of secrecy that has prevailed since Mr. Truman was in office. Give us information on this, the greatest secular news story in the history of Man. I sincerely believe we are mature enough to accept the facts.

Here's a letter that mentions neither the term UFO nor flying saucers but which, nevertheless, received the same tired old USAF form-letter reply assuring us that Project Blue Book records remain openly available, offer no evidence to support the hypothesis of the extraterrestrial origin of certain reported UFOs, and serve as no justification for a renewed, federally funded public UFO-investigation program.

2-120.

February 15, 1977

Dear Mr. President:

I am tired of the Air Force, NASA, and their agencies covering up information dealing with life on other planets! I have read in several books and have heard from a few very reliable sources that the moon is hollow. I am no expert, but if I recall, these people and authors said that from mathematical equations in order for the Earth to keep a moon of that size in its orbit, the moon would have to be hollow. I have also heard that when the astronauts, and even the cosmonauts, took seismographic readings the sounds rang as if in a bell! I want to know about this! Why don't the papers ever print this? It is not just the Albuquerque papers, for I have lived in Portland, Lincoln, Denver, Alexandria, and Pennsylvania because my father works for the Forest Service.

The Air Force has continually found "excuses" to explain strange events or sightings. I have even heard that there are beings living on/in the moon. The people support the Air Force and NASA, and we have the right to know what they know. If they think that the fact of the existence of extraterrestrial beings would panic the people, they are wrong. The knowledge might even inspire new thoughts or new inventions. It might even open new fields and create more jobs!

The people are mature enough to handle the knowledge. I have a big interest in space, and I hope to make it my career. I have written this in hope that you will act upon this situation.

2-121.

April 1977

Dear Mr. President:

For some time now, we in Northern California and the southern part of the state have been experiencing a strange phenomenon. It appears to be an infrared light coupled with laser-centered light effects. After serious consideration and thought and experience with this extremely aggravating sensation, a little knowledge of physics, and conference with friends concerning moving (star-appearing at night) lights in the sky and the sighting of a saucer object in broad daylight over a nuclear generating plant (Rancho Seca, seen by three of us), I have come to a definite conclusion—that the industrial giants in this country are playing havoc with the public.

These objects appear to hover and use both infrared and laser light—both extremely injurious to your health, i.e., mine and many others'.

I'm serious about this, Mr. President, and I wish the matter investigated and stopped. If my conclusions are correct, this is willful misuse of nuclear energy to do harm to mankind. My sympathy goes out to the demonstrators in New Hampshire, for theirs is truly an ethical cause in view of what I have seen and experienced.

This engine depends on heavy water as a fuel source, and its inventor has leased it to several large utility firms to test. The object that myself and two friends viewed above the fog of the Sac valley (we were in the Sierra foothills), directly hovering about Rancho Seca, appeared to be refueling.

I can be reached at *[AF-deleted]*.

Mr. President, this devastation—or, to put it in vernacular, burning sensation—in California must be stopped. Thank you, Sir; and I liked your style in Britain.

Chapter 25

Connecting with
the Pulse of UFOpolitik

Author Norman Cousins noted that "The writer is a creator of options. The writer enables people to discover new truths and new possibilities within themselves and to fashion new connections to human experience."

Cousins's insight brings to mind one of the better books about the controversy over so-called UFO abductions. This first-person account, titled Connections: Solving our Alien Abduction Mystery *(Wild Flower Press, 1996), derives from the life-long, sometimes jointly undergone experiences of its two pseudonymous, Virginia-based authors: Beth Collings and Anna Jamerson.*

On June 5, 2000, in the Circuit Court for the City of Alexandria, Virginia, their compelling, courageous story became a key exhibit within the ultimate connective medium—a lawsuit (Larry W. Bryant, et al., v. Hon. James S. Gilmore, III). Crafted as a "Petition for a Writ of Mandamus," the suit centered on the Virginia chief executive's constitutional and statutory duty to "protect the general welfare" of the state's citizenry—a duty that the petitioners interpret as also helping to repel the invasive presence of so-called "flying triangles" as well as incidents of UFO-related abductions by perpetrators yet to be fully identified, apprehended, and brought to justice. After a brief hearing on the governor's motion-to-dismiss, the judge so ordered. He agreed with Gilmore's counsel that any such gubernatorial duty remains a matter of discretionary function.

Which brings us to the Epilogue of "Connections," where Beth Collings concludes: "We [as humans] are unique, yes, but not because we are alone in the universe; we are unique because we crave understanding and knowledge, plan for our future, and embrace the lessons of the past."

2-122.

April 25, 1977

Dear President Carter:

This letter has a twofold purpose. First, we are writing about the terrible problem of the cult activities in our country. The cults are increasing in number daily. They are taking our young people and brainwashing them into doing work for them—not to benefit the individual or the group, but to benefit only the leaders of these cult groups.

Young people are being taken off college campuses and school grounds daily. They are being separated from their families and told that they must forget the family and cut off ties with them. Women are being taken from their husbands and husbands from their wives. They are being programmed against what our country is based on—the family. Many cults are even hiding the children so the parents cannot find them.

Many of these cults have their followers standing on street corners selling products from which the money is going into the pockets of the leaders—or monies are going out of the country to support leaders there. Some are working at regular jobs and turning over all the money they earn to the cult leaders. What is going to happen to these people ten or twenty years from now when they should be productive people in our society? They have not got the education or the training to support themselves. They cannot make decisions on their own—many cannot even decide what clothes to wear in the morning. They are told what to do, what to say, where to go, and when not to go—day in and day out.

Some investigation must be started into these pseudo religious cults.

They are using religion as a front, and are gaining wealth and power—and are tax-exempted. Many of these groups are already into our government, using mind control to get just what they want. Rev.

[AF-deleted] has been doing just this sort of thing.

These cults are very much against deprogramming. They are saying it should be illegal and should be banned. A true, legitimate religion does not fear deprogramming, and does not use coercive mind control tactics to enslave their members. Deprogramming is the only way to free the minds of these enslaved people caught in the thousands of cults in our country. Please! Please look into this problem.

The second reason for writing is that during your campaign in Appleton, Wisconsin, you talked to some people from the UFO Educational Center there. You remarked that you had a UFO sighting and that you promised when you would get into office you would open up all the government files on UFOs. Please be very careful when you open up the files on UFOs. There are many groups in our country that are legitimate UFO groups and report only sightings. Then there are groups like the one in Appleton who are cult groups. They have two different meetings in Appleton. One is for UFO sightings, and the other is for teaching their philosophy. Many of these groups, the Appleton one included, teach that the twelve Apostles of Jesus were spacemen; some even say Jesus was a spaceman. They take passages out of the Bible and make it fit their situation. They lie and are evasive about their answers when asked direct questions.

I believe in UFOs. My son and I had a sighting. We were not able to identify the objects we saw, and to us they were unidentified flying objects. These UFO cult groups are just waiting for something from you to use your name to back their cult works and their philosophy. The Appleton group teaches George Adamski's philosophy. He claims he rode in a spaceship to the moon and that on the moon there is vegetation like that of Earth. He says he saw all of this. George Adamski died in 1965, and our astronauts went to the moon after that and found no vegetation there like what we have here on Earth. But the group still teaches that Adamski saw all this and it is true. This group in Appleton programmed our daughter against her father and against me in twelve hours. It is unreal. There are several other young people from this area that they have brainwashed into their teachings.

This letter only hits on a small part of the whole UFO groups and their activities. We ask that you study the whole problem first. Please remember there are many UFO cult groups in our country; the Appleton group is not the only one.

We realize that the cult situation is hard to do something about with our freedoms, but someone has to start—and start soon. People are enslaving the minds of other people. Hare Krishna, Children of God, Love Hanna, Love Israel, The Way; UFO groups are but a few of the over two-thousand cults in existence right now.

Thank you for your time.

2-123.

March 1977

Dear Mr. President or Secretarial Staff:

I'm writing in reference to a statement you made concerning ufology.

You've said that, once elected, you would release every bit of information our government has on UFOs. Mr. Carter, I'm begging you to stand by your promise. Over 80 percent of the total population of America believes in UFOs, in a more advanced people who run them, and in a higher technology on their part in relation to us. So you'll be satisfying not only the voters, but also 80 percent of the entire population. The other 20 percent will be enlightened and, with us all, will be taught how to react if and when there is an encounter.

The final preceding sentence above is the reason why this information should be released. We must know how to act—what to do, and what not to do. Does a farmer in Iowa know what to do when a cylindrical space-craft, hovering over his corn field, freezes his dog in mid-air with a "green ray"? Or would he know what to do if the space travelers try to examine him and his family? Obviously, the American public knows more than the Government thinks, and can handle the situation. After all, I'm just a twenty-two-year-old ex-college student, and I know about the green ray, the general set-up of spacecraft, and how it works in theory.

Here's a rough sketch:

ELECTROMAGNETIC FIELD (REASON WHY RADIO TRANS-MISSION IS INTERRUPTED WHEN THEY PASS OVERHEAD)

GAS DEFLECTS OFF FIELD AND HEADS DOWNWARD—

NUCLEAR POWER HEATS AND EXPANDS GAS, WHICH RE-BOUNDS OFF FIELD AND HEADS DOWNWARD WITH TREMEN-DOUS FORCE. THUS, A HOVERING EFFECT IS MADE POSSIBLE.

I've read we will be constructing such a craft in about five to ten years (if we haven't already and if these craft aren't being mistaken for UFOs).

It's probable that they have a base here on Earth—perhaps some place like the ocean floor somewhere in the Bermuda Triangle, for instance!?

We've theorized that they are scientists examining us; they're cautious and fearful because of our different appearance. Highly intelligent, they communicate telepathically and have the ability either to hypnotize or control our minds. They can even make us forget an encounter.

Being scientists, they probably have performed dissections and studies on live human beings. I'm not being maudlin, but I know I would do that if I wanted to discern the functions of an Earthling! Furthermore, they should, by now, realize their technological superiority. What does the future hold for us if they suddenly become hostile? If a farmer in the mid-West is confronted with a saucer and beings, he might use his shotgun out of fear. That's just a hypothetical example, of course. But who's at fault? The man wasn't briefed on how to react. The Government hasn't even stated its acknowledgment of their existence—thus, the twenty percent of disbelievers. So how can we expect Mr. Average American to react rationally with reason and logic? Again, herein lies the necessity for total disclosure immediately.

Perhaps Americans can send away for a pamphlet with all the previously classified material in it. In this way, public announcements over TV won't be necessary. The impact would be far less, and the chance of panic would be nonexistent. Furthermore...*[Note: The next several lines are illegible from the copy made available for this compilation.]*

I wasn't going to vote in the election last November, but then I heard about you and your ideas. You've turned a skeptic into a believer. I voted for you. It was the first time I ever voted, and I had to change my party to do so. Please don't let me and all of us down. We came through for you; now, please, please reciprocate.

In conclusion, I would like to volunteer my services in assisting in this field, if you would be so kind as to inform me of any existing organizations that civilians can join. I'm willing to make this my life's work and would do anything to further our attempt to contact and exchange information with these space travelers.

I thank you or your secretary for your time and wish you all the luck in the world!

God be with you, Sir.

2-124.

April 9, 1977

Dear Mr. President Carter:

Sir, in the past ten years of my life I have devoted a lot of my spare time to trying to solve a puzzle.

Some folks say the puzzle does not exist, and others say it does.

Sir, I'm speaking of UFOs. Mr. President, it was ten years in finding out, but, Sir, I have figured out how they fly.

Now, I don't claim to be a big brain of any sort or a super scientist.

But, Sir, I have stumbled onto something that I think could really help the defense of the United States.

Now, it's not a super anything yet, but with the right people working on it, it could be something great. Now, Sir, I'm only a high-school graduate. I will need to have some years of college before I could figure out the right metals to use, etc.

But our government has great engineers and aircraft design personnel.

They could develop my discovery, and they could make it work. In these times of energy shortage and bad words with other countries, wouldn't it be nice to know you have a defense device that would be far advanced and immune to the energy shortage?

Sir, the Wright brothers gave you a wing and a method of lift created by the flow of air on the curved surfaces of the wing. To use this function you must have forward pull, lift, and drag. Thus is created the source of artificial flight.

Sir, my device will run circles around your SST. It can hover over a certain spot indefinitely, and it can accelerate to speeds that will stagger your imagination. It can also operate under water at great speeds, and it can go to outer space and back far more easily than your big rockets.

Now, your personnel and private industries in America developed the wing into a great thing. But the wing is limited to the air, and at slower speed it can be used in water as lifters for boats. But, Sir, if you try to reenter the Earth's atmosphere at a slow speed and hold onto your wings, Sir, you're hurtin' for certin. The design changes of a craft must be so it will repel the heat and not break up. And the heat that is present must be dealt with. The power plant must be so that it will function without fail in all temperatures. Do you have any craft that can do all these things by itself? I think not.

Mr. President, let's talk about one more thing: speed and distance. How big will the rocket be that will go to Mars? How much fuel will it carry, and how long will it take? Mr. President, we have to start a new type of craft now—because to develop metals and control systems takes time. The Wright brothers could not fly two hundred mph on their first flight because their ship was not capable. My first engine will not fly that fast, either. But four years from now it will. It will even out-run your SST. You can go farther and faster than you ever thought possible. And you can do it in outer space, under water, or in an electrical field or a radioactive field such as the Van Allen Belts. It will be something to see.

Now, Mr. Kennedy said, let's be first on the moon. We made it because he stuck out his neck. Now, Mr. Carter, if we go ahead on this spacecraft you will probably be sticking out your neck. So it is a serious decision to make. Think carefully on it, Sir.

Now, number two on my mind: you're probably wondering what it is I want out of all this. Well, you're right. I do want something. I want at least two years of college, and I want to be an officer in the U.S. Navy. I want to work with the big brains on my discovery, and when I'm out of college I want to be an aircraft and submarine designer for our government. With the proper training in college, I can design some craft that can also be used at great depths in the ocean. They can be used for harvesting and living quarters. And the engine will hardly ever fail. I say hardly, because anything made by human hands can at one time or another go haywire. Yes, Mr. Carter, we must at this time look toward the future. Our population will soon double. We will soon run out of gas and oil and energy, period, if we don't develop a new kind of engine.

I will be waiting to hear from you, Mr. President. Please understand that I'm serious about wanting to help, and I think my discovery will help.

I want to be a part of the future, Mr. Carter. I want to see my idea grow. Thank you.

2-125.

January 26, 1977

Dear President Carter:

During your campaign you stated that if you were elected you would release all previously classified UFO documents to the public. I urge you to do this, and if at all possible, send me some copies of these. I realize that in all probability you will not read this, but if it is convenient, and if I am assured you will release these documents, please try to send me copies of some of them.

2-126.

March 7, 1977

Mr. President:

It's been reported that more than one-half of a sample of sober, intelligent people believes that there are UFOs from "out there" now visiting Earth—even that you yourself have seen one!

Number one, have you? Number two, would you urge the Defense Department to reopen Project Blue Book? Number three, is this area considered to be a part of national security still? Number four, what security classification do you think should be attached to unexplained sightings, if any? Number five, what significance do you attribute to the facts that interest in the subject is so high and that there are so many believers? Last, are the Russians ahead of us in UFOs?

2-127.

May 1977

Dear President Carter:

I know you've probably had many a letter asking this of you, but I think every letter is written when people want something done. In Official UFO it was told of how you had seen a UFO. In your campaign you promised to have the Government release all information they had on such. I want you to know I have seen a UFO (no little men, no messages, no trip in a UFO). I just saw a UFO. My phone was bugged after I started writing my sister about UFOs and my sighting. I didn't bother with it 'cause I don't care.

I do care about people who have seen UFOs, aliens, or photographed such; then harassers come along—AF and civilian.

A sheriff who photographed an alien had his mobile home burned and his car blown up. He received threatening letters. AF ridiculed him.

A patrolman who was abducted was later fired for telling his story. People laughed when he tried to give them tickets.

People have disappeared after reporting close contact with a UFO.

The military have a ten-year prison term or ten-thousand-dollar fine for those in the service who release UFO data without their superiors' permission.

I don't expect you to receive this letter or answer it, but if you'll have your press secretary just release a 1-minute statement on whether you are going to release the information, it would ease the minds of fifteen million Americans who have seen UFOs.

I would like to talk to you as one American to another. Just five minutes, I believe, would be sufficient to convince you of this problem. May I call you? Or please call me. I do hope you get this letter.

Thank you. Phone: *[AF-deleted]*.

P.S.: If the secretary gets this, please let me know that at least you got it.

2-128.

March 1977

Dear President Carter:

I believe in UFOs or spaceships from other planets. I have seen about thirty-five UFOs here in Arkansas, and I saw one in Pensacola, Florida, last summer. I'm wondering, just like millions of other Americans: what are you going to do about the UFO situation in America?

What about the supposedly crashed UFOs and the crafts' occupants? Are there two, three, or four UFOs and alien bodies at Wright-Patterson Air Force Base? Are there three UFOs in a cave in Washington? And are there some crashed UFOs in Florida?

OK, President Carter, the United States and Russia are [illegible] compared to the rest of the world; if the alien thinking is not [illegible] that admits [illegible] they will get to be ruler of the world. What if the United States doesn't admit their existence? I think it's time to tell the Americans the truth.

P.S. But, President Carter, the decision is yours (about UFOs),

2-129.

January 25, 1977

Mr. President:

I am writing this letter in hope that you keep your word pertaining to UFOs.

As you said, before you became President, in an interview with the *National Enquirer*—that you will make every piece of information this country has about UFO sightings available to the public and the scientists—I hope you start with the CIA and U.S. Air Force. These two groups have the majority of the information that has been suppressed from public view.

As a field investigator for NICAP, I trust you will keep your word.

Thank you for your time.

Note: After receiving the standard kiss-off reply from Colonel Seminare's office, the above correspondent chose to do battle with that office's Col. Ronald J. Skorepa, USAF:

Dear Colonel Skorepa:

In reply to your letter of March 25, 1977, I am fully aware of the termination of Project Blue Book.

However, as far as the Air Force not withholding information on UFOs, I still do not believe it—especially when there once was a strict Air Force order, entitled AFR 200-2, that stated Air Force personnel are forbidden to talk in public about UFO sightings and information about UFOs is to be withheld from the press until the thing seen "has been positively identified as a familiar or known object." Not to mention the incident at Wright-Patterson Air Force Base—when a UFO was kept in hangar 18 and not even Senator Goldwater could enter that hangar because he did not have high enough clearance! Of course, it was removed later when an investigation was called for.

I do not expect to get any information from your department. However, I would like to say that it would restore confidence in the Government by the people if it was made public by the Government—that UFOs do exist—instead of letting the people find out by themselves.

Thank you for your time.

The following letter writer, a housewife in Fairfax County, Virginia (who recently had started her first job as a clerk-typist for the federal government), chose to direct her rejoinder to the President:

2-130.

March 30, 1977

Dear Sir:

Please locate my original letter to you, and compare it with the reply I received from the Air Force (copy enclosed). The reply is an obvious form letter, which I do not think you could have answered my letter with. What secretary puts the address in the lower left-hand corner?

What secretary stamps the date rather than types it? And who, for God's sake, puts an envelope thru a meter-mail machine when the envelope is franked? Talk about mistrust or credibility gap in the Government, etc.

—seems it is all true, and it starts right at the top, the head of the Government. At least that is where my letter was first addressed.

Mr. Carter is the one who brought this UFO subject up during the campaign; then how much of what he has said during the campaign was serious, how much is he saying now that is serious?

I only volunteered to organize a group. Why, again, why would a UFO question to the head of the Government be answered by anyone remotely connected with National Defense? Again, why can't a UFO question be treated as bisexual bumblebees or the rush-hour on Wilson Boulevard? Why the Defense Department for UFO? There is a strong insinuation that there was or is a concern for our security or defense? If there is no concern, then this is the beginning of mistrust again, for why a response from the Defense Department? Note: it is the Air Force responding—why? Who has proof these "things" are aerial? Why not suspect "them" as flaws on the eyes, and have the AMA respond? Why not suspect "them" as from another planet, and have the Naval Observatory respond? Or have the Smithsonian Institute respond as to a short-lived phenomenon? Why, for God's sake, the Defense Department? Of course, this is logical to you because of Project Blue Book. Again, why did the Defense Department ever begin to investigate the UFO situation? By Colonel Skorepa's letter, the Air Force's involvement was fruitless; maybe they are not experts on the eyes, not experts on the atmosphere, nor experts on other phenomena. So why should the Air Force ever have begun any UFO investigation?

Wherever you are—reading this letter—you know more than I about the waste in the Government, the duplication, etc. For Colonel Skorepa to mention any Government funds being unavailable is to call me ignorant and stupid! My boss makes many personal long-distance phone calls to his son from the Government office phone. I reported this, but as you well know, I might just as well have spit in the ocean. The abuse of the lunch hour, annual leave, etc., only shows the surface problems of most government employees. Yes, I know the argument that unemployment would go up, etc., but the Government is too big to control, and the only result is a high tax bill for everyone.

There are six agencies that work on population control—why six? That means not one is really effective. If it was, there would be no need for another agency to be involved with population control. If Mr. Carter is really concerned about helping America, he, at least, could scrap some countries that we have population control programs in (by checking figures) since our involvement. I mean the percent of growth rate each year. India had 1.8 percent 15 years ago; now it's over three percent. What help were we? We were more of a hindrance!

I did not mention funds in my letter, but if the Government employees were honest, and did an honest day's work, and completed honest annual-leave slips, and took honest lunch periods, there would be less employed by the Government—less to keep watch over, and much more efficiency. Some of the most efficient organizations function with volunteer workers. Check out the DAR, Girl Scouts, church groups, etc.

I would like an honest reply to my original letter and to this one, also.

2-131.

Shelton, Nebraska
August 1977

Dear President Jimmy Carter, or whoever reads this letter or deals with UFOs:

This may sound like a weird story to you, but I hope you have the time to read my letter about my vision. I am not an important person. I am just a plain, simple housewife.

But I am concerned about this vision I am having. I can feel something to be good and evil. I have been having this vision for about five years. I see three craft in my vision. I am sending you a model of the craft that I see in my vision.

I also see certain things inside it, but I'm still working on it.

Because of what I can feel out what it is that I can't see—like a blind person.

You also told the public... *[Note: The remaining portions are either illegible or incoherent.]*

The incidents reported in the following letter are also recounted in an article in the Winter 1978 issue of True Flying Saucers & UFOs Quarterly, *titled "Yes! Virginia, There Are Such Things as UFOs," by Wendelle C. Stevens.*

2-132.

Virginia Beach, Virginia
February 20, 1977

Dear President Carter:

This letter is written in regard to two separate incidents, involving UFOs, that occurred in Virginia Beach, Va., in the fall of 1975—one involving my family and the second Mrs. *[AF-deleted]*, whom I did not know at the time, but have since met and visit often.

My family's experience has had a great influence upon our lives. We know UFOs do exist, and feel that all people are entitled to know the facts that former presidents have covered up. You are the first "ray of hope" that we have had, not only in this area of investigation, but also hope for our country, in general.

The UFO situation has become so commonplace that only handfuls of small-minded individuals could even doubt their existence. We could not allow our names to be used in pages of newspaper coverage, because of "labels" previously placed on persons coming in contact with UFOs, owing to the fact that we are both business professionals. My husband owns his own contracting company, and I am a licensed Real Estate Associate.

I will not go into detail and make a lengthy, boring letter to someone of your high esteem, but will say my husband, myself, and our six-year-old son were "hovered over" in a church parking lot for over an hour, by a soundless, hypnotic aircraft of unknown origin, within three hundred feet of the front of our car. This craft was slate-gray in color, with undulating white, amber, and green lights, and could move up and down, sideways, stop still in mid-air like a ballerina. A very odd ray or beam was turned onto our car which turned the inside a "bright glowing orange-gold." This craft disappeared before our eyes, then paced us home down a heavily traveled boulevard, and finally hovered over our home, before it slid down, barely over trees in our back yard, and down to the lake behind our home.

Mrs. *[AF-deleted]* and her two children also experienced UFOs for a period of a month in November of 1975, of such a close nature not only in distance from her, but in time, that a local paper carried her experiences also. Mrs. *[AF-deleted]* and my family had never met, until I called her months later to assure her that myself and family, if no-one else, could understand what she was going through, and we were consequently brought together by our experiences.

Mrs. *[AF-deleted]* was able to get twenty-two photographs, and although taken with a small Polaroid are invaluable at this point, as she has visual proof. Mrs. *[AF-deleted]* had a small bell-shaped UFO in her yard about fifty feet from her. She lives in the same general area that we resided in at the time of our experience. We are both in agreement that these are the weirdest events that we have been exposed to, and both felt that they would return. There have been so many "mind-boggling" events to this date that it would take too long to put into this letter.

I only pray, as does Mrs. *[AF-deleted]*, that someone will investigate the Virginia Beach sightings, as the sightings have become numerous in this area; and whatever these things are, they are obviously "here to stay."

We realize that you are confronted with numerous other high-priority problems, but we sincerely feel that this area of United States security should be given some much needed attention.

Thank you very much for your time and consideration, and we anxiously await a reply.

2-133.

3 September 1977

President James Carter:

I understand that you have sighted a UFO. I, too, believe to have seen a UFO. I saw three bright objects moving in a southeasterly direction.

Mr. President, I hope that, now that you have seen a UFO and you realize what you saw, you will open up the Project Blue Book files to inform the public on what is happening over our nation. I also hope that you will form a new committee to investigate the subject of UFOs. I do not think it is right for the subject of UFOs to be so easily explained off as weather balloons or swamp gas or some other natural phenomenon.

Mr. President, I trust that you will support me on this issue because you yourself have seen a UFO and you know that the government must be more open on this subject to the public.

P.S. I have enclosed the negatives of the three pictures I took; they are #10, #11, #12. Mr. President, I would appreciate if you could handle these negatives.

As has been shown, an appreciable number of citizens choose to enclose various documentation with their letters to the President, the following two examples of which lead off with a letter apparently from the sheriff's office of Cascade County, Montana (May 19, 1976) and wind up with a letter from an unidentified chronicler of related events.

2-134.

Enclosed are summaries on all the reports this department has received on hairy creatures. I would appreciate it if you would let me know your ideas and comments on this information.

Since August, 1975, to date we have received 122 reports of UFOs and unidentified helicopters. Most of the UFO reports have been nighttime sightings with the exception of a few daytime ones. The information received consists of seeing strange, extremely bright lights and hearing strange sounds. We do make contact with the people reporting them but have not been able to obtain any evidence.

We have had quite a number of cattle mutilations also. Some have died of natural causes and then were mutilated. A number of them have been the mysterious surgical kind. The mutilation varies from just the rectal area cut out to the lips, an eye, ear, lower jaw, or teats cut out too. We have not been able to connect the cult, hairy creatures, or UFOs with these mutilations.

I have not sent copies of the UFO and mutilation reports as the files are quite large and it would take a lot of time to prepare these reports like we did on the hairy creatures. If I do get something really different from the regular reports I will send it to you.

I hope this helps you out in your investigations. Please keep in touch. Thank you for the reports you sent.

Dear *[AF-deleted]*:
Well, since I wrote to you we have had two more killed. I was out on a calf kill last night. They cut the nose, lips, tongue, and nipples off this calf.

This one was killed approximately five hundred yards from a rancher's house. I can't tell you any more than that. It looks the same as the rest.

As far as I know, these hairy creatures don't have any part in mutilations. They are in our area, but I never saw any tracks or reports of them around these kills.

I don't know what you got for facts on these UFOs, but they are flying around here. People see them all the time. And sometimes we get mutilation; then it completely stops, and then they will kill three in one night.

We are going to have a meeting and try to get a different plan going this summer. As to how to stop this for sure we don't know. We aren't getting very good results the way we are going now.

One of these days I will get some copies made and send you a bunch of stuff—okay?

2-135.

April, 1977

Dear Mr. President:
I am a senior at *[AF-deleted]* College and am the traffic manager of our college radio station. While listening to another FM station in our city, I heard some very disturbing information. My focal point is this: the station played a short announcement from a syndicated show, called the "Odyssey File," that the United States Air Force was responsible for a cover-up that dealt

with two beings from outer space who were found dead. In further checking, I found out that "Odyssey File" is put out by the Public Affairs Broadcast Group, 260 S. Beverly Drive, Suite 210, Beverly Hills, California 90212.

If this particular episode is factual, I think the American people have a right to know, and should be informed. As an understanding individual, you I'm sure can see that public opinions cannot be redistributed or abandoned, but must be dealt with head-on, or trust will disintegrate. Thank you very much for your valuable time, and I look forward to hearing from you.

2-136.

March 7, 1977

Dear President Carter:

This letter is written because of the expressed interest you have shown in unidentified phenomena.

In January, February, and March of 1976, I taught a course entitled "UFO" at the Community College in *[AF-deleted]*. This course offered the students a broad overview of past, present, and future dealings with worldwide unidentified phenomena. Enclosed is a copy of the diploma issued at the end of the course.

One of the members, Mr. *[AF-deleted]*, of the above-mentioned class, and myself decided to pursue this interest further. We have set the wheels in motion for the establishment of an in-depth, concentrated organization entitled "PROBE" for the sole purpose of discovering and exposing the mystery behind unidentified phenomena. We think of ourselves as taking a different approach. Unlike other organizations, we are not biased in our knowledge reference unidentified phenomena. We have discussed the possibility of eight theories, as follows: (1) outer space, (2) center of the Earth or beneath the Earth, (3) time warp, (4) another dimension, (5) something we don't know about yet, (6) hoax-created in the minds of many people, (7) Government, and (8) demons or supernatural, including angels.

Recently, I spoke with the sheriff in one of the largest counties in *[AF-deleted]*. PROBE and what is hoped to be accomplished was explained to him. He was enthused and offered us all the cooperation he legally could so that he too would have a part in solving the unidentified-phenomenon mystery that has prevailed for over thirty years.

We realize from what we have studied and have read and heard in the media that this is a very dangerous subject that could cost us our lives, but we are determined to discover and expose this mystery to the public, regardless of the consequences.

The interest that the public and the intense interest of ourselves have shown in this subject has prompted us to request consideration for a personal conference with yourself regarding the subject of unidentified phenomena.

If you are interested in what we represent, feel free to contact me by return mail or telephone.

JB/lf—Enc.

References: J. E. Hoover (received personal letters from him); Mike Douglas (talked to in the past by phone); WHO Radio (been a guest speaker); KSO Radio (been a guest speaker); Drake University (may teach a course); Air Force Base, Omaha, Nebr. (talked to by phone); Betty Hill (talked to in depth ref. her UFO experience); Major *[AF-deleted]* (talked to and received materials from him); Contactees in contact with UFO (talked to them ref. their UFO experience); 1965, saw UFO in Warren County; Civic groups (given lectures).

2-137.

February 20, 1977

Dear Mr. President:

My eleven-year-old son David is writing a report on UFOs, and to assist with this we purchased several books and obtained several from the library.

Major Donald E. Keyhoe, USMC (retired), in his book "Aliens from Space," refers to secret Washington archives, official scientific findings, and lists the names of many individuals who have seen UFOs and whose credentials confirm in our judgment the existence of UFOs.

I am now seeking clarification from the Administration to clarify whether or not such objects do in fact exist, or are they merely the figment of so many's imagination?

David has been a staunch supporter of you and continues to believe you are the most honest man he knows—your deep sense of integrity and your absolute convictions on the desperate need to return this country to normalcy comes through every time we see you on T.V. or read about you in the press. This instills respect, confidence, and a belief that you will prove to be the greatest President in history.

David received a letter from you prior to election, which is framed, as well as your picture that he received two months ago.

I fully recognize the need for National Security; and to assure the full commitment to this need, you as President cannot reveal much that the public is asking for at this time; in fact, I don't believe I ever realized the full impact of your responsibilities until the news media revealed certain incidences which were unknown to you prior to assuming the Presidency.

Recognizing all sensitivities associated with your office, I am asking for some measure of information to satisfy his inquiry. Both David and I will be profoundly grateful for any information—not only to help with this major assignment but also to provide continuity of faith in government, which David is now aware of through a close association with you; and at his tender age I want this faith to continue.

If time permits response to this request, please send it directly to: *[AF-deleted]* at the above address.

May God bless you richly and abundantly with good health so that you can serve for the next eight years.

Part Three:

The Younger Set
Speaks Out

"And a Little Child Shall Lead Them"

Chapter 26

What Can We Learn From UFOlogy, and Who Cares?

(1). "Education is a progressive discovery of our own ignorance."—U. S. historian Will Durant. (He also noted: "Knowledge is the eye of desire and can become the pilot of the soul.")

And Durant's aphorisms most assuredly apply to the role of "adult education" as well as to our youth's. Over the years, a few UFO researchers have been privileged to bring their authority, knowledge, and experience to the classroom—most notably in this or that junior-college-level or university-level course on UFOlogy.

But, aside from the academic pay dirt in formal UFO research/teaching, young people the world over have the opportunity of acquiring solid UFO knowledge beyond the pages of any textbook, encyclopedia, or lecturer's notes. First, they simply may learn from becoming more observationally attuned to atmospheric activity (i.e., keeping their eyes to the skies!). Then, they can draw upon the real-time networking advantage of sharing their first-hand UFO experiences with others (especially via the Internet). And, third, they can gain perspective and support from studying and disseminating published reports of youngsters' UFO encounters.]

(2). When the late Dr. Edward U. Condon, head of the University of Colorado's embarrassingly inadequate "Scientific Study of Unidentified Flying Objects," wrote the conclusions and recommendations of the purported final U. S. Government solution to the UFO controversy, little did he anticipate the longevity of his propagandistic remarks. And little did he comprehend how a portion of those remarks—quoted below—could be so wantonly disregarded by his target audience:

> "Therefore. we strongly recommend that teachers refrain from giving students credit for school work based on their reading of the presently available UFO books and magazine articles."

Plus: to preserve the youthful flavor and candor of the letters in this part, I've made little effort to edit them for errors of format, syntax, and spelling.

Several letters from the Suncoast Middle School in North Ft. Myers, Florida:

3-1A.

March 18, 1977

Dear President Carter:

Our sixth-grade class has been studying stars and space science. Part of a classroom discussion we had centered on a speech you made promising release of information about UFOs and other phenomena.

One of my students already wrote a letter to you a few days ago. These are the rest of them. The children took it upon themselves to do this, and it is not a class project.

I personally would like to see the release of all UFO information and other unexplained phenomena that the Government has.

I would appreciate any answer you or an aide could make to the children's letters.

I voted for you, and I like the job you are doing.

3-1B.

Dear Mr. President:

When they were voting for the President of the United States I didn't know who I wanted for the President, but when I heard some of your speaches I wanted you for President. And that promise in that one speech that you would tell people all the news about UFOs and I know you have information as to whether there are aliens on other planets. If you have such information that has not already been released to the public, I would like you to send some of that information. And if you have any information on big foot, or the lock ness monster, I would really like that information, also. I am in 6th grade at Suncoast Middle, and we are studying unexplained phenomenon.

3-1C.

3/17/77

Dear Mr. President:

I am in the sixth grade at Suncoast middle school in North Ft. Myers, Florida. I would like to know if you will keep your campaign promise about the UFO information. If you would please send that information, it would be very much appreciated by me and my classmates. We are studying about the UFOs in our science class.

3-1D.

Dear Mr. President:

The Suncoast Middle School, Sixth grade Science class, would like for you to send us the UFO information you promised that you would release when you became President. We are very interested in knowing more about outer space. We are studying the stars and planets and would like to know if all of the evidence about UFO information is true, also if there really is a museum where a so-called Martian is captive.

3-1E.

Dear President Carter:

I am in the sixth grade at Suncoast Middle School in North Fort Myers, Florida. I would like to know if you will keep your campaign promise about the UFO information. If you would please send that information, it would very much be appreciated by me and my classmates because we are studying about UFOs in science class.

3-1F.

Dear Mr. President:

My name is *[AF-deleted]*. I am in the sixth grade. I go to Suncoast Middle. And my science teacher's name is *[AF-deleted]*. And in science we are building a rocket. Is it true that they found burned up men from outer space? Are you keeping your promise about releasing the information on UFOs?

3-2.

March 30, 1977

Dear President Carter:

Following my teacher's advice, I am writing you today, urging you to please do whatever you can to look into the UFO phenomenon, and perhaps have a Congressional Committee undertake a new, serious investigation of this problem as soon as possible.

Surely there are lots of "gray areas" in the UFO problem that as of this moment still remain to be explained either by an investigation committee or by the U.S. Air Force.

I, personally, am not satisfied with the results of the Condon Committee Report. There seems to be simply too much concrete evidence around the world that points out that UFOs are more than mere results of overactive imaginations. I, along with many others, feel that a lot is being held back by the U.S, Air Force for one reason or another, and the general public hasn't been told all the truth. Surely, a thorough new investigation would be to the benefit of mankind, and that is why I urge you once again to do whatever is in your power to get to the bottom of this problem.

I realize, of course, that you must be a very busy man, Mr. Carter, with urgent problems at hand; and also your presidency is still very young, but I'm sure you do agree with me that the UFO phenomenon can be ignored no longer and calls for immediate action on your part.

This is the first time I have ever had the urge to write to a U.S.

President in my life. I hope my letter won't end up in the waste-paper basket. I have faith in the Carter Administration.

My sincere thanks for whatever you may be able to do about this problem, and best wishes to you while in the White House.

3-3.

Dear Sirs:

I am a student of [AF-deleted]'s class of Webster County High. In General Science we are studying UFOs. I was wondering if the people in the White House are withholding information on UFOs for fear of panic throughout the U.S.A. Also, if you people have any contact or knowledge of life on other planets.

Please answer my letter, for this is very important to my classmates and I. We are very concerned about our lives and what's happening.

Thank you.

3-4.

May 19, 1977

Dear President Carter:

I am a student at El Morro Elementary School in Laguna Beach. I am learning to debate. My topic is UFOs. I think that UFOs exist. I would very much appreciate your opinion on the subject and/or any other information that would help me with this report.

3-5.

May 18, 1977

Dear Mr. President:

I am a student from El Morro School in Laguna Beach, California. We are doing debates in our class. I'm doing mine on UFOs. I think and believe there are such things as UFOs. I was wondering if you could possibly find the time to write me and tell me your personal opinion and maybe some information on the existence of UFOs.

3-6.

May 18, 1977

Dear Mr. President:

My name is *[AF-deleted]*. My partner, *[AF-deleted]*, and I are doing a debate on UFOs.

We thought you might be able to give us your personal opinion and/or any information you might have. Anything at all would be greatly appreciated!

3-7.

May 10, 1977

President Carter:

What are your views on UFOs? In a filmstrip I saw in my space science class in school, part of a *National Enquirer* headline from June 8, 1976, quoted you about having seen a UFO. It also quoted you regarding the making public of any UFO files if you were elected.

No one in my class at Lutheran High School West has heard any news on this subject. We would like to know what has been done involving UFOs.

We would appreciate any answer.

3-8.

Dear Mr. President:

I am a sixteen-year-old girl. I come from a very small town with a small population of 220. Our school consists of only sixty students in high school and forty-nine in grade school. We don't have any problems with drugs or murderers. We are very proud of our school and appreciate all the help we get from our government.

In our English class we are required to make research papers through much hard thinking. I have decided to make my paper on flying saucers or UFOs, and I thought you might have some information on UFOs. I would be very grateful to you if you could send me the information. The papers have to be done by March 10, 1977, so if you could possibly get them sent to me as soon as possible I would be very, very grateful.

Via its correspondence control sheet dated May 16, 1977, Colonel Seminare's office processed the above letter in the following vein: "Please FAA—she wanted info for a March 10 high-school paper. It's a little late! No answer would put the WH in a better light than a kiss-off two months old."

This Rhode Island constituent chose the congressional route for his/her inquiry:

3-9.

Dear Senator Pell:
I am doing a 4th quarter report, with the topic on UFOs. Could it be possible for you to send me some information on my topic? I would really appreciate it…

3-10.

April 1977

Dear President Carter:
My name is *[AF-deleted]*. I am a senior at Mona Shores High School. For one of my classes, I am required to do a report with a minimum of one hundred and forty hours. My project deals with the topic of unidentified flying objects. This area fascinates me along with many others.

I was reading in the *APRO Bulletin* where you allegedly told a *National Enquirer* reporter that, "If I become President, I'll make every piece of information this country has about UFO sightings available to the public and the scientists. I am convinced that UFOs exist because I have seen one." I would like to know when you plan to make this information available, now that you are President. If you cannot do this, could you please tell me the real reason why you cannot.

Thank you for your valuable time and effort. I know you are an extremely busy man.

3-11.

March 11, 1977

Dear President Carter:
I am writing this letter in hopes that you may be able to send me some information on UFOs. I would also like to have you send me more information on your summer work force for teenagers in this country.

Also, if you have a list of jobs the government has to offer.

In my Lands & Events class we have been talking about your stand on dissidents in other countries and your human rights policy, and I would like you to send me a copy (if you have one) of that report. And now back to the UFOs: you made a statement during your campaign about letting all files on UFOs go to the people of this country. Please send me the address of the office I could get in contact with.

I met some of the most important people in 1976, such as your Vice-President, and Vice-President Nelson Rockefeller and your son Chip when he was at my high school here in Everett. Cascade High School sends their good cheers for your new grandson.

Your friend.

3-12.

March 16, 1977

Dear President Carter:

Here at the *[AF-deleted]* Junior High, we have a club, "In Search of Ancient Mysteries," and of late we have been investigating the question of Unidentified Flying Objects, and whether or not they really do exist.

We have reviewed Project Blue Book, and feel that there might possibly have been a government coverup regarding some of the sightings. We have also been very impressed with your record in office to date, in that you seem to be a person who is open, and can be trusted; and that is why we now write you this letter.

As students in the process of learning, we would value your opinion on this matter. Were you given any sort of briefing on this subject matter when you assumed the Presidency?

We certainly do realize how busy you have been of late, and we do not mean to take very much of your valuable time; but if you or one of your staff could respond to our request, it would be immensely appreciated.

Thank you very much.

3-13.

March 14, 1977

Dear President Carter:

I am ten years old, and my birthday is April 1. I am doing research on UFOs because I saw one Thursday night and Friday night, March 10 and 11, 1977. I got some pictures of the UFO and half my classmates saw it. I wrote this letter to you because I saw a magazine saying you saw one too. Can you please tell me what should I do if I encounter it again?

3-14.

April 6, 1977

Dear President Carter:

I am a student at the Williamsport Middle School (Williamsport is about six miles outside of Hagerstown). I am writing to you because a few students and I are forming an investigation on aerial phenomena, that is the study of UFOs (Unidentified Flying Objects). We are very serious about this operation and are hoping that the National Investigations Committee on Aerial Phenomena (NICAP) can assist us.

Back when you were running for President, I think I read something in the paper where you had seen a UFO. If this is true, I was wondering if you could fill out the following sheets preceding this letter to help us find out what the phenomenon was or help to explain it. If a question doesn't apply to what you saw, you can just leave it blank. There is no hurry in getting these back to us, so you can take your time in answering them. If you are ever in the neighborhood, feel free to stop in and visit us. Thank you for your time.

3-15.

Dear President Carter:
For my school project, I am writing about UFOs.

There have been so many stories printed about UFO sightings from the Air Force, astronauts, and private citizens. I've also heard the military has withheld information from the public for years. |

Could you please tell us if there are any plans for the future, as far as disclosing military information on UFO sightings? I have wrote to you before about UFO sightings.

Thank you for taking the time to read the letters.

3-16.

Dear President Carter:
I believe that UFOs exist even though my parents kid me. I am twelve (12) and have a center called Research of Unexplained Phenomenas. We (friends in the center) are collecting information on sightings along with photos. I read in an Official UFO magizine that you didn't laugh at people who saw UFOs because you had seen one yourself. You are the only person I trust for giving me the truth about the UFO mystery. Before you became president you said that you would make every piece of information on UFOs available for the public. I would appreciate very much if you would tell me the truth about what the Air Force found out when Project Blue Book was in use. We could use some sightings and photos of UFOs also. If you have any addresses of UFO information we would thank you for them.

Thank you.

3-17.

Dear President Carter:
My name is [AF-deleted], and I'm fourteen years old, I am a UFO enthusiast or a junior UFOlogist, take your pick.

I'm writing about you and UFOs. I read in a UFO magazine and heard on the radio that you had seen a UFO. I didn't think it was some kind of publicity stunt or anything. I also heard that you're planning to put a lot of secret UFO things out in the open. I think that's okay. I think you should. But, I want to warn you that some Republicans might try to hold that against you to throw you out of office. Now, I just heard on the radio that you're sending out a space ship with pictures, sounds, and things like that. I think that's great. It's a very good idea. I heard some of the things on the radio.

I would like a response from you if you're not too busy. Sorry for being so sloppy.

P.S. Did you ever think of joining a UFO organization?

3-18.

April 20, 1977

Dear President Carter:
I want to join the committee to study UFOs. Could you please send me any information I need?

I have been interested in UFOs for two years.

3-19.

March 17, 1977

Mr. President:
Does the Air Force or any other agency have documented proof that the unidentified flying objects in our skies belong to someone who doesn't inhabit our planet?

3-20.

Dear President Carter:
I would like to know, Mr. Carter, what the world would do if a space ship came down here.

Would there be communication or what?

3-21.

May 29, 1977

Mr. President:
During the presidential campaign you promised, if elected, you would let the American people know the truth about the flying saucers or UFOs.

Okay, so what is the truth?

3-22.

February 2, 1977

Dear Sir:

I am a high school student who has been interested in the subject of Unidentified Flying Objects for many years. Though I have never had an encounter
with one, I do know people who have. And I as well as them would like to
know what the United States Government has found on the subject.

I have read that you have had an encounter with a UFO and in public
interest would release the U.S. Gov'ts findings. But since then, months ago,
I have not heard of anything from you on the subject.

There are many people in this country who are directly or indirectly
involved in finding out what this strange phenomenon is, so why not give
the people the information the gov't has on this most puzzling of subjects?

3-23.

March 23, 1977

Dear President Carter:

I am a student at Axtell Park Junior High School in Sioux Falls.

Awhile ago you gave an interview to the *National Enquirer* on your eyewitness account of a UFO. In this interview you stated that if you were
elected you would make public the reports and information the government has on UFOs that is being kept from the eyes and ears of the public.

I know there is something out there, and I am sure millions of others
think this way.

I myself have never closely seen a UFO, but I don't understand why
you wouldn't want to explore the matter further, you being an eyewitness.

I realize that you might be very busy and not have the time to see to
it, and if you think knowing will cause panic, think what not knowing is
doing. People don't know if these beings are friendly or are invading us.

I think you are doing a great job as President, and hope to see you doing
something about this problem.

3-24.

May 16, 1977

Dear President Carter:

Last year there was a television special on UFOs which was presented on
Channel 6 of Milwaukee. On that special they were talking about that when
you were elected you would release information to the concerned people.
I happen to be one of those concerned persons, so could you please send
me some true information about UFOs? I have read most of the books

about them, and I'd like more. I am also a freshman at Hartford Union High School, so please send me some information.

A concerned person...

P.S. Thank you.

3-25.

Dear President Carter:

Do you remember the promise that you made during your campaign—you would release all UFO information? That is why I am writing you. Please send me as much as possible.

Thank you.

P.S.: [The writer's sketch of a futuristic, swept-back-wing craft.]

3-26.

Dear Jimmy:

We are a large group of 19-20-year old citizens from Peabody, Massachusetts, who are very concerned about information being withheld from us dealing with UFOs. In one of your previous statements, you announced to the American people that all information would be made public regarding this topic. We feel the reason for all the cover-up is that people will panic. At this day and age people have to know what's going on.

Please read this letter with concern, and make us feel like we are a part of the country.

P.S. We are glad you are President, and know you will help the country.

3-27.

Dear Mr. President Carter:

I think you are one of the best presidents we've ever had. You're doing a good job so far.

I recall that when you were running for president, you said if you were elected you would tell us about the mysteries of the UFOs. When do you propose to unveil this to the public?

I am fourteen years old and my name is *[AF-deleted]*. I'm very interested in these kinds of things.

3-28.

Dear Mr. President:

About in the year 1969 the plan blue book was never seen again. It was about the mysterious UFO (Unidentified Flying Objects). They're have been more sightings this year like the one in Los Angeles. The strange brightly lit objects that at least a half dozen persons saw speeding across the southern California sky. Seven air men at March Air Force Base sighted two objects. The diamond shape objects, glowing silver with a blue stream behind them. They were observed for about fifteen section. The March air base sighting occurred at 3:28 a.m., Tuesday. Mr. President, I'm concerned about this fact and more surly that other people are too. I wish that you would continue operation Blue book once more.

P.S. I wish you would send pictures of your family.

3-29.

Dear President Carter:

I am concerned about something called UFOs. The letters "UFO" stands for unidenified flying object. UFOs have been plagueing this naition since it was born, and I would like to know what they are because I have heard strange storys about them and I would like to know which ones are true. During your campain you said that you would open up on UFO files. You still haven't. I have proof that you said it because I have an newspaper clipping that said you would. Will you please open up the files?

P.S. Enclosed is clipping from *Miami Herald.* Please return clipping. Please reply.

3-30.

Dear Mr. President:

In an interview with Malcolm Balfour for the *National Enquirer* you said: "If I become President, I'll make every piece of information this country has about UFO sightings available to the public and the scientists."

If you are going to do this, when will it be? I am very interested in UFOs, and like to read all the information about them I can.

3-31.

March 7, 1977

Dear Mr. President:

My name is *[AF-deleted].* I am twelve years old and have two sisters. We live just outside of Los Angeles.

To get right to the point, I am very interested in UFOs (flying saucers). I read any books, watch any movies, and read and collect UFO articles. Shortly before you were elected, I was reading an article about you and why you believe in UFOs, published in the *National Enquirer.* In it you said if you were elected you would make all the info. on UFOs available to the public. If you haven't done so, when will you, and if you have where can I get it?

Recently two very bright UFOs were sighted over Los Angeles, and I was wondering what you do when they're sighted. I have, over the years, collected quite a stack of info. on UFOs. One of the most interesting articles was after firing a lazer beam off the moon, to calculate the distance between the Earth and the moon, the second shot missed. We then picked-up an S.O.S. signal near Jupiter; could that have been a UFO?

Anxiously awaiting your reply.

P.S. If possible, please send me some UFO pictures.

3-32.

Dear President Jimmy Carter:

My name is *[AF-deleted]*. I am 12 years old, and I go to St. Cornelius School in Chicago. I am very interested in UFOs. I was reading the *National Enquirer* newspaper, and there was an article about you seeing a UFO, and also it said that you said that if you would become president you would make all information about UFOs made public. I am requesting that information.

Thank you.

3-33.

Tempe, Arizona
June 7, 1977

Dear Mr. Carter:

I have been investigating UFOs on my spare time with one other friend.

We are ten and eleven years old. We have two cameras and other equipment. We have not been too successful in my reaserch, so I am wondering if you have or you know where I can get some information about UFOs. If you have any info. please send it to me, or send me the address where I can order it.

Chapter 27

Look Up!

Any youngster favored (or disfavored, depending on the circumstances) with a "close encounter" of his own will realize that such an experience can indeed be one's best teacher.

Imagine, for example, how the young witness in this account views the issue of UFO reality today:

On March 19, 1968, in Beallsville, Ohio: "Gregory Wells was walking home from his grandmother's house, carrying a jug of water, when he heard a loud noise like a generator. Then he saw a huge, red, football-shaped object about 150 feet away. It had four red flashing lights along its side. A tube came out of the bottom and aimed at Gregory. A red beam from the tube hit his right arm at the shoulder, set his jacket on fire and knocked him to the ground. His mother and grandmother came to his aid and saw the red object fade away. The doctor at the hospital said the two blistered spots were second-degree burns." (Source: "A Catalog of UFO-Related Human Physiological Effects" (1996), by John F. Schuessler (director of the Mutual UFO Network, Inc., now headquartered in Morrison, CO 80465-0369).]

3-34.

Sunday, 3 July 1977

Dear Mr. Carter:

My name is *[AF-deleted]*. I am thirteen years old. I live in Irving, Texas, about a mile from Dallas. It's a little bit hot down here, but that's Texas weather for you.

What this letter is about is I am interested in UFOs. I plan to be an astronomer. I'm quite interested in space and communication with other planets. There's bound to be someone else in that vast outer space.

Well, anyway—I read before you were elected President you would release information on UFOs. I haven't seen much about that since I read that. I want to know if you could write me a letter because I want to hear from the President to know what is going on. Could you send me a letter concerning UFOs? If so I would be very happy.

Well, that's about it. So I will say good-bye.

Your friend…

3-35.

Dear Mr. President:

My name is *[AF-deleted]*, and I am very interested in the government in relation to the UFO controversy. I would very much like to see at least some of their files opened to the public. UFOs have been a part of my life for 8 of my 15 years here on this earth. I have always wished that some day the government whitewash would end and the files opened to the public. I heard your campaign promises and to my delight, opening the government's UFO files was one of them. I know you are probably busy, but this is very important to me.

UFOs are real and are from other planets or even other dimensions. If the government were to admit that, a great many people who hushed up because of government and local ridicule might relate their sightings, which would help us solve the mystery and even make friends with whoever flies them.

If you have already started, I would like some information on what you have uncovered. If you have not started, please do so as soon as you can. I will be awaiting some action.

P.S. I would like it if the information from the files were printed in book form, or put into a series of books if there is a lot of material.

Thank you!

3-36.

Mr. President:

I am deeply concerned about a promise you made about releasing all UFO information from government files. The people of the United States had entrusted you to become the leader of our nation; so you should pay back that trust. Don't sweep this promise under the rug and so do not betray the people; help them. Your decision may change history by letting the people realize there are other inteligent civilizations in space. You will give every one new hope. The cover up of UFOs has gone on long enough!

Although I am only fifteen years old and I may not know much, I know what the government is doing is very wrong. If we get in contact with these beings we could possibly advance technically and mentally hundreds of years. We could cure deadly viruses and feed hungry people. All the American people need is trust. People must know the truth about UFOs.

You must not go back on your promise.

3-37.

Dear Mr. President:
I saw two flying saucers (this is what they look like) [via an attached sketch]
last night, June 20th, at about 8:30 p.m. I heard that you are interested in
them.
    Love…
    P.S. I am seven yrs. old.

3-38.

April 12, 1977

Dear President Carter:
I am twelve years old. I was reading *UFO Report,* and it said, "If I become
President, I'll make every piece of information this country has about UFO
sightings available to the public and scientists." I've got a center, RESEARCH
of UNEXPLAINED PHENOMENA, and we are doing research on Bigfoot,
Abominable Snowman, Loch Ness Monster, and UFOs. I would like more
cover-up [follow-up?] on when you saw the UFO in 1973 in Georgia, and
I would like to know what you really think about UFOs.
    We were wondering if you would send us some information on UFOs
and some photographs and some sightings (1970–1977) if possible. And if
you have any information on any of the others please send it to us.
    Thank you so much for your time.

*Occasionally, a letter to former President Ford finds it way into the Air Force's as-
sortment of UFOlogical letters to President Carter.*

3-39.

July 13, 1974

Dear Mr. President:
I saw you last night on television, and you said that inflation was the largest
concern of the American People. I do believe that it is the largest concern
for *most* of the people, but there are people like me, people who seek truth
from the government. Now we have a leader whom we can really trust.
    Before I get to the main part of this letter, I would like to tell you a lit-
tle bit about my self so you can really feel there is a person behind this letter. I was born in Grand Rapids, Mich., and lived there all my life until a
few short months ago. I am thirteen years old and very involved in many
things.

My grandfather *[AF-deleted]* told me he was a friend of yours, and he also told me he taught you how to swim.

Now to the important part of the letter:

When you were a congressman you said that there should be a study on UFOs. As to date there has been no study of this type. The only thing the air force has used these so-called studies as a way to "debunk" the sightings. There is no doubt in my mind that UFOs exist. UFOs have been reported by policemen, by scientists, by famous astronomers. Even by Governors. The Governor of Michigan and the Governor of Ohio both claim to have seen these elusive objects.

Now that you are President, you have the power to disclose the existence of UFOs to the public.

3-40.

February 7, 1977

My dear Mr. President:

I am a high school student, and I am very interested in the subject of Unidentified Flying Objects (UFOs). I have read many books on this subject, and I have discussed it with knowledgeable people, and, invariably, the question of Air Force concealment of UFO information has come up. At one point in your campaign I understood that, if elected, you would make public this information. I am wondering if you are still intending to release this information. Since most of the American people believe in UFOs, I think it would be to their interest to release this information. If there is no information concealed by the Air Force, you could clear up this matter.

3-41.

TO: Mr. James Carter, President of the United States:

My name is *[AF-deleted]*. I was wondering if you really seen a UFO? I also was wondering if you gave a statement about seeing a UFO to a UFO magazine?

I would be sincerely grateful if you answer me.

3-42.

February 26, 1977

Dear President Carter:

My name is *[AF-deleted]*, and I will soon be twelve years old. I am very much interested in UFOs, and have spent about four years studying them.

I read about you seeing a UFO in 1973.

During the election you stated, "If I become President, I will make every piece of information this country has about UFOs available to the public."

Last year I read that the U.S. Air Force was supposed to let the facts be known about UFOs by December, but didn't. I would like to know the true facts about UFOs, or why they didn't reveal the truth about them.

My address is *[AF-deleted]*.

P.S. Keep up the good work!

3-43.

Dear President Carter:

I like your family very much. I admire the way you are, and I think if every one was as sincere as you they wouldn't be no wars and every one would be nicer to each other. I would of voted for you as president but, I couldn't because I am only sixteen years old. I wrote a letter before to you. But I think it didn't come so, I wrote you other one. I like you to help the aerial phenomena research organization of Tucson, Arizona. This organization is for investigating UFO sightings, and people who had seen UFOs are interviewed by this organization. There is this book called project blue book, and it is written by the C.I.A. This book tells that UFOs had been out sight the white house and Capitel building. Can you please answer for me this question? If UFOs ever come back to Washington, D.C., do you think they would like to have communication with you? If so in what way? If not in what way?

Here is my address *[AF-deleted]*.

3-44.

May 21, 1977

Dear Mr. Carter:

This is the second time I've wrote to you. The last time the staff assistant answered my letter, so if you can't answer my letter can the Vice President or the Secretary of state or the Secretary of Defense? I don't mind who, but just somebody impotant!

I would like to know what anyone thinks about UFOs. Please give me an answer even if its a little card like what I just received.

3-45.

March 6, 1977

Dear President Carter:

According to an article entitled "EXCLUSIVE—Jimmy Carter: The Night I Saw a UFO" in the June 8, 1976, issue of the *National Inquirer,* you witnessed a UFO in Thomaston, Georgia, in 1973. According to the article, you and about twenty people watched it for ten minutes. I have been interested in the mystery of UFOs for a number of years. I have not seen one and do not necessarily believe that they represent extraterrestrial space-craft. I do believe that there is serious work being done by scientists and reputable civilian UFO study groups in the U.S. and the world.

My question is, Mr. President: Do you believe that the government should fund future UFO investigation projects somewhat like the Condon Committee, which studied the problem at the University of Colorado for the Air Force in 1968–69? My feeling is that the Condon Report, released by the Air Force in early 1969, did not satisfactorily get to the bottom of the UFO mystery. The article in the Inquirer stated that you are "convinced that UFOs exist because I have seen one." I would take that to mean that you believe UFOs exist as a rightful phenomenon unexplainable in terms of contemporary physics and does not fall within the scope of misidenti-fication of natural objects.

If you could find time, I would appreciate it if you could tell me if the government has any plans which could be directed in the future to solving this problem once and for all. I might remind you that UFO reports are made nearly every day to various newspapers in the country, to police au-thorities in local communities, and to various civilian UFO study groups, for example, the Center for UFO Studies headed by Dr. J. Allen Hynek, for-mer civilian consultant to the Air Force's Project Blue Book (which stud-ied UFOs from 1947–1969). The UFO problem is a persistent and contin-uously intriguing one for the citizens of the United States and those handsful of scientists who are taking their own time and money to look into the phe-nomenon.

Thanks for your time.

3-46.

March 24, 1977

Dear Mr. Carter:

My name is *[AF-deleted]*. I'm writing in concern about what Mr. Ford said while he was in office. He said that he was going to lift the veil of secrecy on UFOs. But I've never heard anything about it. What do you plan on doing about this?

3-47.

Dear Mr. Carter:

My name is *[AF-deleted]*. I'm fifteen and am in the ninth grade.

I would like to ask you a question. What I would like to know is, do you believe in flying saucers and men, or rather human beings, living on other planets? The reason I would like to know is because some people at school I know say there are, but the government won't say because they think it will cause everyone to panic. Personally I would like to know for certain.

The way I see it, either there are or there aren't, no maybe. Also, did you watch the "Outerspace Connection" on television? It was on Thursday, March 3. It really gave me something to think about. And, oh yes, about everyone panicing, I don't think it would happen; most people are more civilized than to run around like Chicken Little. I know I wouldn't panic, because it would only confirm my own suspicions.

P.S. Could you also tell me the correct address for the National Association of Rocketry?

3-48.

May 28, 1977

Honorable President:

I'm a young man twelve years old and very interested in astronomy.

You stated that you would release informating that the government had on UFOs.

I will appreciate if you can send me whatever you can on the subject, or please let me know where to write to get this information.

3-49.

May 9, 1977

Dear Sir:

I live on a farm near Warrens, Wisconin. I am fourteen and attend Tomah Jr. High School.

I am interested in UFOs. I read in an article that you were going to release the government files on UFOs. I was wondering if this is true, and if so, when? I think the American people have a right to know this information. I think the Government should have more trust in the American people's ability to accept this information.

I know you are busy with the problems of the country, but I would like to know if you are going to release the Govt. files on UFOs this year.

Thank you.

3-50.

Dear President Carter:

I could not get you by phone. So I have decided to mail you this letter. I have a question. President Carter, when will you give the public the government information on UFOs? You said you would disclose it—but when?

My phone number is *[AF-deleted]*.

Sincerely, *[AF-deleted]*: (Age 12).

3-51.

Dear Mr. Carter:

In *Official UFO* you said, "If I become president" you would make every piece of information available to the public and scientists. Well, I'm the public, and when I grow up I want to be a scientist. But right now I would like to prove UFOs are true. I believe in them, but other people don't. I would like very much to have some information on UFOs.

Very serious...

3-52.

Dear President Carter:

How are you? I hope you are okay. I'd like to ask you a question. Was there really a UFO flying over the White House? Anyway, we had our own class election, before the real election, and you won. It was 1,211.

It was fun. After Easter, we're going to hatch duck eggs. I hope you can come to our school. Our school is right across from the Chalmers.

Anyway, getting back to my question, I hope you will write me and answer my question. My address is at the heading of the letter, and my zip code is *[AF-deleted]*. Hope you write back!

3-53.

March 10, 1977

Dear Mr. President:

Ex-President Ford backed a UFO investigation. Are you going to continue this investigation? Are you going to expand the investigation to other mysteries, such as Bigfoot and the Loch Ness Monster?

Thank you.

Note: The Correspondence Control Sheet (May 10, 1977) accompanying the following letter contains this message from Lieutenant Colonel Powell:

"I think this is a student hoax letter or he is a *[AF-deleted]*. A.F. cannot address the matter of 'antigravity ore.' Further, he seeks no answer. Please FAA."

3-54.

March 22, 1977

Dear Mr. President:

The mysteries of flying saucers are over. They are true!

Hint: there is/are planet/s which have an ore. An ore so opposed to gravity we humans cannot and never will be able to measure it (opposition to gravity). This repelability is what makes the saucers move faster than the speed of light.

The steering system or degree of navigation is controlled by the volumetric flow of direction of the liquified ore "

Sincerely yours, Student, MSAC.

3-55.

Mr. President Carter:

Mr. President, I have been a Jimmy Carter fan ever since the campaign began. I hope this letter gets to you because to me this is very important. I read in the *National Enquirer* about your UFO experience, and that if you were elected you would let out information on UFOs. I would like to know if this is a for-real statement of yours. If this is for real, I wish you would find time to write back and tell me about what you saw, because I believe in UFOs. I have studied them since I was in fourth grade. I am in eighth grade now. I am glad that you won because if Mr. Ford won I would have been afraid that this country would be done. Some day I hope I will meet you in person.

P.S. Sorry about the wording. I know it isn't the best.

3-56.

Dear Mr. President:

I was reading about UFOs in *Official UFO magazine.* And I read the article about you seeing the UFO at Thomaston, Georgia, in 1973. Plus it said that you would make information available to the public. I'm doing a report at school and would like some information on UFOs.

I'm a sophmore at Jefferson Senior High, Delphos, Ohio.

Thank you very much.

3-57.

May 22, 1977

Mr. President:

Being a rather curious fifteen-year-old, I have a question for you concerning one of your campaign promises, which was: "If I become President, I'll make every piece of information this country has about UFO sightings available to the public, and the scientists."

My question is: Have you made any plans to carry out this promise, and if so, how? In my opinion the release of this information (beginning with that of the National Archives) would be of inestimable benefit to not only the American public but also to the world.

3-58.

Dear President Carter:

I would like for you to remember a promise that you made. You said that you would give out information on UFOs. I would be pleased if you could send me some. [Note: (S)he includes a sketch of a flying saucer headed from space toward planet Earth.]

3-59.

March 21, 1977

Dear President Carter:

How are you doing? My name is *[AF-deleted]*. I was reading the *National Enquirer*. It said that you saw a UFO one night, and you said that if you became President you would tell everyone that UFOs are for real. I also beleve in them, and when you tell everyone would you wright me a letter that you did tell them this? And I can wright to you from someone that likes to see you some day, or you can call me at *[AF-deleted]* and ask for *[AF-deleted]* and when you call tell them you are okay, just tell them you are a frand.

3-60.

Dear Mr. President:

I am writing you concerning the phenomena known as UFOs. I am a third-year college student majoring in astronomy and have had a deep interest for years in the subject of UFOs. I wrote to President Ford on this subject almost a year ago and never received any response from him; so therefore I voted for you in the election. All I received was a ridiculous letter from NASA concerning UFOs and about how they did not exist and were all explainable. This answer from NASA is of course very hard to believe, and so I am writing you to request that you attempt to open up a brand new investigation of UFOs which would shed light on the truth concerning this phenomenon. I am sure that millions of Americans would like to see a new investigation started; one which "would not" involve the Air Force or the Central Intelligence Agency, but instead a team of highly expert scientists. Thank you.

3-61.

Ann Arbor, Michigan
March 5, 1977

Dear Mr. Carter:

I am writting you to find out when you are going to reveal the secrets of UFOs. Because you haven't siad anything about it. I am ten years old and would like you to write me back. I know your busy but I'd like to know.

And don't forget that you siad if you became President you would reveal all the secrets from the files. My address is *[AF-deleted]*.

3-62.

Mr. President:

I read somewhere that you would try to release all UFO reports. I am pretty interested in UFOs, probably because my grandmother said she saw one. I was wondering if you were going to do this. I think people should know what's going on with UFOs to a certain degree. Would you please write back and tell me?

3-63.

Dear Mr. Carter:

My friends have been teasing me about seeing UFOs. One of my friends said that you saw one of these UFOs during election time. They are saying that it was changing color of red, blue, white, and green. Last Friday my friend called me up and said to look east in the east, and I saw the thing.

3-64.

July 9, 1977

Dear Sir:

My friend and I think we saw a UFO. We are not sure, but it had a yellow and kind of white light that was blinking. And it wrote UO. If you can tell me what it means, you may write to me. But if you don't believe me you don't have to write to me.

    P.S. I am nine years old.

3-65.

Dear Mr. President:

Even though I am only twelve years old, I supported you during the election and tried to see when you came to my town. One of the things that led me to support you was an article in the June 8, 1976, issue of the *National Enquirer*. In this article there was an interview with you stating that you had seen a UFO in 1973 and that you promised to release all the UFO information our country had to the public. Being a supporter of UFOs and the theory that the Air Force has an exclusive file on it, I and some of my classmates were wondering if any of this was true. If you have the time to answer please do and send an autographed picture of yourself.

3-66.

March 23, 1977

Dear Mr. Carter:

My name is *[AF-deleted]*. I live in Irving, Texas, just outside of Dallas (big D). I am thirteen years old, and I go to Travis Jr. High School, named after William B. Travis.

What I'm interested in is the subject of Unidentified Flying Objects. I read once, before you were elected President, that if you were elected you would release information concerning UFOs. Is that true? I'm really very curious. I am really interested in the study of space exploration. In fact I plan to be an astronomer one day. Space is really a vast unexplored territory. I think it is really fascinating to think there are others like us in the giant outer space. People waiting to communicate with us. So many stars that they're uncountable. I have a twenty-eight-inch telescope here at home that I use ocasionally. We could look at the sun spots with the little fitter on the lens. We could look at all those stars too.

What I am really getting at here is that could you send me any information on UFOs, because I'm studying UFOs for a hobbie. Well, that's it, but if you could I'd really would appreciate it. Thank you.

Your Friend...

Epilogue

Upon reading this book, a French-styled Yogi Berra might have this to say: "The more things stay the same, the less likely they are to change."

Indeed, its content raises the perplexing question of how come, after more than twenty years, the state of UFOculture remains so predictably stagnant and static. Has the dynamism for the sought-for Carter UFO D-Day (Disclosure Day) served merely as a sort of "crying wolf" catharsis for Mr. and Ms. Joe Sixpack? Must public apathy reign supreme over public inquiry? Or have these D-Day advocates lost their cause, their cozy dream of reform, to that ultimate American convention (born of our craving for instant gratification): "out of sight, out of mind."

If they indeed have lost their cause, then let this book help them re-ignite it.

Ten or fifteen or twenty years from now, when someone chooses to compile a similar collection of citizens' UFO-related letters to, say, Bill Clinton or George W. Bush, let her use this book as a navigation tool. Over time, as these unwitting "people's White House correspondents" become more sophisticated and knowledgeable, they will have added their fair share, and more perhaps, to this time capsule of sociopolitical history and commentary. As such, their collective contribution, like this one from the Carter era, might come to be known as a citizens manifesto for greater UFO freedom of information and accountability.

And from their continuing quest for UFOtruth in the Court of Public Opinion, you doubtless can expect to see some measure of unintended humor and unexpected pathos.

So, how about it, Mr. President (and/or Ms. Presidential Candidate): will you choose to break the mold by helping fulfill Jimmy Carter's celebrated promise?

Readers eager as I to locate any of the Carter UFOcorrespondents would be doing us all a favor were they to spread the word about this compilation.

Imagine if even just one thousand of those unaccounted-for nine thousand letter writers were to step forward to share with us the contents of their missives! The result: more *recorded* history…more fuel for the sought-for paradigm shift in the citizens-government confrontation over what the UFO presence means to society (and vice versa). And, perhaps understated in a between-the-lines perusal of this book: a renewed opportunity for officialdom to discover and acknowledge the depth of UFO reality by merely reading the reams of UFO-related documentation generated by various government agencies during the past fifty-odd years.

So please pass on to me your various leads, research tips, and other material deemed worthy of your attention and mine. My postal address is 3518 Martha Custis Drive, Alexandria, VA 22302-2001; e-mail: *overtci@cavtel.net;* telephone: (703) 931-3341.

Footnote: Then comes Clinton…

Grant Cameron has published a three-part report on certain FOIA-obtained records pertaining to the *Clinton* administration's flirtation with the UFO-E.T. controversy.

You may access the report (as well as the ensuing e-mail listserv discussions thereof) via a series of messages that Cameron initiated July 8, 2001, on the sub-website of "UFO UpDates Mailing List" (for *ufomind.com*), starting with the following URL:

http://ufomind.com/ufo/updates/2001/jul/m08-019.shtml—which now has been superseded by the website of *http://www.virtuallystrange.net.*

Appendix A

Harry S. Truman's UFO Americana

If you can judge by the various letters written to him by citizens during his terms in office, President Harry S. Truman truly was "The People's President." And nowhere is this judgment more apropos than when you consider the letters sent his way by persons convinced that the subject of "flying saucers" deserved his direct, serious attention.

The collected letters—or at least that portion that somehow escaped referral to the Department of Defense for reply—now reside at the Truman Library in Independence, Missouri. There, they share the shelves with such missives as (1) citizens' requests that Truman lift the embargo on arms shipments to Palestine; (2) a women's group's telegram seeking a personal interview with Truman to discuss the status of proposed legislation aimed at setting up a U.S. Customs Border Patrol so as to improve the enforcement of anti-smuggling laws in relation to narcotics; and (3) parents' pleas that their sons be released from military prison so they can rejoin their families.

Amid that potpourri of issues and concerns major and minor to a president who united the nation during wartime transition, what's so special about the correspondence on things that go swish in the night? For one thing, Truman might have been the only president ever to have received a formal briefing on the "UFO problem" from Air Force intelligence experts— if you can accept that revelation as voiced in a 1956 book by former USAF "Project Blue Book" chief Edward J. Ruppelt. For another thing, Truman resided in the White House during the famous UFO-sighting "flap" near Washington, D.C., back in 1952. Third, it was Truman who was instrumental in establishing the U.S. Central Intelligence Agency, which to this day insists on denying public access to some 57 of the UFO-related documents that surfaced some years ago via litigation under the U.S. Freedom of Information Act.

Then there are the letters themselves—a cross-section of views, concerns, suggestions, and explanations about a problem so touchy (and sometimes zany) that only a few citizens dared confide in their president. Lucky for them (and him), in retrospect, that this man Truman was so attuned to the American psyche that he was able to weather the growth of UFO interest with just the right mix of detachment and solicitude. (Maybe his approach has served ever since as the model for presidential response to the UFO problem.)

Although most of the letters wound up being referred to the Defense Department (Air Force) for direct reply to the writer, a few did remain in the White House files. Apparently, each of them underwent indexing upon arrival—under the writer's name, address, and date. A White House staffer synopsized each letter in a cross-reference log. Here are some excerpts quoted from the log; for most entries, I've added a commentary from my perspective as an historian of the "politics of UFOlogy":

Pioneers Petition the President

Kenneth Arnold of Boise, Idaho (April 6, 1948): In a telegram, the man whose UFO encounter of June 24, 1947, sparked the coinage of "flying saucers" as a household word had this advice for Truman: "Your Honor, I understand there is enough evidence on hand by our intelligence and the people of your great country to announce that flying disks, flying saucers, and other reported strange missiles that are being seen by reliable people throughout the world daily are aircraft from outer space. You know we are not making or flying these aircraft and the United States is the most scientific nation on earth. Why should not America be at least the first to announce this great discovery?"

Although the White House never acknowledged the telegram, Arnold felt obliged to communicate once more: On December 13, 1951, he sent a copy of his booklet "The Flying Saucer As I Saw It." At the time of the telegram, he was 31 years old. He died in January 1984—never to see the resolution of a public issue that rages on throughout the world.

Meade Layne of San Diego, California (April 7, 1950): Writing as the founding director of Borderland Sciences Research Associates, this True Believer in extraterrestrialism announces: "It is our earnest hope that, as a matter of public interest and policy, you will find time to examine the enclosed booklet. It is not necessary to point out to your Excellency that an extremely difficult situation may develop at any hour, in connection with the phenomena referred to in this booklet.

"Allow us to assure you that we serve no selfish interests in this matter, and stand ready to comply with any request for information or service which may be in our power to give."

The 38-page booklet, which remains part of the Truman papers, is titled "Flying Discs — The Ether Ship Mystery and Its Solution." This hodgepodge of metaphysical discussion and interpretation on the origin, purpose, and scope of the reported flying saucers ended up being referred to the National Academy of Sciences. On May 1, 1950, the academy's executive secretary wrote back to Truman's secretary, stating that Layne's organization apparently deals with phenomena outside the field of the academy and suggesting that if Layne's communication "is to be given serious consideration it be referred to some philosophical organization." With that, Truman's secretary, then William D. Hassett, sent this reply to Layne: "Your interest in making available to him [Truman] the enclosures which accompanied your letter is very much appreciated and you may be sure they will be given careful attention."

Leon Davidson of Arlington, Virginia (September 7, 1952): This tenacious, indefatigable   prober-polemicist requested, as described by the correspondence log, "a list of the official statements or press releases made by the President, or the White House, on the subject of Flying Saucers since 1947. States if the statements are long, a mere reference to the date of issue would be sufficient." In later years, Davidson won fame for his persistence in prying loose from the Air Force a copy of its Project Blue Book Special Report No. 14, which he reprinted for wider distribution in a never-ending campaign to prove that most of the "saucers" were man-made, experimental devices. His persistence in going after CIA UFO documentation gave that agency heartburn long before its current headaches over the power of the Freedom of Information Act.

Robert Spencer Carr of Clearwater, Florida (July 31, 1952): From the log: "Writer encloses miscellaneous material relative to 'flying saucers'—suggestions for contact. Respectfully referred to the Department of the Air Force for appropriate handling."

It was Carr who, back in the early seventies, traveled the lecture circuit and radio talk-show route in a short-lived effort to convince the public that the government has all the information it needs about the saucers — based on the USAF retrieval of crash-landed discs and some of their crew members. That contention thrives in some UFO-research circles today, of course.

The Roots of Official UFO Secrecy

Carr's fixation with retrieved saucers might have got its impetus from the notorious 1950 book by Hollywood columnist Frank Scully, *Behind the Flying Saucers,* which was cited by a man in New Orleans (November 19, 1951). From the log: "Requests President's comment re this. Threatens to publicize his letter if he does not receive an answer. Critical of the Pentagon. (consideration and appropriate handling.)"

Then there's a fellow from Cleveland (August 9, 1952): "The writer relates a personal experience which happened in October, 1947, near Reno, Nevada, at which time he saw a formation of shining globular objects from which something, perhaps a parachutist, catapulted to the earth. He disapproves the theory of interterrestial [sic] bodies and advances his theory that the source of these objects is Eurasia and suggests that they are being used as a means of enemy infiltration. Whatever the source, the writer feels that as full a disclosure as possible should be made by official Washington since these saucers may present a serious military threat about which the American public deserves to know."

Someone (gender unknown) from Waurika, Oklahoma (August 26, 1952), enclosed clippings: "One article [was] by a Navy officer who said he knew the location of a saucer but was not permitted to tell where it is as the United States and Mexico hid it. Also refers to article about a man in Florida who claims his hair was singed by a flying saucer. Would like an explanation regarding these articles."

A man from Chicago (October 29, 1952) "refers to the Air Force report re flying saucers as well as article by Robert S. Allen on this subject dated Sept. 26. States he does not believe that such matters should have to be investigated by private citizens. He hopes the secrecy of the Air Force will be lifted, etc."

From Dinuba, California (July 30, 1952), a man "urges that the Air Force inform the public as to the results of the investigation."

Then, a woman from Tucson (July 28, 1952) "opposes the secrecy in re to the Flying Saucers. Believes the public should be given a complete report."

Finally, from Baltimore (September 13, 1950): A man "refers to article entitled 'Flying Saucers' appearing in the October 1950 issue of *Pageant* Magazine, and feels the American people should be told the truth about the saucer reports. He asks if a cover-up attempt is being made on the part of the Air Force and Department of Defense."

Echoes of *The Roswell Incident*

One White House file-record sheet identifies letters from eight separate persons—all written during the time frame July 5–9, 1947, which coincides with the reported crash-landing of a disc(s) near Roswell, New Mexico (as recounted in the 1980 book *The Roswell Incident*, by William L. Moore — Grosset & Dunlap, New York; and thereafter in several other Roswell-focused books/articles/docudramas). Each of these letters was "respectfully referred to the War Department for consideration."

To Kill or Not to Kill

A woman (with others not named) from Los Angeles (July 29, 1952) requests "that the Air Force not fire on the 'flying saucers,' as they have not attempted any harm upon any persons or properties."

Likewise, another woman, from Ocean Park, California (August 1, 1952), "opposes the recent order from the War Department to fire upon the 'flying saucers.' Gives her views re the 'saucers' and offers suggestions re same."

From Albany, Georgia (July 28, 1952), a man "urges the Air Force to refrain from attacking the so-called 'flying saucers.'"

In her letter from Hollywood, California (July 29, 1952), a woman "comments on reports of the so-called Flying Saucers and suggests they may contain highly intelligent humans and that an effort should be made to contact them in a friendly manner."

Echoing that sentiment was a man from Indio, California (July 30, 1952): "Referring to the report that our armed planes have been ordered to shoot down a flying saucer for investigation, the writer suggests that we had better cultivate the friendship of the space visitors and perhaps save ourselves from annihilation. Says that a friendly gesture would be supplied if the President were to issue a proclamation ordering our military and all private citizens to welcome space visitors and treat them with the utmost consideration should they choose to land among us."

For his part, an irate New Yorker (July 29, 1952) "requests by what authority orders to shoot down the so-called 'flying saucers' were given—states that the makers and operators of these devices are vastly more powerful than the United States—such orders would be equivalent to a declaration of war. Requests and urges President to immediately countermand these orders. States further, that unless he is informed promptly, that such orders have been countermanded, his letter will be given to the Press."

A telegram from a man in Glen Ellyn, Illinois (July 29, 1952), "suggests that no offensive action be taken against the objects reported as unidentified, which have been sighted over the nation—(Flying Saucers)—offensive action might result in grave consequences—alieniating [sic] US from beings of far superior powers—suggests friendly contacts."

But then we have the sentiments of a resident in The Green Killaloe, County Clare, Eire (June 22, 1952): "Writer states she read about Flying Saucers seen over New York. 'Don't be too easy with them, bring them down, show no mercy.' Comments that to make airplanes noiseless, cover their engines with felt and rubber."

Miscellany

The draft of this report contains too much material to include with this printing. Sections omitted here are titled "Inventors Invite Investigation" (several letters proposing this or that means for duplicating saucers' construction/propulsion); "UFO Curios" (referring to some three-dimensional items sent to Truman); "The Theory File" (letters showing the wide range of citizens' theories on the origin/purpose of the saucers); "Words of Wisdom from the Children" (letters that show the sincerity—and intensity—of society's younger seekers of UFO knowledge).

Wanted: UFO Pen Pals

A male graduate student in journalism at the University of California (Los Angeles) (April 5, 1950) wrote this inquiry to Truman's secretary, Charles G. Ross:

"I am currently engaged in research for a graduate dissertation which will attempt to analyze the sociological and psychological implications of the flying saucer phenomenon.

"In the light of the forceful radio commentary by Henry J. Taylor and the article which appeared in the *United States News and World Report,* both of which declared or implied the saucers are aircraft of unusual design developed in the United States, I was interested to learn the reactions of Mr. Truman to the reports.

"I understand that the Navy and the Air Force have issued qualified denials to the reports.   Does the White House feel such reports are baseless?

"I wish to thank you in advance for your interest and help.   You may be assured that I will appreciate any information you may be able to give me."

Ross's reply of April 11 contains what turns out to be form-letter phraseology from the Truman White House: "The president has expressed no opinions concerning these reports other than that he has no information of any kind about flying saucers."

And So It Goes...

Many of these UFO-oriented letters, of course, have something in common with the hundreds of other letters sent to any given president: the naive expectation that somehow the president himself not only will read them but also will respond to them.   That form of faith in the paternalistic, omnipotent majesty of the Oval Office has carried over, for example, from the Truman days to the Jimmy Carter era of UFO awareness. Incidentally, the content of the Truman letters is echoed by the scores of UFO-related letters received by the Carter administration.   Would Carter's staff have received far fewer such letters had Truman chosen to read his UFO-related correspondence and thus decided to transfer official UFO investigation from military hands to civilian control—in an aim reflective of his move to assure civilian control of nuclear weapons?

Appendix B:

A Presidential Statement on UFO Reality?

For several years now, the following monograph has circulated among re-searchers and activists worldwide—both in hard copy and via various post-ings on the Internet.

Let's suppose that, within the next several years, the growing pressure on the federal government to level with the public about UFO reality ac-tually succeeds. The full measure of that success, of course, would consist of a formal announcement from Washington.

And who better to make it than the president of the United States? Ac-cordingly, CAUS Washington, D.C., director Larry W. Bryant proposes that the president deliver the following speech, timed to coincide with the an-niversary of the Roswell, New Mexico, UFO crash-retrieval case of July 1947.

Presumably, the White House press office will have given the news media advance notice of the general topic—but not the key element—of the speech. Thus, the news-wire advisory to editors might read:

> "Tonight, at 9:00 o'clock Eastern Daylight Time, the president is sched-
> uled to address the nation from the Oval Office of the White House. In-
> formally referred to as the 'Citizens of Earth' speech, the president's remarks
> are expected to reveal new developments in space research, to include mat-
> ters involving unidentified flying objects."

JULY 7, _____ (9:00 p.m.)

FROM: Washington, D.C.

The Oval Office of

The White House

An Address by the President of the United States

Fellow Americans…and fellow citizens of Earth:

Earlier today, I invited three senior members of the White House press corps to join me and the Secretary of the Navy in a round-table discussion of what I'm announcing to you this evening. In making the announcement, I ask that you stay tuned to this TV or radio station for thirty minutes of recorded highlights from the discussion.

Now, perhaps I should use the term astronomical announcement. Because what I'm revealing today certainly has profound implications for all mankind.

It was nearly sixty years ago this week that two so-called "flying saucers" collided during a thunderstorm near Roswell, New Mexico. A few days later, the resulting wreckage, with four humanoid occupants, was retrieved by military authorities.

What little we can surmise about the occupants' origin and mission stirs both our imagination and our compassion. By their sudden and violent demise, these small, vulnerable beings—cosmic pathfinders, perhaps?—have left us with a mystery that both invites and defies solution. Unable to return, or to be returned, to their home planet, they epitomize the grim risk confronting every space traveler.

Ever since July 1947, leaders from within and from outside the federal government have chosen to let the "Roswell Incident" lie in limbo—a political hot potato that would grow hotter whenever they tried to deal forthrightly with it.

Now, with the passage of five decades, that difficult issue has begun to cool. The turnabout is due in part to acknowledging our own advances in space technology and travel. For, today, who can say for sure that our march into space has not been duplicated elsewhere, and with greater success?

My purpose here tonight is not to find fault with past leaders as to when and how to tell the whole story about the Roswell Incident and its aftermath. Rather, as one who only recently has learned the story, I want this occasion to be one of mutual reassurance and recommitment.

We citizens of Earth must reassure ourselves that, as a community of nations, we can deal effectively and justly with unannounced visits by life forms beyond Earth. And, in the process, we must recommit ourselves to the principles and ideals that preserve our species and its civilization.

Are we up to the challenge, in light of this news that mankind truly does share the universe with advanced inhabitants of other worlds? If I had any doubts about that, I would not be here before you tonight.

As we rise to the challenge, let us rely upon the cooperation of a free government and a free press to inform, to inspire, and to lead us in coming to terms with this singular event in human history.

By an executive order to be issued tomorrow, I am directing that all official records pertaining to the Roswell Incident—and to any other such spaceship-retrieval case—be transferred to the Library of Congress. There, under guidance from officials of the Department of the Navy (which has had custody of the records for a number of years), researchers, scholars, scientists, and just plain citizens will have full access to what used to be the Ultimate Secret.

Tomorrow evening, I will address a joint session of Congress, where I'll present my proposal as to how our government should deal, from now on, with the reality of these extraterrestrial visitors.

In the meantime, I'm asking that the Navy secretary conduct a press conference tomorrow at noon in the auditorium of the National Press Club in Washington. There, reporters will have access to a packet of background material that includes photographic and technical data derived from analysis of the retrieved spacecraft.

Tonight, MY duty is to affirm your right—and to renew everyone's opportunity—to take part in the decisionmaking on how and where we should proceed from here. YOUR duty is to help keep the event in proper perspective—and to build upon it in the realization that we, indeed, are not alone in the universe.

As I welcome your understanding, I thank you for your patience. And may God bless the citizens of Earth.

To order additional copies of this book,
please send full amount plus $5.00 for
postage and handling for the first book and
$1.00 for each additional book.
Minnesota residents add 7.125 percent sales tax

Send orders to:

Galde Press

PO Box 460
Lakeville, Minnesota 55044-0460

Credit card orders call 1–800–777–3454
Fax (952) 891–6091
Visit our website at *www.galdepress.com*
and download our free catalog,
or write for our catalog.

www.ingramcontent.com/pod-product-compliance
Lightning Source LLC
Chambersburg PA
CBHW070856250626
47159CB00003B/1087